AF352251

Comedia Series● No – 32

# PHOTOGRAPHIC PRACTICES:

# TOWARDS A DIFFERENT IMAGE

Edited by Stevie Bezencenet and Philip Corrigan

Comedia Publishing Group
9 Poland Street, London W1V 3DG   Tel: 01-439 2059

Comedia Publishing Group was set up to investigate and monitor the media in Britain and abroad. The aim of the project is to provide basic information, investigate problem areas, and to share the experiences of those working in the field, while encouraging debate about the future development of the media. The opinions expressed in the books in the Comedia series are those of the authors, and do not necessarily reflect the views of Comedia.

First published in 1986 by Comedia Publishing Group
9 Poland Street, London W1V 3DG.



First published 1986

ISBN 0906890500

British Library Cataloguing in Publication Data
Photographic practices
  1. Photography
  I.  Bezencenet, Stevie   II. Corrigan, Philip
  770   TR145

Cover design by Stephen Devane
Cover illustration by Christopher Corr

Typeset by Photosetting, 6 Foundry House, Stars Lane, Yeovil, Somerset
BA20 1NL (0935) 23684

Printed in Great Britain by Unwin Brothers Ltd., The Gresham Press, Old Woking, Surrey

Trade Distribution by Comedia

# Acknowledgements

As well as all those people with whom I have talked in the preparation of this book, I would like to acknowledge the support and encouragement of the following individuals: Jo Spence, Ed Barber, Jenny Matthews, Judith Williamson, Stuart Hood, Owen Kelly, Charles Landry, John Bradshaw, Charles Craig, Simon Watney – who was there at the critical last moment, and Haim Bresheeth – who was always there.

*Dedication*

For Katie and Haim

# Contents

Simon Watney

# Introduction

The central institution of photography is, of course, the camera. Far from simply duplicating what we might think of as 'ordinary vision' every photographic image is the result of a complex yet determinate institutional convergence between photochemistry, optics, the various marketplaces of capitalist and mixed economies, and the equally various sites of photographic production, distribution and consumption. It is only in the context of our particular alignments to these institutions that we exercise individual control of any kind on the medium. Yet we are all familiar with the dominant voices of photographic criticism which speak only of the individual photographer, in terms of self-expression and technical competence. To return the study of photography to the analysis of institutions is already to effect a significant break with such voices, and the values which they embody. The question of values is important, since there is an ingrained tendency to equate institutions in a narrow sense with 'property', to the neglect of their wider discursive aspects.

This is a book about the institutions of photography in a particular geographical area – England. It is not, however, concerned with the institutions of 'official' photographic culture, but rather with the work of groups committed to widening and expanding the use of photography throughout society. The sheer range and diversity of photographic practices described here signifies a profound cultural struggle between the interests of the photographic industry, and rival definitions of what photography could become – a technology for increasing rather than restricting our understanding of ourselves and one another. Hence the emphasis on institutional categories and areas of practice which cross over barriers of class, race, gender, age and sexual orientation. This range and diversity also graphically illustrates the increasing tension between the institutions of 'official' State culture, and the needs of those constituencies which it habitually overlooks and ignores.

Like any other branch of production, photography has its own political economy. The question of funding is fundamental to every level and aspect of the emergent photographic culture to which this collection of essays and working papers bears witness. Funding comes from a wide variety of conflicting social sources – the Arts Council of Great Britain, Trade Unions, Local Education Authorities, the European Economic Community, Local Authorities, private sponsors, individual museums and galleries, multinational corporations, and so on. It would be naive to expect these institutions to line up and agree concerning their expectations or demands of working photographers. Most sponsorship is limited to traditional notions of production and exhibition – single framed images, in galleries, produced by 'named' photographers. It is precisely this approach which is currently being questioned throughout England, and the United Kingdom as a whole. The idea of 'photography' as a unified subject is under strong attack. As John Tagg has written, 'what alone unites the diversity of sites in which photography operates is the social formation itself: the specific historical spaces for representation and practices which it constitutes. Photography as such has no identity. Its status as a technology varies with the power relations which invest it. Its nature as a practice depends on the institutions and agents which define it.'[1] It is these power relations, institutions and agencies which *Photographic Practices* maps and records.[2]

Such records are of particular importance since the sites of oppositional photographic culture are widely dispersed, and it is difficult for groups or individuals to gain a national over-view of the achievements of the last decade. This book works both as an historical record, and as a resource, allowing the reader to compare projects with aims, and aims with particular audiences and funding bodies. It is also a timely publication, given the dramatic transformation (and frequent contraction) of sources of photographic finance for the types of work described and proposed. Whilst the central control of funding by institutions such as the Arts Council has largely given way to devolutionary pressures, the subsequent developments have been extremely uneven. In this respect the North-East of England has advanced furthest in terms of the construction of a progressive and comprehensive photographic culture, encouraging the regional specificity of local cultural traditions whilst acknowledging the need for greater diversity of community uses.[3]

Funding informs all areas of photographic practice, and is frequently subject to what is known as the 'Mozart factor' in Arts Council jargon: namely, the tendency for sponsors to prefer 'prestige' projects, defined against the criteria of State culture, rather than the types of educational, distributive, and community projects outlined in the Sections of this book. This problem is exacerbated by the absence in Britain of tax concessions for business interests which might otherwise support areas of cultural production beyond the safe confines of 'South Bank' culture. Such factors, however, cannot prevent the momentum which has been gathering steam ever since the Arts Council announced its first annual budget specifically for photography in 1973. For photography cannot be miniaturised by *fiat*, no matter how restrictively State funding is allocated. The dramatic transformations within British society since World War Two refuse to be contained within the ossified traditions and received wisdoms of 'official' photo culture. The 'Different Image' to which the subtitle of this book refers is the reality of contemporary Britain, a plural reality which traditional image-based professional photography remains unable to comprehend. The democratisation of photography in England is one of the most remarkable and significant achievements of post-war culture. *Photographic Practices* offers us an opportunity to reflect critically on these achievements. It is also (I think) an inspiring publication in its own right, which will help support a generation of photographers in the face of the difficulties and complexities of contemporary cultural production. For how we think about the categories of education, distribution, publication, exhibition and community audiences will, in turn, determine the emergence of new strategies, new practices and new democratic institutions of photography.

# Photography and education

Stevie Bezencenet
## Photography and education

## Introduction

Photography within the education system is generally understood to mean the control of the process of the production of images. This activity may be complemented by technical, historical and stylistic investigations, and variously considered as a craft, art, recording medium, scientific study or a subsidiary element of media studies. This is generally the case in the secondary school sector, where photography is treated as a low-status, hobby-like subject, or irrelevant to the traditional curriculum altogether. It is not accorded the significance of the high-status, discrete core-curriculum subjects, which are characterised by their traditional, if fragmented, relationship to the student's cultural and social experience.

The primary and FE/HE sectors are another matter – the former tending towards an integrated curriculum, where the relationship of photography (when it *is* studied) to the other subjects is more coherent. As for the further and advanced educational sector, it acknowledges the subject in a diversity of ways, and at a variety of levels. Since the 1960s, photography as an academic discipline has been validated by its degree status at under-graduate, post-graduate and research levels. This process of 'sanctioning' was echoed in the secondary sector (GCEs and CSEs) in the mid 1970s and is beginning to filter backwards into the primary sector. However, the developments of the sites of study do not guarantee that the subject is being taught in the most socially beneficial manner.

If we consider education to be a process of acquiring and investigating 'knowledge', in order to achieve a competence and pleasure in critically understanding social differences, then photography can have a substantial role within such a system. If, however, we accept the more traditional view, that education is the acquisition of predetermined and specific 'subjects', historically constructed in an exclusive manner ('really useless knowledge'), then we would have to relegate photography as a minor and irrelevant skill.

The momentum within progressive photography studies today is one which questions and 'refuses' such a limiting role for the medium. Practitioners and teachers across the educational spectrum are working through debates concerning the potential of the medium as an aid in understanding ourselves, our broader social territories and the world at large. Donald and Grealy maintain that:

'The school curriculum is a crucial area for the construction of a popular, national culture and for the moulding of the imaginative relations to it of groups and individuals.' (p. 98)

And if we consider ideology as the practice of reproducing social relations within the sphere of signification and discourse, then the study of photography as part of the statutory education syllabus would seem to help in the production of 'really useful knowledge'. Our individual and collective ways of making sense of the world are based on representations – generally constructed by others. These representations, in contemporary society, are frequently visual and generated by the lens media, of which photography is the most accessible and most public. Therefore, in order to understand how events, ideas and relations are made meaningful for us – we need to interrogate the means of representation, who controls it and for what purposes.

This is not the same as the conventional idea of practising photography. Rather, it is a method of study which considers the taking/making of images as a part of a wider process – that of visual literacy. The ability to read and write has always been considered the basic criterion of education – the control and understanding of words, in the service of communication. Information forms today are rather more complicated than when that concept of skill was created, yet our educational system has failed to adapt its curriculum accordingly. Images are treated as the province of the art class or the illustrative mechanisms for all subjects. The standard use of the photographic image is one which produces an image which presents information, as if we had seen it with our own eyes; as if there was no medium or author intervening between the making and the viewing stage. (This is a so-called 'transparent' use of the medium, where realistic visual codes and devices serve to inhibit our understanding of how the image has been constructed, and in whose interests.)

If we consider how we encounter photographic images within the statutory education system – if we begin to add up all those textbooks, which stand as reference, providing the basis of our 'knowledge' – then we might begin to doubt what we have been taught. We might wonder if all such images are as neutral as they appear to be? Take one subject – History. The totality of the images we each carry and the way that they have been interpreted for us is only one of the problems. What of the absences? All the pictures which might speak of alternative histories or enable different interpretations – did they never get made; or have they merely been 'left out'? What is being suggested here is that we do not 'take-for-granted' what is on offer, but that we question the traditional curriculum, its forms of elitist knowledge and its processes of containment, through a method of critical questioning and testing, in relation to our own experience. The realist photographic image may well be one of the forms of limited and reactionary representations, but it can also be a tool for progressive analysis. We need to engage in a process of deconstructing the 'naturalness' of those images, ideas and values on offer from within the pages of our pasts, and to appropriate the power of photography, by constructing new visual forms. Unmasking old meanings is not sufficient – there is an increasingly urgent need to create new records, new meanings and social possibilities.

This process could begin with schooling. Why not an integrated programme of study, where imaging processes form part of the analytical 'tool-kit'? There would be a problem. We would begin to have a population which had an altered relation to the consumption of 'news', 'entertainment', 'advertising' and so on ... and anyone who has tried to write a course for the M.S.C. will understand that it is not in the service of the *status quo* to have a debate-based study – it leads to too many questions.

## Recent history

Since the 1960s it has been possible to study photography at an advanced level in a diversity of ways. Though the first degree course was not validated until 1973 there were many art colleges, polytechnics and other institutions offering two- and three-year full-time courses in the 'subject'. What this subject was had been broadly interpreted to include: science, documentary, industrial, portraiture, expressive, fashion and photojournalism among the possible angles as the basis for study. These courses were practice-based, with varying concessions to theoretical and technical areas. It was possible until the beginning of the 1980s for both the staff and students of these courses to persuade themselves that they were engaged in a vocational activity, with the likelihood of relevant employment at the end. Photography was taught as a set of skills utilised in the creative production of 'good photography', with the emphasis on pictorialism – the reduction of the world to a well-composed frame.

It was not long before the Council for National Academic Awards (CNAA) was giving degree status to most of the three-year courses around – in 1985 there were 10 such under-graduate courses in Great Britain, with over 40 other courses offering it as a component or option, at degree level. Though there is clearly a substantial increase in the provision here, still, some of the more well-known colleges have up to 15 applicants for each place. Though there are still many two-year courses (BTEC) as well, the status of the degree and the more 'academic' nature of the studies serves to privilege the '10' and generally enables the degree courses to maintain their standards of intake.

Within these courses, Photography has increasingly been aligned with Film and Video (or Television), and the marriage has not always been an easy one. The assumption that the common characteristics of camera-based media make them academically sound partners has been disproved by many years of negotiation on most of the full-time courses. A compromise is usually reached where all students undertake a common first year, in both theory and practice, specialising for the latter two years. This is more useful for the theoretical studies than for the practical areas and one of the London courses (London College of Printing) has decided to separate the disciplines altogether, dividing the combined course into two degrees as of 1985. At a formal level there will be the loss of those useful crossover debates between the two sets of students. However, it does mean that the staff are better able to construct a programme of study over three years, which focuses on the significant, yet diverse areas of knowledge considered necessary for the student. The advanced courses are becoming increasingly concerned with photography as a critical practice with the practical work being produced within a theoretical framework, rather than the two areas of study maintaining the strained distance of their respective heritages.

At the secondary level there have been several changes since the late 1960s. The development of media studies as a significant (though marginalised) subject within the curriculum led to the study of the mass media and images in general, in a way which was new to the system. A questioning attitude encouraged by teachers enabled students to begin to 'make sense' of their social environment, as well as problematising it. However, any radical advances tended to be contained by the restrictive nature of the secondary school curriculum, which put subjects into boxes, as if they had no relation to each other – instead of allowing productive analytical relations to be made between them. Apart from this development, there was the formal study of photography as an examinable subject in a manner which, until recently, reduced its capacities to that of technical, recording or expressive medium – with an emphasis on technique.

There are many exceptions to this tendency and they serve to identify the potential of the medium to be employed in a variety of ways, over and above the straightforward image-making tradition. This is partly because of the theoretical disciplines which teachers have utilised in the creation of teaching programmes, thereby broadening the defined areas of study. Photography need no longer be restricted to those areas of knowledge in which it is directly implicated; indeed, some of the media studies (and sometimes cultural studies) courses are broad enough to be an adequate substitute for the rest of the entire curriculum. This might sound rather far-fetched, but the references made to history, economics, technology, cultural production, the media, social forces, psychology, linguistics, etc., which characterise the best of the syllabi in question are far more useful to the average student than the specialist subjects, which do not necessarily help them to become more thinking and active members of society.

It is less easy to identify changes in the primary sector, due to the integrated nature of the curriculum. Photography is widely used at a craft and experimental level, but less so in the manner proposed here – though changes are occurring in this area as well. One of the best examples of this is a project sponsored by Ilford, Hampshire Education Authority and King Alfred's College in Winchester, where Chrisi Bailey (research fellow) is based. The project began in May 1984 and is intended to run for seven school terms – Ilford's brief was:

'to research and develop curricular programmes through the use of light sensitive materials and photographic processes as agents of learning, and to assess and evaluate how these may enhance learning, across the total primary curriculum'.

The Project is concerned with the place of photography in the 'communication of information about ideas, attitudes and experiences', believing that introducing children to the making of images (often without cameras) will be of help in the general process of interpreting visual information. The programme includes in-service training for local teachers from the six pilot schools, leading to the teachers taking control for themselves and working out how to integrate the Project into the general school work. This relationship between industry and education is becoming increasingly common as the government cuts bite deeper and teachers are forced to investigate the benevolent potential of other funding sources.

# The rationalisation of the education system

In the name of economy, efficiency and a greater relevance to the 'needs' of modern life, this government (and Labour before it) is responsible for the gradual dismantling of liberal tendencies throughout the education system.

Since 1974 successive governments have been responsible for restructuring the secondary sector, due to a decrease in the funding allocated and of projected student numbers. A process of closures, transfers and amalgamations of resources caused disruption in the short term, combined with a lack of concern for long-term strategy. The liberal tradition of education, namely a concern for the development of the individual, is becoming replaced by an industrial attitude, where the criteria of 'production' becomes reduced to the most cost-effective way of creating syllabi, work practices and structures, which 'produce' students who could more directly serve the needs of industry.

It is easy to identify this tendency across the entire educational spectrum, from the general cutting of public expenditure in this sector, to the rise of the power of the Manpower Services Commission and a recent suggestion that humanities should only be taught in the Universities, leaving the Polytechnics and Colleges for 'vocational' subjects. Progressive forces within teaching have become marginalised as the structures of 'privileged schooling' are being rebuilt and the criteria for assessing the viability of the public sector are becoming increasingly mechanistic. Currently we are undergoing a process of dividing up the field into the 'mental' and the 'manual' in a manner which will consolidate the divided nation we are becoming.

'It is true, of course, that deep damage is done as soon as education is understood as providing "what industry wants or needs", in the terms that it wants it (docility and discipline) and at the level that it wants it (within the existing horizons of skill and attainment). This reductionism – seizing the opportunity provided by recession to impose what otherwise would have had to be done by brute force or dull compulsion – is what is really going on in the youth training and other MSC-inspired programmes. (It is interesting that the state – a Labour-dominated one, please note – had to construct a new apparatus, the Manpower Services Commission, and retire an old one, the Departmant of Education and Science, in order to fit up education and industry in a desperate tandem.)'

*(Hall, 1983)*

Though the MSC is only a small part of the system, it is a growing one – one which is in the process of expanding its share of non-advanced, work-related study from 11% in 1984, to 25% in 1986/7. First of all this means that there will be a resultant decrease of funds controlled by Local Education Authorities and, secondly, it is an index of the current conservative attitude towards training as a replacement for education. The White Paper of 1984, 'Training for Jobs', could easily be read as an attack on Further Education within the Colleges, as it proposed the need 'to relate the courses more closely to the needs of the customer and in the most cost effective way'. At other times, the 'customer' might be thought of as the student – clearly, not in this case.

The contradiction at the centre of this ideology is so blatant that it can be overlooked – training for what? The decline of our traditional heavy industry and the replacement of worker by machine in all sectors has created the high levels of unemployment today. The systematic destruction of the employment potential of the steel, shipping and coal industries, amongst others, can hardly help create a market-place with the potential to take on so many new trainees.

There is a significance in this tendency for the future of photographic education. The study of Photography, Film and Television is an expensive process – the unit of resource (how much allocated to each student place) is never enough, as they are industrially-based media with production incurring costs which cannot be controlled by the educators. Measuring such courses by the standards of others (Business Studies) might allow us a greater proportion of resources, but if they are measured in pencils, then the production costs of silver-based and time-based media seems excessive. The arguments have been made and won many times for this area of arts education – but the aspirations of the new courses could be fundamentally undermined by applying the new concepts of efficiency. Already, courses are running on a decreasing funding level and at the degree level become trapped between the contradictory requirements of their LEA, the National Advisory Board (NAB) and the Council for National Academic Awards (CNAA).

It has become necessary to consolidate those advances made during the 1970s within the system *and* to look elsewhere for support (Industry, the Independent Sector, the EEC, etc....) in order to create a series of networks that cannot easily be dismantled. Education as a form of social control can be transformed in some 'spaces' into one of social understanding – and, despite the marginalisation of enthusiasms, attitudes and work practices developed in the last two decades, there is a diversity of progressive structures and projects in existence today.

# The actual and the potential

Within the confines of the educational framework there have been many advances, both for photography as a discrete subject and as a component of broader areas of media studies, cultural studies, current affairs, etc. It has been widely developed as an integrating factor within the curriculum and as a means of relating the students' 'lived'. experience with their formal syllabus. (The Cockpit is a good example of this approach.) And the links between photography and film have been beneficially exploited by many teachers creating an educational space for a critical practice. The potential for the expansion of this area of study would seem to be in those possibilities of making relationships with institutions and frameworks outside the statutory education system.

In 1985 the Arts Council of Great Britain published a report by Jim Hornsby, 'Independent Photography and Photography in Education'. It is an extensive compilation of the range of projects which have been state-funded and which have attempted to work with a range of educational institutions in the pursuit of imaginative visual practices. Hornsby makes a distinction between the 'educational' and the 'educative' – maintaining that the former refers to activities within the system and the latter may be said to refer to 'many, if not all' arts activities. The report emphasises the artistic status of the medium over any other, but does usefully describe the details of many projects which have far wider concerns than this. (Readers should refer to this document for specific information on schemes over the last 10 years.) What does become clear is the potential for constructing links between different social formations – a process which requires elements of commitment, energy and understanding to have a chance of succeeding. (In March 1985, the ACGB organised a conference, 'Photographers in Education', in an attempt to investigate this potential. A large body of people participated from all parts of the country, yet the day was not a success, for the groundwork had not been sufficiently laid. Suspicion and resistance oscillated with openness and radical suggestions throughout the proceedings – indeed, the Director of a major photographic organisation expressed the view that: 'this conference has been arranged for the educational sector to use photographers as a cheap source of labour'.)

There could never be an expectation that the 'independent sector' can compensate for a shortfall within the educational one, which has an overall budget of over £12 billion, as opposed to under £1 million for the state-subsidised photo-sector. What was being floated was how each system could benefit from the activities in the other – an exchange of ideas, practices, funding, and so on. The difficulty was that the brief was both too broad and too specific. Too broad because it quickly became impossible to conceptualise the diversity of possible relationships across the whole spectrum of education; yet too narrow, as the exclusion of other types of social organisation (the community movement, the trade unions, industry, local authority institutions, etc.) meant that we were only considering part of a possible answer.

Instead of conceiving how education can 'make use of' the subsidised sector, perhaps we should reverse the idea. How might photography organisations and projects benefit from a relationship with education and what reciprocal effect could there be for courses? How about teachers on secondment to projects, and galleries as an extension of the classroom? Of course this is already happening and the recent Arts Council stress on the importance of the 'educational' element of their clients' activities has ensured that new ways of bringing the two sectors together are being developed all the time (see Funding for details of projects). There has been a vital circular effect between these areas of production since the early 1970s and, despite the 'disorganising' taking place within the educational system (in the name of 'rationalisation'), it is time for us to help ourselves by supporting all those practices in photography that have helped create the radical and divergent photographic culture from which we all benefit.

Terry Dennett and Jo Spence
# Ten years of Photography Workshop

As a group which has been involved in many debates within photography and the politics of representation as they have emerged recently in this country, we feel slightly strange in writing about ourselves. Ever since Photography Workshop was formed in 1974, from the shared photographic and political interests of its founder members, it has either been ignored *as a group* (most of its work is attributed to single members) or else rejected outright (as in the case of our working hard to found, run and then write for *Camerawork* magazine). And one of the ironies of the left and women's movement must surely be this: that groups which are set up and do innovative work usually split into differing political segments; these segments then go on to found new dynasties, or just quietly fade away. In time, the original differences, cracks, fissures and explosions come to be neatly laundered over, erased from the memory of those involved because they are too painful, not fully known to those who came later because 'nobody told us about it' and, finally, mythologised through the accounts of others writing about them from outside. It is surely contradictory, then, that very little is actually known about most groups who are involved in the politics of representation; that, although they themselves raise fundamental questions about representation, the question of how they represent *themselves* is almost always ignored. This prevents the emergence of any serious mapping process becoming discernible from 'outside'. It also prevents the development of dialectical or polemical discussion in any real sense and means, too, that we go on 'inventing the wheel' over and over again.

In this sense, then, Photography Workshop is an unusual group. It started with two core members and 10 years later it still has the same two core members. And this is *our* account. The drive for the work of the group has always come out of the obsessions, bitterness and passions of these two members, sometimes collaborating with others, or working together, or working alone. We believe it is this passion and determination to survive in the face of all criticism that has helped us to be here today. However, in the course of this survival the group has changed drastically. We started with the ultimate in 'independence' – poverty – moved on to the use of voluntary labour, donations, ploughing back the earnings of members; we always housed ourselves in our own home and very latterly decided to apply for a grant. We have ended up with a combination of all these things. We now have a small grant from the Greater London Council for very specific purposes, still work voluntarily, and are very poor. But nobody tells us what to do – we can make a lot of noise or be silent if we need to. But we don't have to behave like performing seals for the grant-funding bodies. Throughout we have always attacked particular types of opportunistic radical-professionalism and have tried to open up the very big question of how to rework and redefine the term 'amateur'.

The question of labels hangs around all groups: we have found it strategically useful, for instance, that one of our core members has been blandly labelled as a 'feminist photographer' (a very generalised term), whilst on the other hand we are often called vulgar marxists (when we know we are not). In fact, much of our work has been about history, both of the individual subject – 'Who am I?', 'How do I know that?', 'How did I get to be that way?', 'How will new knowledge of the past affect my future activity?'; as well as being  interested in the broader political perspectives of belonging to a class (however fragmented or ill defined), or understanding how our race, age and gender shape our conscious and unconscious desires. We have been interested, too, in the relationship between these questions and the institutionalised bases of photographic practices.

What follows is a progressive chronology of our work for the past 10 years. We have tried not to ascribe motives, beyond our initial aims, and to be as descriptive as possible about our attempts to help in the broader cultural and political struggles to change society. We do not see this as a trumpet-blowing exercise – our history as a group has been fraught with mistakes, but each of them has taught us to grow and to know better how to survive and to share. Underneath everything has been a desire to pass on information and to make it possible for others to realise their political and personal potential in the widest sense. Above all else we think it is important to say that the 10 years' work brought us a total of £8,000 from funding bodies – which works out at an incredibly low annual average. The rest we raised ourselves. We think that working on this scale should be seen as a useful political activity because we always hope that a point will emerge when there are enough small groups within photographic practice to become federated, so that we can all increase our power base through the making of alliances.

Photography Workshop Limited is an independent educational, research, publishing and resource project. Founded in 1974, it carried out an extensive programme until 1979 of workshops on photography – lecturing, research, exhibition production and publishing. In 1980 it became a registered charity and non-profit making limited company (registration no. 280873). Its programme since 1980 up until the present time has been based around an extensive research and retrieval programme, archival details of which are below. Photography Workshop has helped many groups in the community, labour and women's movement, and adult education, towards a better understanding of the progressive potential for making and using photography.

The Workshop's research programme has, until recently, been carried out on a self-funded basis, without grant aid, through donations, sales of literature, lecturing, teaching fees and exhibitions. It currently includes work on visual representations of labour, race, gender and sexuality in the popular mass media. We also carry out a programme of extensive research/retrieval into the technological and social history of photography, as well as into the cultural history of the labour movement. Our overall perspective is towards the use of such material in community and educational/arts projects/workshops in London and elsewhere.

We have been instrumental in helping to set up a number of other projects: these include the setting up of the Half Moon Photography Workshop and the magazine *Camerawork* jointly with the Half Moon Gallery Ltd. (later to be called *Camerawork*); initiating and working with the Hackney Flashers Women's Photography Collective; publishing the first serious collection of essays on photography, history and politics in this country (*Photography/Politics: One*); publishing the broadsheet *The Worker Photographer*, as well as various teaching jackdaw kits and posters.

At the same time, members involved in research have systematically written up their work in a variety of educational magazines, as well as setting up or collaborating in teaching workshops, lecturing throughout London and the home counties and trying, with the aid of slide shows, to make accessible a variety of differing approaches to photography. Such approaches also entailed the making of small teaching exhibitions, as well as writing in cultural and art journals.

The Workshop has also produced a variety of permanent and temporary touring exhibitions, and has much partly finished work now in the pipeline. These exhibitions (many of which can be interchanged or juxtaposed with each other to suit particular needs) have been used in arts centres, community and youth projects, as well as within a whole range of formal and informal teaching situations, weekend and day schools and at conferences. We have established a wide network of users throughout the country as well as in London.

At the moment, because our voluntary staffing situation is so overloaded, we have placed several of our touring shows with the Cockpit Gallery Holborn, where they are used extensively by educational, community and youth projects.

A brief chronology of projects from 1974 to 1983 follows.

## 1975

Working with children using do-it-yourself, home-built cameras and photographic equipment (the 'discovery' method). This culminated in *The Home Made Show:* alternative and low-cost technology in photography. It was done by Terry Dennett in collaboration with the South Island Children's Workshop.

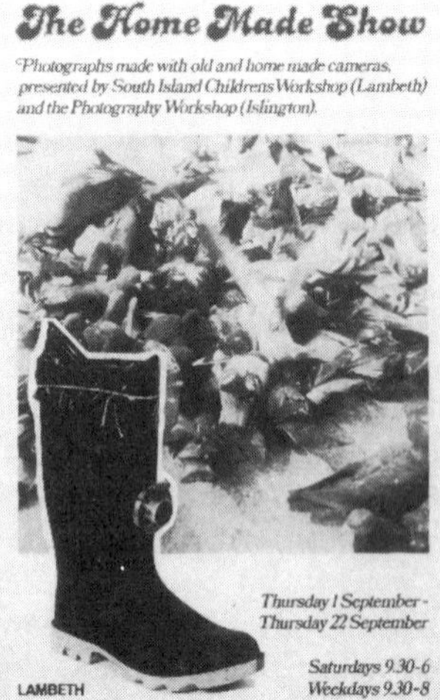


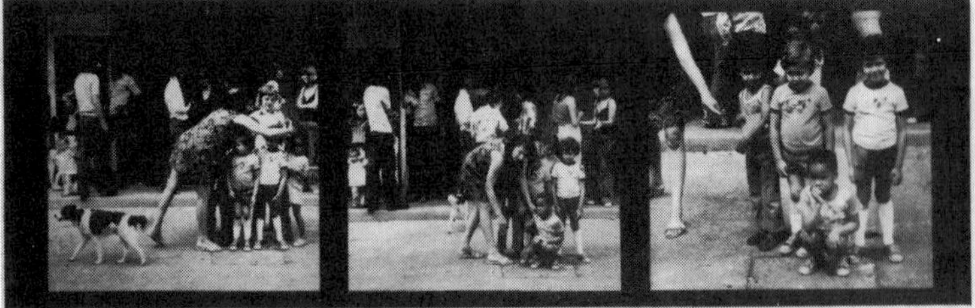


Looking at representations of children in British photography: a collaboration between Children's Rights Workshop (of which Jo Spence was a founder member) and Ikon. This culminated in the touring show *Children Photographed.*

Photography Workshop was set up in 1974 and immediately became a programme of workshops to teach photography to children, outside of formal schooling. In those early days most of this work was done at weekends within the adventure playground movement, in free schools and in independent children's projects. At the same time we began to research the 'hidden history' of the cultural activities of the labour movement and the trade unions, particularly centring upon the period of the General Strike in 1926. Out of this came a travelling exhibition.

In 1975 the Photography Workshop temporarily merged with the Half Moon Gallery Ltd. Out of this merger came the Half Moon Photography Workshop and the production of *Camerawork* magazine. Various other shows were researched and produced by us at this time, but are not shown here. At HMPW an Education and Photography group was set up, which convened and ran four weekend workshops on 'Photography and Youth'. These brought together such apparently disparate elements as critical input from commercial educational television, the BFI Education Department's work on the semiology of the image, work on literacy and with welfare agencies, work with handicapped children, and drew upon the advanced ideas from existing youth projects in the field, such as Blackfriars Settlement.

# 1974-76

*The Thirties and Today* was produced by the Labour History Research Group of Photography Workshop under the umbrella of HMPW. This exhibition is still available from us.

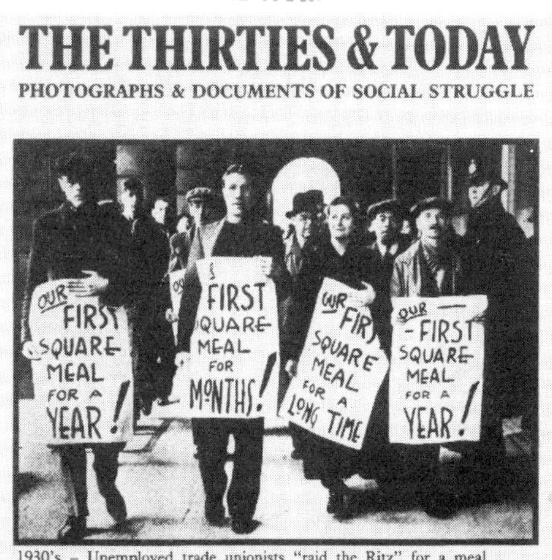

1930's – Unemployed trade unionists "raid the Ritz" for a meal

# Photography Workshop's original statement of aims

To provide an ongoing research, information and advice resource, and to publish and distribute in whatever form most useful, such research, basic bibliographies, etc.

To continue to establish a permanent, readily available, non-commercial photographic archive which will also encourage the depositing of negative and slide collections and thus ensure their continued use after the owner's death.

To continue to establish a register of slides and prints available for loan at minimal cost for campaigns, lectures, educational projects and community arts use.

To positively encourage self-reliance in photographic users and makers, with the aim of working towards group activity, collective practice and the pooling of resources and information as a general principle in contemporary photography.

To systematize the investigation of alternate chemical and photo technology so as to develop a basic independence from monopolistic companies. (This is an essential first step towards demystifying technology.)

To initiate projects and promote interest in the critical use of photography and various media as educational and communicational tools.

To self-publish concise educational worksheets on various aspects of photography, which can also eventually be put together as a teaching aid. Also to make available technical and useful information in poster and broadsheet form.

To promote the collection of existing local and photo history from all sources, including public and private institutional archives, old personal and family photographs, long-established local commercial photographers, local history and conservation groups, local newspaper files, and with special emphasis on the family album as a valuable social document.

To encourage the photographic recording of personal, group and local history by people themselves, with or without the assistance of professional photographers.

To encourage the preservation of existing industrial and commercial photographs and work records, and to guarantee their safekeeping as documents of historical and political use which are readily accessible.

To continue to help to participate in the setting up of short-term groups to carry out specific documentary/mediation projects, as requested by educational, community and sub-cultural groups. Additionally, to act as intermediaries in the exchange of details between those wishing to teach or learn photographic skills.

(*Note:* Some of these aims have been realized – others not.)

## 1977-79

Photography Workshop was involved in the calling together and early coordination of the Hackney Flashers Collective, an agitprop group who produced exhibitions and posters around issues of women, work and domesticity – moving away from simple 'window on the world' techniques to ask questions about mediation and ideology. They also produced a teaching slide pack and a much-used bank of images on class and gender. One of their exhibitions was included in the *Three Perspectives in Photography* exhibition at the Hayward Gallery after being used extensively throughout the country.

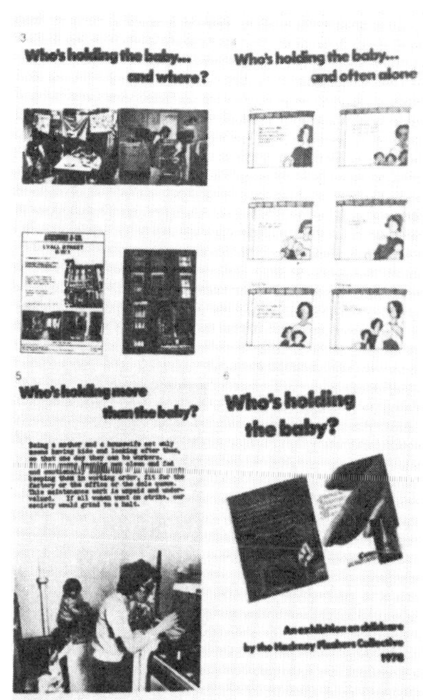


'The previous photographs were positive and promoted self-recognition but could not expose the complex social and economic relationships within which the women's subordination is maintained...'

## 1977-78

Critical autobiographical work on a 'history of self' in relation to a 'history of photography'; questioning the function of family photographs in the production of knowledge about our lives. This laminated exhibition was produced for the *Three Perspectives in Photography* exhibition at the Hayward Gallery and later made into a TV arts programme by BBC2/*Arena*. (Both the above exhibitions are still available as laminated touring shows from the Cockpit Gallery, Holborn.)

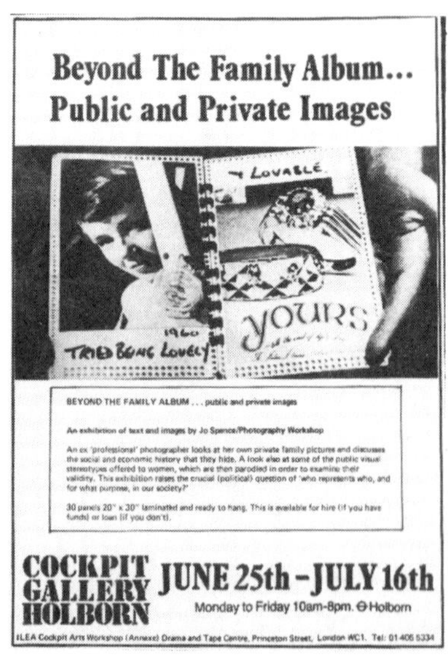


The re-emergence of Photography Workshop after the split with the Half Moon was very productive. As well as working on the two new publications, we set up a series of evening classes on *Feminism and Photography* in collaboration with the Cockpit Cultural Studies Department.

## 1978-79

*Photography/Politics: One*, which was self-published, was distributed for us by Southern Distribution. We printed two editions and had a wide readership in all English-speaking countries, as well as throughout Europe. The book was produced by four editors who worked over a period of 18 months on a voluntary basis, with the final calling in of a designer. As we produced the first English language socialist 'annual' of photography, we are obviously glad to have

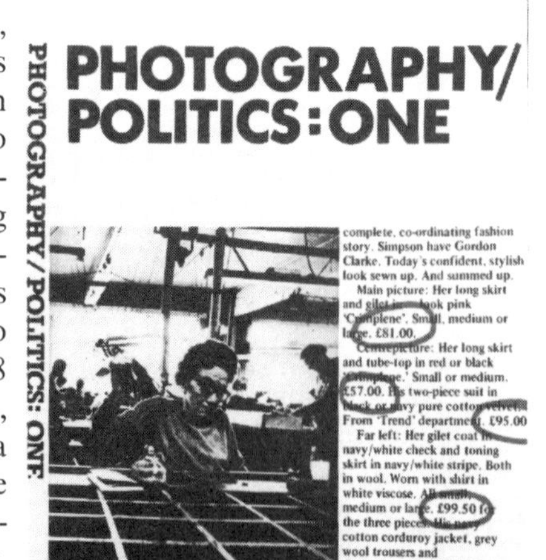

done this work. In retrospect, though, we would never want to get involved in this type or scale of production and finance again. The cost of printing was paid for out of Jo's severance pay from HMPW, and the rest came from donations and forward subscriptions.

'*Photography/Politics* breaks important new ground, not least in its quiet demonstration of the total inadequacy of traditional approaches to photographic media and their effects upon our lives...'

Time Out *review*

## 1978-79

*The Worker Photographer* was produced by a small voluntary group working within the labour movement, under the Photography Workshop umbrella. It attempted to open up once again discussions started within the socialist movement of the 1920s and 1930s about the class nature of photography and its specific forms and importance as a weapon of cultural struggle.

It had some success in showing the 'hidden story' of labour photography and journalism, exemplified by the concepts of the amateur 'worker photographer' and 'worker correspondent' and was responsible for the re-introduction of these concepts back into the language of the radical movement in Britain. On a practical level, however, it was a premature experiment from which no further journals or stable groupings developed, to our knowledge.

This exhibition is still available direct from us.

## 1980-82

An extensive period of research, workshops, lecturing, teaching, preparation of teaching materials. As an example, we produced:

*Remodelling Photo History:* a collaboration between two photographers. This was done, initially, for inclusion in a show on British Photography prepared for the Massachusetts Institute of Technology, later touring America. We also made a small, laminated version for use for teaching in this country, which is still available direct from Photography Workshop.

This work attempted to look at the broader institutional base of photography. In looking at various photographic discourses, we endeavoured to foreground their inter-connectedness through our reworking of photographic styles and genres. This was a conscious move away from the (autobiographical) idea of *images of self* into the more psychoanalytic and post-structuralist-based disciplines which have examined *self as image*.

'We wanted to get away from the dry didacticism which pervades so much worthy work on photographic theory and to provide, instead, a kind of revolt from within the ranks ... This is a tiny statement which should be seen in the tradition of "worker photography" – our

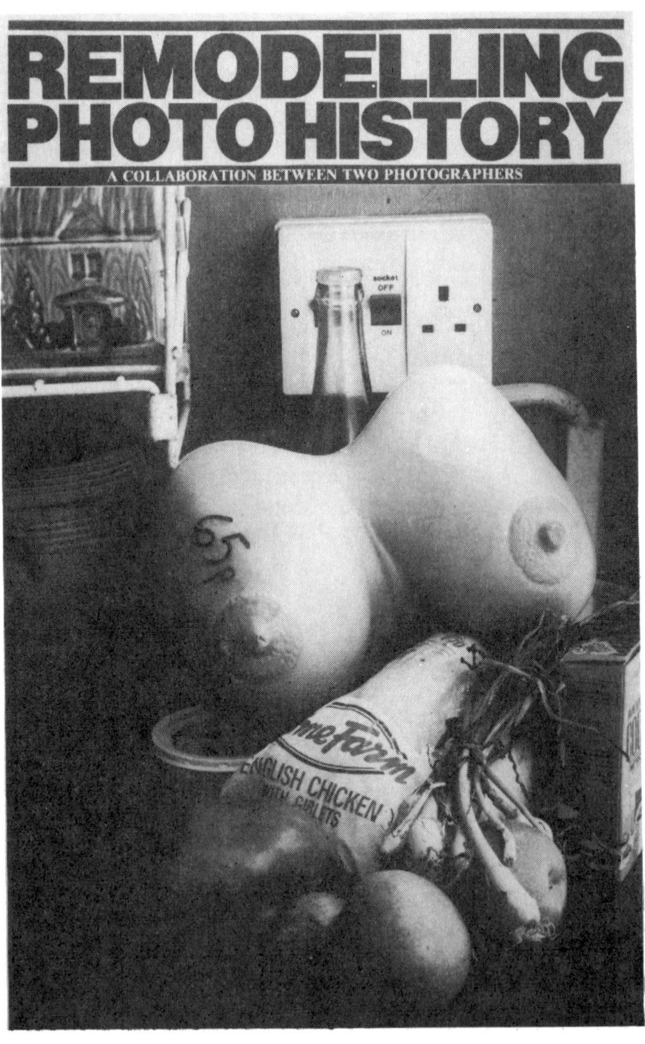

workplace being photography itself, as a production process in which we are daily involved ...'   *From* TEN.8 *magazine*

We are very glad to have been asked to contribute to this collection of accounts of how different groups work. Most publications don't ask groups actually to speak for themselves, but lash together sets of so-called facts which are then threaded through with a (now invisible) pre-existent argument which the researcher or writer already had, and which then structures the dominant point of view in the writing.

Accounting for group work is in itself difficult, and this is no exception. Photography Workshop has always been small. Two of us set it up and we remain at the end, long after other small groups have come and gone. So this is our view of events. We have never tried to hide our political leanings (towards challenging a class-dominated society): we are not popular frontists, not ultra leftists, nor separatists. We believe that different strategies are needed at different times, and so our work has often been interventionist, as with our decision to join up with the Half Moon Gallery in order to gain a wider platform for our views through the journal *Camerawork*. But because we adamantly stuck to our views for the period we were there, by challenging the dominant view of documentary photo-graphy and the sexism and racism inherent in all existing photography, and because we tried to introduce notions of ideology and technological determinants into the work we produced and published, and because we always insisted that we bear in mind that we live, work, have pleasure and are ripped off in a class society, we were eventually expelled from the Half Moon Photography Workshop, and Jo was fired from *Camerawork*. However, this did not mean the end of Photography Workshop. This is the nature of small, interventionist groups; they form alliances and work where it seems politically useful, they don't overload themselves with enormous organisational structures, nor do they court large grants from funding bodies which often mean that they can end up doing what the funding bodies 'think advisable' at the moment. They just quietly get on with their programme, as we have done, now dormant, now active, now in a major gallery, now with a factory-based group, now in an Adult Education Centre's evening classes, now writing for *Screen* magazine. Whatever and wherever it was expedient – and we will continue with this policy. This has always meant that we have seriously considered who we were preparing materials for, and so have formulated 'ways of speaking' and 'ways of showing' which were most suitable to each audience.

# 1974-84: Setting up an archive

The Workshop has now accumulated a very large body of work which forms a more than rudimentary archive. This consists of 35mm colour transparencies, 35mm black and white and colour negatives, black and white and colour prints, a collection of xerox reprints, pamphlets, books and audio visual aids. The work has concentrated on several different areas.

1.  The collection of 'popular' and ephemeral images from children's books and comics, certain thematic issues from newspapers, advertising, hoardings and posters, specialist and trade journals (our particular concern here has been to keep evidence of the everyday activity of the printed mass media, especially in regard to sexist materials depicting women and children).

2.  Research project materials which document the social and cultural history within the labour and trade union movements, with particular emphasis on photography, theatre and their own media. We have also conducted numerous interviews with cultural workers from the 1920s and 30s, and these form part of this archive.

3.  A resource which concentrates on the social and technical history of photography from the 1870s onwards (currently researched up to the 1930s), which will continue right up to the present period as and when we are able to do this work. This material is being culled from various public and private collections within the Greater London Area, many of which are themselves very under-staffed. Thus the possibility looms that the retrieval of such materials might be prevented in the near future by the lack of facilitation to researchers who need access to such material. Our retrieval programme is totally understaffed within our own project and at the moment we have a huge backlog of material which has been recorded onto negative but which is awaiting printing, indexing and housing.

4.  A book/pamphlet/reprint collection, which also includes a small collection of postcards and radical cartoons.

5.  Copy negatives of archive of the *Workers' Film and Photo League*, with xeroxes of supporting material, frame stills made from original films, etc.

6.   35mm slide collection of ephemera and advertisements of present period, concentrating on material which would be useful for discussions of sexism, racism and class bias.

7.   Cartoon collection:

   1.   This concentrates on contemporary cartoon publishing in the popular mass media (again concentrating on those which are sexist, racist and show class bias, as we have found these to be extremely useful within educational and media projects).

   2.   From the labour and trade union press (largely radical and socialist cartoon material).

8.   Postcard collection: this has concentrated on the collecting of materials which indicate that the postcard is itself a form of social history, particularly of people's 'life and labour'. Through the use of this and the cartoon collections we have been able to demonstrate in workshops the mechanism through which cartooning and caricature have their 'effect'. The basic mode of stereotyping to be found in both collections highlights certain arguments very effectively when teaching about mediation, and the visual representation of social reality.

We feel that the materials we have and are collecting can make an important contribution to many labour, trade union and community publications, by improving their visual appeal and helping to change the ways in which ideas are presented, which is usually through dense pages of type.

# Postscript

In 1982 we sought a total grant of £15,000 towards salaries and the promotion of the archive (other running costs to be met, as in the past, through our general fund-raising activities). In June, 1983, we received a grant of around £6,000 from the Greater London Council for which we are very grateful. However, we have decided not to apply to them for further funding as we are very unhappy about the bureaucratic ways in which funding is done, the interminable delays and intrusions, the uncertainties of their commitment to continuing grants, and the forthcoming political situation.

# 1974-1984 The setting up of the archive

From our Photo History Collection: examples from the photographic trade press at the beginning of this century give a clue to the exploitation of working women within a still-emerging mass image industry.

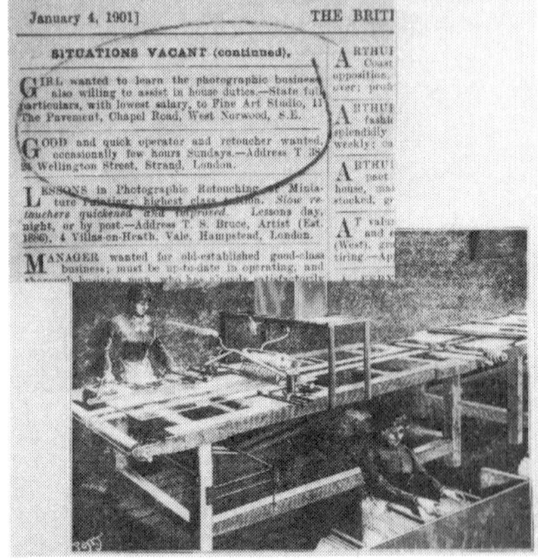

We would emphasize that this material does *not* form the basis of a commercial archive, but that we only charge a small search fee for the cost of making prints. In many instances no copyright is involved, so there is no question of material being used commercially. The archive exists, rather, as a resource for researchers, educationalists, cultural workers and people engaged in a variety of artistic and educational pursuits. Much of the material takes as its focus the need for groups to be aware that *they can represent themselves* through photography, images (both moving and still) and language. In the past we have found that the non-commercial nature of the archive has meant that it is especially welcome to those seeking materials who have little or no funding (e.g. projects by the unemployed, nursery campaigns, etc.).

# 1983

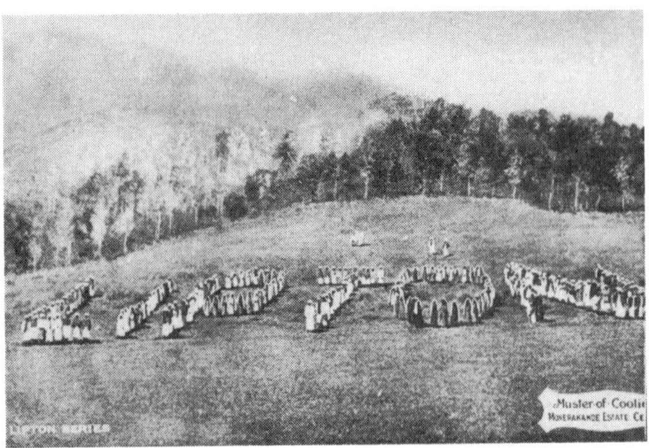

From a series of picture postcards published in tear-out booklet form, purchased in our local market. It shows a 'Muster of Coolies' spelling out the name of their employer on the hillside of the tea plantation in Ceylon.

An example of a cartoon from an American labour journal of the 1930s.

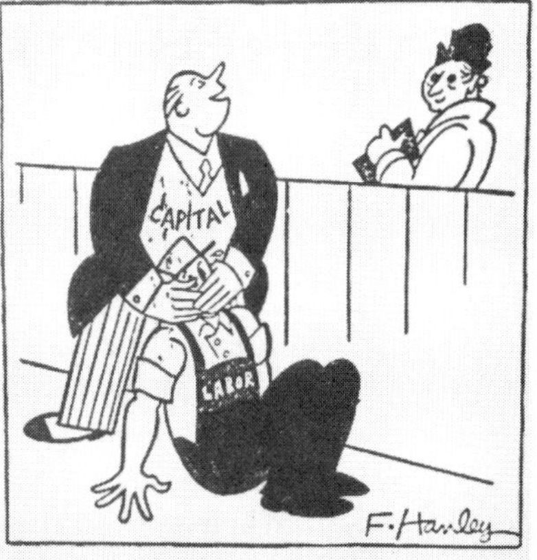


"*Oh, good morning, Miss Perkins . . . yes, everything is allright.*"

'We have begun to realize that the most promising fields of enterprise for our ever increasing community, the most profitable markets for our wares, may some day be found in places which are now the darkest corners of the earth; and that the half-clothed savage, just emerging from the brute condition, is a human being capable of being educated, in the near future, into a customer for British trade and a contributor to the world's wealth . . .'

*From the introduction to* The Living Races of Mankind, *published by Hutchinson and Co. early this century (part of the Photography Workshop Library).*

# 1984

*The Crisis Documentation Project* now in progress back-to-back with *Fairy Tales and Photography.*

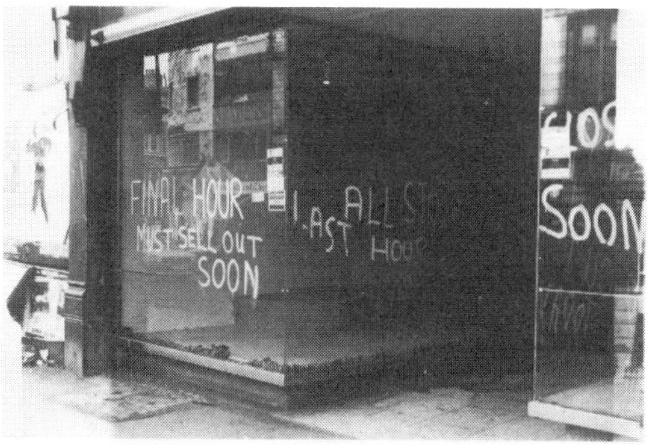

'The starting-point of critical elaboration is the consciousness of what one really is, and is "knowing thyself" as a product of the historical process to date, which has deposited in you an infinity of traces, without leaving an inventory.'
*From* The Prison Notebooks
*by Gramsci*

'In 1928 they said a depression could not happen, can you believe those same voices in 1983? This is what happens in the downwave. Whole countries go bankrupt. Banks large and small go bust. Companies crash, whole industries disappear and millions lose their jobs. House prices tumble. Building societies shake, office blocks become unsaleable, land values slide, and share prices slump. People live differently, think differently, wear different clothes, watch different films, hum different songs, and see sex differently...'
*From* Downwave *(Surviving the Second Great Depression) by Robert Beckman.*

The everyday Fantasy/Reality of the High Street

*Autumn, 1983, Terry Dennett/Jo Spence*

Andrew Dewdney and Martin Lister
# Photography, school and youth culture: the Cockpit Arts Project

*Practices and perspectives on photography in education from the
Department of Cultural Studies at the Cockpit Arts Workshop**

(Opinions and statements made in this article do not necessarily
represent the views of the Cockpit Arts Workshop or the Inner
London Education Authority.)

The Department of Cultural Studies was formally established in
September, 1978. Between 1976 and '78 it operated under the title of
Art Department and prior to that it was the Visuals Team. It is one of
five teams which comprise the Cockpit Arts Workshop, which is
maintained by the Community Education and Careers branch of the
Inner London Education Authority. The Cockpit has been in
existence for 15 years and operates from a purpose built theatre-in-
the-round in Marylebone, London, and at an annexe in an old school
in Holborn. The Cockpit has a history of changing orientations to
and definitions of Arts in Education and the Community. Its earliest
definition was around integrated performing arts. At present the
other teams are Music, Youth Arts, Theatre-in-Education and
Theatre Events.

The current work of the department is covered by the following
areas:

Practical photography projects with young people in schools,
timetabled as part of their school work and undertaken in
collaboration with their teachers.

Practical photography projects with young people out of school.

The running of the Cockpit Gallery Holborn for showing the
photographic work of young people or the work of individuals and

---

*This article contains extracts from a pamphlet entitled *Cultural Studies in
Schools published by the Department of Cultural Studies, 1984.*

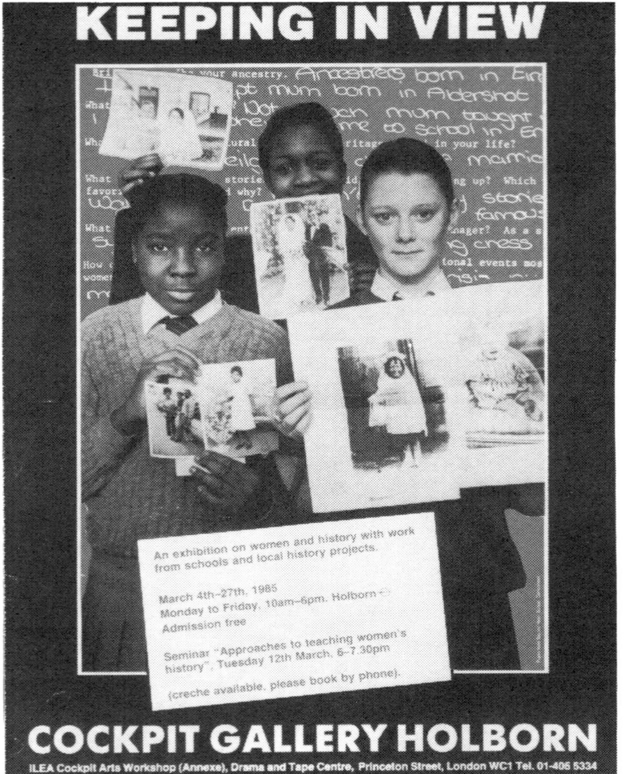

KEEPING IN VIEW
An exhibition on women and history with work from schools and local history projects.
March 4th-27th, 1985
Monday to Friday, 10am-6pm. Holborn
Admission free
Seminar "Approaches to teaching women's history", Tuesday 12th March, 6-7.30pm
(creche available, please book by phone).
COCKPIT GALLERY HOLBORN
ILEA Cockpit Arts Workshop (Annexe), Drama and Tape Centre, Princeton Street, London WC1 Tel. 01-405 5334


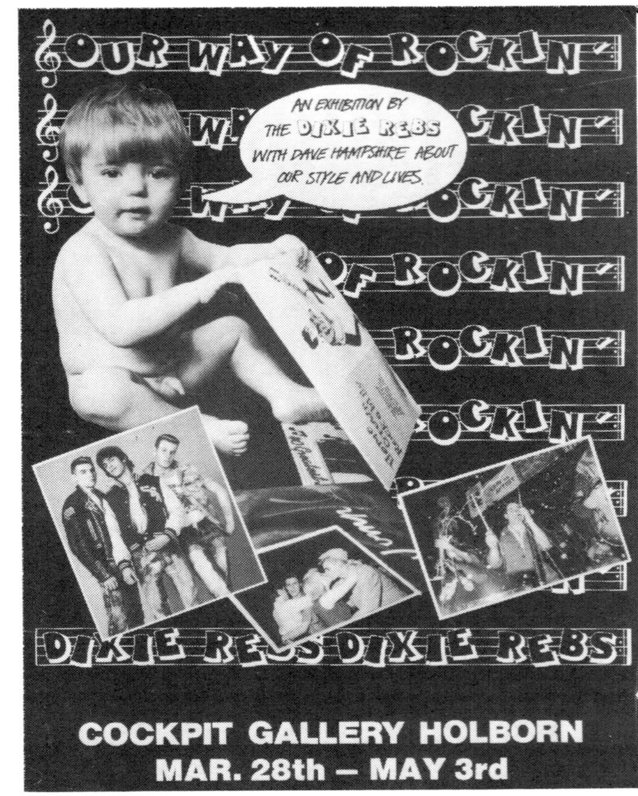

OUR WAY OF ROCKIN'
AN EXHIBITION BY
THE DIXIE REBS
WITH DAVE HAMPSHIRE ABOUT
OUR STYLE AND LIVES.
DIXIE REBS DIXIE REBS
COCKPIT GALLERY HOLBORN
MAR. 28th — MAY 3rd

groups which we consider of relevance to young people and those who work with them.

The provision of a Touring Exhibition system for travelling work to youth clubs, community venues, schools and colleges.

The publication of young people's photo-text work.

The publication of a bi-annual journal, *Schooling and Culture*, to constitute an audience and network of cultural workers who can share their experience, analysis and practice.

# The Work of the Cockpit Cultural Studies Department

> Without conscious and active engagement with the content of young people's resistance, teaching is bound to reproduce more than it transforms.

*Negotiating the curriculum*

Cultural studies does not exist as a distinct curriculum subject. What do exist and have to be met by us are definite assumptions about the value and distinctive features of the subject discipline which we are going to work within. In English, for instance, it may be a stress on a group's needs to acquire basic literacy skills, or to comprehend the meaning and conventional means of a set text. In social studies it could be to gather and organise facts and opinions or to describe a taken for granted aspect of roles in everyday life. So whenever we set out to work from a subject base we have to make connections and build a reasonable framework which allows for extension and redefinition of the conventional curriculum subject.

Basically this can be done in two ways. Firstly, by taking the concerns of the area of study and its mode of work, say reading, writing, discussion and note-taking, and finding ways of integrating and extending them into forms of practical, expressive work. This will also usually involve work on some form of public, or at least audience-orientated production – a pamphlet, a display or exhibition, posters, video, film or tape-slide.

Secondly, and this is made possible because of the awareness and interests of the teachers who seek joint work with us, by looking for approaches to issues and study material through cultural experience and in contemporary and popular ways.

When considering the broad proposition of a cultural studies within secondary schooling it is important to remember that our own work in this area is always the outcome of a specialist agency coming into a collaborative relationship with a teacher and a group of young people in mainstream schooling. This is, in itself, a determining factor upon what is possible and achievable. There is no blueprint for cultural studies as a straightforward curriculum option. Which is why we've set out to define an approach which is, we believe, applicable across the curriculum and in relationship to current timetables and curricula arrangements.

The work we do is carried out within present conditions and limits, with subject teachers, timetabled groups and available resources.

At one time we made contact with teachers and prospective groups of young people through our project publicity, which was circulated to all ILEA schools. This has steadily become unnecessary as a network of contacts and collaborators has been built through projects undertaken and our working relationships within a number of schools and related agencies has developed. The majority of work we do is now generated through this historical and contemporary network.

We depend upon collaboration with teachers who are concerned to develop their subject practice. We work where there is a real possibility and a will to make the space and the structure in which pupils' lived experience and cultural practice can become the raw materials of an educational project. This amounts to a generous definition of where such projects can be situated in current schooling. The majority of our work has been taken up with non-examinable options, either in relationship to exam groups, but more consistently by non-academic groups. The competitive examination system is still the backbone of the curriculum, currently being stiffened by central government and, in more complex ways, extended by local authorities. The range of certification is currently expanding and defining newer forms of assessment. Work in schools which develops from and responds to local and immediate experience is usually marginalised for those young people who are bounded by the competitive system which, of course, in some ways or another they all are. For a significant proportion, however, certification is not a continually valued emphasis. So in differing degrees all subject teachers are presented with the problem of engaging young people's immediate interest in their subjects. Thus teachers have come to have an inevitable autonomy within some parts of their subjects with some students, for some of their time. This is the usual space for the cultural practices we have developed to date.

There are more than casual reasons why a cultural studies practice has been particularly appropriate and taken up within certain subjects and for a certain age group. In principle these are not reasons which exclude other interests, but they do create a specific profile to much recent work. The overall characterisation is one of a concern for the exploration of developing social identities. This connects a number of subject interests in the arts and humanities. In English and in Social Studies there is an obvious interest. A further developing interest has emerged through the increasing number of vocational preparation courses which include a concern for future adult roles and responsibilities. All this has been work for upper secondary pupils where there is a closeness to adult worlds beyond school.

We work over a number of time scales, assessing what is possible and what our approach should be according to the amount of continuous time we have available. The majority of our work has a two-year time scale. We meet a group for the first time at the beginning of their fourth year and work through until the end of the fifth with possible extensions for some pupils after they leave school, become unemployed, or take up some form of vocational training. In terms of the length of each working session we have to negotiate half days. Any less time than this has proven to be unworkable. This is largely due to the amount of time that is needed for young people to organise themselves around project work which involves a range of connected practices, to organise their materials, to pick up things where they left off, to carry out practical tasks and have time to consider and talk, to interact with other members of the group, as well as finding time to concentrate on a piece of work in hand. In most cases we work both in school and at an off-site base, either a community darkroom close to the school or at our own central London base which has a teaching darkroom. The practical reason for this is the absence of darkrooms in schools large enough to be used by a group of 10 to 12 people (the usual half-class-size groups we work with) even when, as is usually the case, work is planned so that not more than half of the group need to use the darkroom at any one time. Having secured an off-site base, we make use of the opportunity to shift the more formal and schoolish relations of teacher and pupil to both more casual and adult relations in work. The group often change out of school uniform in the break between leaving school and arriving (if that's possible and if they wear a uniform in any case). Teachers' first names are used, somebody makes tea or coffee or goes out to bring some in. The pressures and backdrop of the school are absent for the time being. None of this means that some teacherly cajoling and occasional laying down of the law can be completely avoided. In all cases, as the group comes to value the work, the working relations and conditions, these conventional roles have rarely to be adopted.

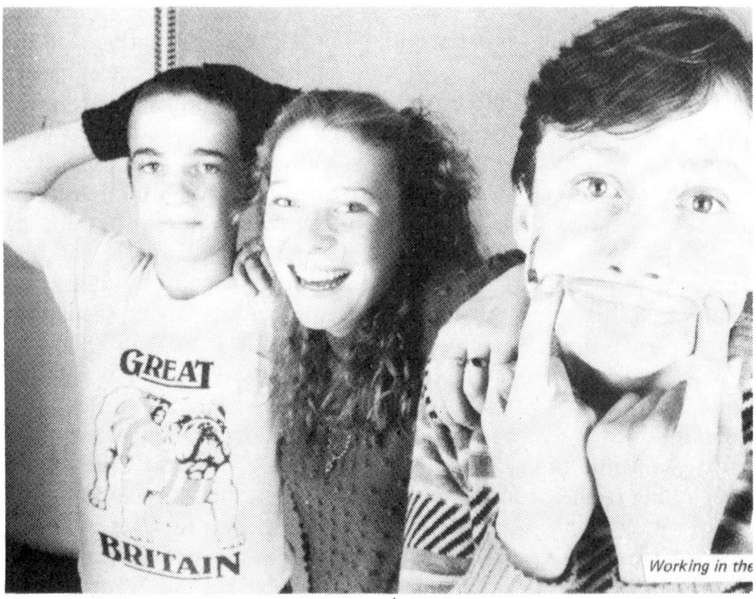



*Working in the studio*

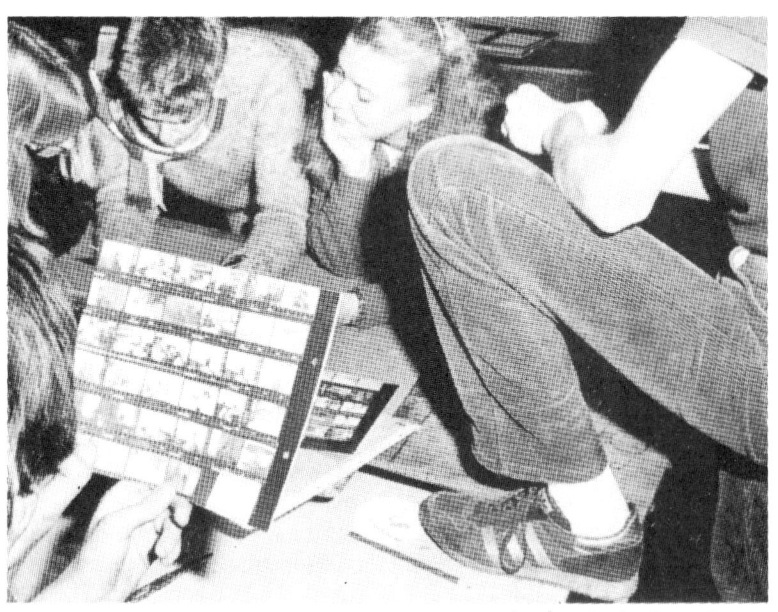

*Selecting what to print in the darkroom*

# Photography and cultural studies

There is some difficulty involved in explaining and locating the place of photography in our work. This is apparent because we describe our work and its range of concerns as Cultural Studies, while, at another level, we are most often seen working as teachers of photography. What is the relationship?

If we define our work as developing a serious educational practice of cultural expression or, in another emphasis, as finding ways of basing general educational practice on young people's views and experience, then we have also to say that photography is *not indispensable* to such a project.

However, through a practical involvement with a wide range of visual media (as educational practices), both autographic and mechanical, we came to recognise a number of important qualities which are either specific to, or especially present in, photography.

This led us to give photography a central place in our work of recent years and has meant both a large material investment in the process and increased involvement in its theory and practice. It is, then, true to say that it is through photography that our larger educational project has been given shape, specificity, and practical form. It is now hard for us, as we work, not to see the larger educational project and its practical form as indivisible. Yet, hopefully, the point is made that, in principle, the practice of photography could be relinquished without a fundamental undermining of the larger project. This is important because it must be clear that for teachers or cultural and educational workers who might wish to develop a similar orientation to our own, other expressive and representational forms might be more available and appropriate.

Having made this important proviso it still remains for us to say 'Why photography?' In doing so we may appear to be working back on the recognition of other possibilities of practical forms for cultural studies. It may be that in the contemporary realm of cultural power, popularity, and complexity, photography is something of a paradigm case.

*Why photography?*

In our work we need ways which young people can use to represent, make present and (re)construct what is normally lived out. In short, we need to find ways and means of making texts for selected and privileged aspects of the everyday.

*1. There are some historically determined or intrinsic features of the photographic medium which are important in this:*

*(a) Continuous availability*. It is relatively *immediate* and mobile. Within many  contexts and locations while out and about in their worlds, the young person 'as photographer' can respond to events and objects of significance. Given the opportunity, this selection, framing, and first encoding of an event/object can be processed and printed within hours. It can be a *readily* and *continuously* available means of representation which can be integrated into the patterns, routines and practices of everyday life.

*(b) Commodity*. Photography is organised as an industry which produces and markets commodities in a highly aggressive manner. The technological hardware is as fetishised as anything in our culture, cars, sports equipment, clothes. This again gives the practice a popular currency which young people are aware of and are attracted to.

*(c) Popular*. Photography is a leisure pursuit, a hobby, a practice within the family, something known to most of us as a serious, skilful pastime which connects as record, documentation and celebration, with valued experiences. If we do not have our own practice we are likely to know this through friends or relatives who do. Young people are included in this aspect of popular culture.

*(d) Educational currency*. In several ways photography has a place within educational contexts. The main ways are: as an artistic and creative medium (examinable), as practical science, as recreational craft, as a remedial practice (especially with regard to literacy), as a tool for documentation (urban, social studies, field trips) and integrated project work. Apart from these practical uses of photography, photographs are also studied within schools. This is most developed within the study of contemporary media and communications, either as a fully constituted media studies, or as a part of progressive English work. Overall this means that from a school's point of view, photography has a wide, if diverse and peripheral, credibility as an educational practice. Equally, if not more importantly, this means that there is one more way in which pupils perceive photography; as reasonable and legitimate schoolwork. So it is a practice which has a wide cultural span and can simultaneously be understood as educational, popular, domestic, recreational, vocational, practical and (through dominant connotations) glamorous. On reflection, we think it will be agreed that no other representational or expressive practice has the same kind of cultural ubiquity. Take writing. It has wide social utility, a young person will certainly meet it as a school practice and will scarcely avoid its use in everyday life. It

has been developed to a very high degree of expressivity within the dominant (traditional and radical) culture but it is highly unpopular. The majority of people do not write about events in their lives but they do, more or less frequently, photograph them. Less still do we typewrite, typeset, reproduce and show what we write to others in everyday social situations; but we do have printed, enlarged, framed, or stuck in albums our photographs and we do show them and talk about them with others. This may seem trivial as a comparison of practices with different histories but it is crucial, as one observation among many, when considering the connectedness of educational practices to young people's everyday worlds and situations.

*(e) Central to reprographic processes.* The photographic process and image stands at the centre of a range of secondary reprographic processes: photo-silkscreen, offset litho, electro-stencilling, video, slide-tape, photocopying. Even more important is the very fact of its infinite reproducibility from negative to print. The single negative image is always available, as and when uses and new contexts arise for its use in re-combination with other materials and images, in juxtaposition, as historical record or point of reference.

*2. Photography and the photograph have special qualities as cultural practice*

*(a) Dominant culture.* Photography is a major means by which society produces and reproduces images and is therefore met and assimilated by us all as the means by which a dominant reality is represented. We are familiar with and responsive to photographic conventions and their representational power in everyday life. Photographs constantly refer to popular mythologies of glamour, excitement, the exotic, wealth, power, sexuality, ambition, etc. In popular culture the photograph, and the idea of the photographer, has many of these connotations. As a means of representation, ideas of photography's power and glamour are not lost on young people.

*(b) Mechanical reproduction.* Unlike most autographic processes it does not require a long apprenticeship to achieve reasonable and powerful results. This is especially the case if a technicist and craft approach is rejected in favour of a careful selection and application of the available technology in a way which stresses immediacy and allows for development of technique and convention *in use.*

*(e) Image and style.* As a contemporary form of representation, photography has also got a close connection with other cultural and

symbolic practices of young people. Photographs can be highly rhetorical, highly partial, they are selective, manipulated and constructed. In a photograph, material objects, stances, gestures, signs and qualities are lifted from their contexts. They are separated from the uneven and contradictory flow of events which check, qualify and cut their meaning down to size.

In a photograph the symbolic functions of objects and actions have a chance of being larger than they are in life. This may have similarities with certain forms of theatre. It's a quality which recommends photography to many young people because it can serve as propaganda in the 'guerilla warfare' of style; as the presentation of identity in and against the world or in conformity with peers, subcultural groups and popular mythologies. The photograph can be to style what, in the sphere of high culture, the painting is to individual sensibility.

## Territory

Human beings are territorial. This is no less true in London today than it was for our hunter gatherer ancestors. The thing to know is how and in what ways modern groups are territorial. The concept has a special relevance for cultural studies as a partial explanation for some current cultural identities, and particularly in the under-standing of youth cultures. It was invoked in the sociological explanation of teenage gangs in the fifties, of studies of football supporters and in studying spectacular youth subcultures. It was also very usefully employed in the study and project of *Knuckle Sandwich*.[1] In our own work we have continued to see territory as an active force in the formation of cultural identities and practices, particularly in respect of youth.

From September 1982 onwards we were continually looking at how the school-based projects could be extended, in a number of ways, beyond the school site. Here we were responding to a need coming through the work young people were doing with us. The basis for this was in the continuous practice of giving cameras to be taken home and then printing and developing those pictures in the school allocated time. The pictures that came back recorded and reflected in some ways the activities and life of young people after school and at the weekends. From the thousands of contact sheets we've looked at we have been able to see that the two main social contexts for the photographs are family and locality. Family is, of course, a highly significant social context in and by which cultural values and beliefs are formed. (Something that we've already spoken of and which runs through all the practice as an important touchstone.) The first snapshots of family invariably tend to be the representation of the parental culture. This is not surprising since the dominant and popular photographic practice is family snapshots. But within these photographs we often also find an area of representation within the home which is not straightforwardly parently centred and encompassed. These are photographs, recurringly taken in young people's own rooms, usually the bedroom. They are photographs of the things found in the room, of themselves and friends within it. Posters and photos on the wall, other wall decorations, object, clothes, possessions, records, stereo players, cassettes. These pictures seemed to us to have more in common with the pictures taken in the second category of location, where most of the pictures of friends occur. As we considered this, the more the concept of location/locality seemed inadequate to encompass what was being represented. It wasn't just the physical area near the home that defines the scope of the photos being taken. It is, in detail, a much more selective route through it. The concept of territory much more accurately describes what is being represented, because it is not simply connections in a physical area that can be recorded by the camera, but an active selection through a locality. The selection process can be understood as an active shaping of symbolically important references or signs. Territory opens up a view of the photographic practice as an active symbolic practice within and towards youth cultures and allows us to see the photograph as more than a snapshot. Collections of young people's photographs now take on the significance of a map of an effective cultural world. Here territory is closely related to the importance of identity. Territory is a context for the creation of identities.

So, for us, the photographs taken in free time make embryonic connections between young people's position in the family and, through territory, the wider society. Routes can be taken through the selection of photographs; on the streets, around the estate, shopping centres or precincts, having a laugh with mates, biking, skating, popping, breaking, cruising, styles of looking, styles of dressing, styles of standing, styles of posing, styles of being. Messages sent, on clothes, on walls, in videos and in pictures. In all, a myriad of images which make sense once you see that a valued world is being actively mapped and celebrated at some level or other. The world through territory, through subculture provides the content of work done in school on photographs.


*What relationship does this work have to schooling?*

Meanings and experiences beyond school can become the subject of work in school through our photo-practice. But the question then becomes what the meaning of doing this work in school is. More precisely it raises the question of who the photographic work is for. The work is school work – 'doing photography', what the photographs show is often areas of young people's lives which are not sanctioned by school, or, those meanings which form a part of resistance to school.

In the first instance the work on meaning is for the young person or group. They work for themselves, making sense of their worlds in the act of representing it. But this is only half of the process, because the world being represented refers at every level to other people beyond the school context. It has always seemed evident to us, and is a pressure we experience from young people, to return the photograph texts to these worlds. This presents a further set of problems to be solved, or at least confronted. The major understanding in this problematic is that there are no easily identified public cultural institutions within the effective worlds of young people. Returning photographs to their effective context is initially understood by young people as taking single images (snapshots) of family and friends back to them, to be put in albums, framed or put on the wall. These are all private uses of photographs within a popular practice, and valued as such.

There is, however, a further audience for photographic work as the mapping of territory, which will include and overlap with family and friends, but is distinguished by being general and public. It is a public audience who are not hailed or constituted so far in looking at photographic exhibitions or reading/viewing material produced by local groups. The local library or museum does not figure highly on most young people's cultural map, whereas the youth club/disco/pub/shopping centre does. The question of audiences for young people's work is a vital one and raises related questions of the kind of cultural institutions and forms of production which are appropriate to young people, where they have control over, and investment in, any public outcome of work produced. So far it seems to us that there is no general answer to the issues raised when young people become producers of valued cultural productions. Each audience, each form of work, will be reached for as work is undertaken. The one general area it does raise, and to which Cultural Studies can contribute, is the area of initiatives and discussion of community education and neighbourhood schools, as well as in institutional networks for young people's work as an educational resource.

*A limited institutional answer*

From September 1982, we started to give a more systematic

framework to our work around and in relationship to understanding territory. The geographical drift of our projects had been to South London over a number of years, the main focus of which was ILEA Division 8, the London Borough of Southwark. We decided that we should concentrate all the projects in one part of the borough. An area bounded by Peckham, Camberwell, Elephant and Castle and the edge of Bermondsey. The geography crossed a number of distinct social/cultural areas and, as we were to discover, a number of distinct youth territories. It included seven ILEA secondary schools, with four of which we had an established relationship. Our initial and modest framework for 'The Southwark Project', as it rather bureaucratically became known, was to establish an institutional network across statutory/voluntary youth and arts projects for the promotion and exchange of cultural work by young people. Initially we confined this to photographic and related text work.

The three levels of initial development were:

(a)  To establish a network of people who worked with young people, teachers, youth workers, arts workers, to exchange working methods and approaches;

(b)  To establish a network for the exchange and distribution of students' work;

(c)  To discuss within (a) and (b) the possibility of and interest in establishing an independent form of cultural institution based on and for the locality which centrally included young people.

This framework has remained an important one for the teaching projects over the last two years. As an example here, we hope that it has suggested how insights gained through the application of the concept of territory to the work young people were producing with us, has led to an overall framework for a cultural studies network. How that, once having established a practice based on young people's experience, important institutional questions are raised and can be followed through. The three essentially related moments in a cultural studies approach to working with young people that can be drawn from the following example are:

(a)  establishing a dialogue with young people where they can bring their experience forward in ways they value and can control;

(b)  having a theoretical framework within which that experience can be understood in relationship to society;

(c)  following through the social and institutional implications and requirements for the successful resolution of expression.

As we have mentioned briefly before, there is an obvious relationship between our application of the concept of territory to youth cultures and the concepts of community and neighbourhood, both of which have been applied to schooling initiatives. They are much broader in scope, insofar as they attempt an inclusive view of class and generation, whereas territory is generationally and class specific, defining exclusive membership of a group. Our approach, however, does allow for a bridge to be made across generation. Photographic practice has always been a powerful choice of medium because of its contemporary popular reach. This applies equally to parental culture, where photography plays an important role in recording the history of families. The history of photography parallels the contemporary school generation's great-great-grandparents. The importance of the photograph as an historical record of working class and popular culture suggests clear and obvious links with the kind of interests developed through community education.

The exploration and expression of youth territories seems to us a substantial base from which to make the link with the experience of other generations and groups. It is also our view that territory provides a basis for young people to understand the relationship they have between family and society. Territory functions to define social membership, to create bonds and loyalties, and connects with youth cultures in defining and exploring social identities. The concept of territory is usefully employed in relationship to understanding cultural reproduction, how it is that any one generation and group of young people acquire adult status and cultural identity. It therefore should command our attention in the same light that schooling does as a social institution of cultural reproduction.

In September 1983 four separate groups from four institutions, three schools and a Home Tuition Centre, all within our area in Southwark, started working with us. All the groups started with a common approach of establishing practical photography, based on their popular interests. The locations of the groups overlapped. Routes between home and respective school intertwined. Consequently it was not long before similar, if not the same, objects, people, places and events appeared across their photographs. Since all the groups had occasion for working at the darkroom and studios at our base, they also began to see each others' photos in casual ways. Photographs would be left pinned on walls or left around on desks. Obviously they were interested in these photographs. They showed areas they knew and, much more importantly, people they knew.

The local popular youth style in this area has, for some considerable time, been soulhead (soul boy/girl). In the last year this has been worked up into a very haute couture style. Upwards of 10 new boutiques have opened in the Walworth Road, East Lane and the Old Kent Road, over the same period. From the outset, style had been an organising interest in their photography. At first it was a casual and disorganised presence in the photographs they were taking to map and celebrate their interests. Over the first term they took cameras home, went on local trips photographing what took their interest, and used the studio. Through a combination of these occasions, style emerged for all of them as a key area to represent. For Steve this was initially a straightforward task. He was a skinhead, his mates were skinheads. It wasn't going to be difficult to aspect the style of skinheads. What was going to need sorting out was what being a skinhead meant and how people would respond to the image he presented. Roy was more casual in his relation to celebrating his style. His style was, in any case, more casual, less spectacular. For Donna, organising her photographic work around her style was the beginning of a quite particular exploration.

It was not difficult for Donna to do what the others were doing. Itemising the elements of her style, isolating it, becoming aware of it, representing it through her clothes, jewellery, the poses she struck. Donna, however, understood her style to extend from herself to her friends and to her location. She didn't put it just like that, but she did insist on seeing her style as related to others, in the direction she wanted the work to take. More than this, Donna wanted to see the photography group as having a group outlook. The photography project was also a friendship group for her. So quite a lot of things kept coming together for Donna in the photography and, as the year progressed, she started to pace the work for herself, the rest of the group and us. From her first work on style she moved to an album of friends and then to photographing the locality in which she met her friends. She moved, in effect, to photograph the territory of the Walworth Road style, the estate of the scagheads and the break dancers. Donna didn't live on the estate or technically in the heart of Walworth. She lived on the fringe of the area in Camberwell. Also, Donna was not at any of the local secondary schools within the area. She was, at the time, a pupil at the local Home Tuition Unit. Her mates were at one of the local schools (she was to go there as a sixth former the following year).

So these streets were not only the boundary of the area where the young people lived and went to school, not only the place to buy the latest fashions, but also the place to wear them as well. Being a Walworth Roader became a new, locally identified style for the spring and summer of 1984. The actual style is unashamedly borrowed from the latest international fashion collections, particularly French and Italian – the two highest currencies in dominant terms. The style is opulent. It speaks of leisure for the leisured class. It is a style of the French and Italian Riviera in high summer. The tops and trousers are generously cut from printed cotton, often with the label of the designer forming the sole motif. Jackets are again generously cut from soft leather, accessories are cheap, although gold, real gold, is as ever part of the style. It is a style, as Frankie says, of relaxed appearance. It is a style, as soul has always been, which crosses race and sex. This high and opulent fashion paraded itself up and down the Walworth Road, crossing the river occasionally to Covent Garden, where the same clothes bought on the Walworth Road were being sold at slightly higher prices. But prices were high throughout. This style paraded up and down a street in an area with one of the highest youth unemployment rates in the country. But the confidence of the style says exactly that life should look as if it was being enjoyed, even if it isn't.

The style of dress is connected to the currency of spectacular dancing. Popping, breaking and robotics have been taken up over the same period that the style of dress has been worked up. Dancing is no longer confined to evening discos or dance floors. The ghetto blasters provide the portable and free-ranging sounds and the immediate occasion for street dancing. The locals have become quite accustomed to groups of adolescent boys carrying around the portable dance floors, improvised from vinyl floor covering (usually in the region of 6′ × 6′). New outdoor venues have been created, and word of mouth can bring upwards of hundreds of young people to a dance competition held in the car park of an estate. Covent Garden has a special relation to these local South London events and, to a certain extent, superseded the local venues. Covent Garden is big tourist business. It is also a shopping precinct which encourages and organises street entertainers. Earlier in '84, working-class male youth, particularly West Indian youth, were going to Covent Garden with their ghetto blasters to do busking in the form of individual or paired routines of robotic dancing. Effectively mime routines as automatons. This was discouraged by the police, who continually moved them on. Later they shrank to the edges of Covent Garden and continued their performances, but with less obvious emphasis on 'busking' as such.

With the development of breakdancing, Covent Garden became known as a venue, just as South Bank did for skateboarding. Somewhere along the line officials or entrepreneurs have seen the tourist dimension of 'local culture' and had a large mural painted on the hoardings behind the spot where the dancing occurred. The mural brought together a highly-graphisised version of the graffiti signatures of the breakdancers, as well as the obvious ikonography of ghetto blasters, trainers, arms and legs, etc. In a cruder form these signatures can be found on any London estate stairwell. Covent Garden thus provided a well-orchestrated theatre and wealthy audience, which was, nevertheless, free for working-class dance performers and their fashionable following. It was the nearest thing to being on TV, to achieving the image of *Fame*, to achieving a glamour image. Covent Garden was a special excursion out of territory, taking the subculture with it.

If this coordinated set of expressions of a working-class youth culture is in part a response to unemployment, or the threat of it, then there is also a dark underside. Over exactly the same period as the style we've described emerged from the more general soul-smoothy (someone who listens to soul music), the same area, same large estate, saw the spectacular emergence of heroin use amongst young working-class people. The scagheads were exploring an escapism with tragic consequences. The rituals and habits of the scagheads are well known to the youth of the area. The scag habit exists alongside the style and the music. The difference for them is that the requirements of the habit eventually take them away from a more general peer group, in the restless search for money to exchange for the drug.[1]

The style, the scag, the prospect, or the reality of unemployment, was and still is, the immediate cultural context for the young people we worked with in the '83–'84 school year. Donna, Steve and Roy were in one of the groups. Roy was a Walworth Roader (ex-soul-smoothy), Steve was a Bermondsey Skinhead and Donna was in the process of moving from the latter to the former.

In the last term we proposed that those in the group who wished could present their work in an exhibition of young people's photographic work which would be held at the Cockpit Gallery, Holborn, but would also be toured around the schools people had come from. Donna was enthusiastic to work in this framework. She reworked her style photographs as a panel and went on to document the boutiques in the area. She worked on a montage/collage about the estate and her friends. In this work Donna had mapped out interests and relationship to an area in a direct way, literally by putting photographs together on the same frame. At a symbolic level she was constructing an identity as it was being worked upon in other areas of her life. Donna really wanted other people to see her work. Most importantly of all, she wanted those who went to the school her friends were at to see it. In the event, her work was shown at the Cockpit Gallery and has since not been shown at the school. Donna is still asking for this to happen. We are attempting to arrange this. Steve is also asking for the work he did. He and Roy left before the end of the year for jobs. The three students we've singled out for attention have moved on, along with the rest of the group, to jobs, unemployment, the sixth form or special schooling, as the case may be.

What was evident in the three terms' work was the high degree of serious engagement in questions of their lives; their prospects and likely future, as well as where they had come from. What we realised was how powerfully territory articulated significant meaning. What we needed then, as now, was much more time across the week to explore this with them, as well as a second year, as they practically made the transition to other institutions and work.


# Publication and distribution –
## *Schooling and Culture* Journal

Schooling and Culture is the bi-annual journal of the department. It was founded in 1978 with a print run of 500. Its original aim was to promote critical discussion of the secondary curriculum and example innovative educational practice which was relevant to the everyday lives of working-class students. The journal attempted to apply and translate much of the academic and theoretical work of the *new sociology*, the *sociology of culture* and cultural theory, to the situation of the school. Its earliest project, and its project up until issue 10, was to map out what a cultural studies might be in the secondary school, as well as report the culture of young people as they related it to school.

By the beginning of the eighties it was clear that recession and Tory ideology were inducing a return to restrictive utilitarian goals and authoritarian models in schools. Whilst *Schooling and Culture* (print run now 1,000) continued to promote work on critical and reflexive school practice, it also embarked on the analysis of the new dominant ideologies, as well as monitoring the actual effects of rising youth unemployment. This was launched as *The State We're In* series in the Autumn of 1982 (with a further increase in the print run to 2,000). This has been followed by two further issues, *Against the State We're In*, and currently *Race, Sex and Class*, which try to bring the analysis of restructuring as ideology and practice up-to-date. Throughout the production of *Schooling and Culture* it has had all the problems of other small, independently-produced journals of limited distribution and ever-increasing costs. It is still the case that the journal is hardly ever seen outside London, with little chance of

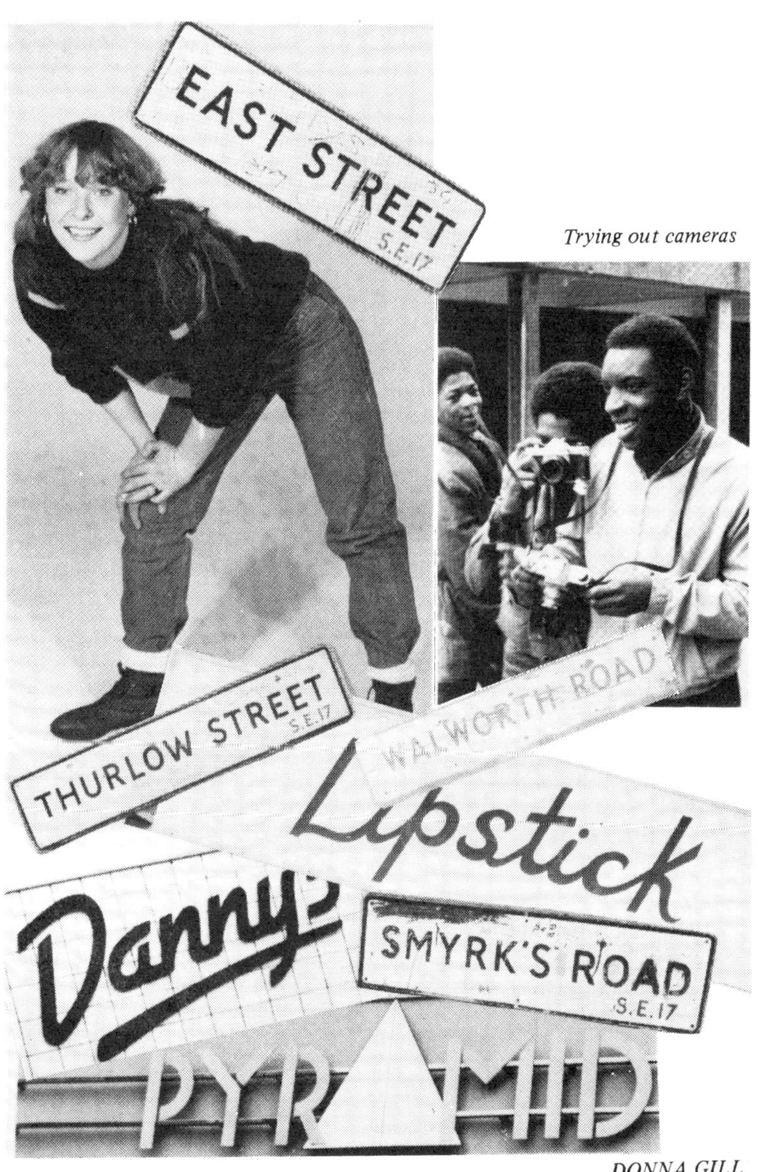


*Trying out cameras*

*DONNA GILL*

international outlets. We have inevitably run up debts, even though
we have sold out of many back issues and continue to sell well. With a
higher guaranteed sale, the cover price would come down, sales
would go up. It is a general problem, although for *Schooling and
Culture* it has reached a crisis point, even though there is a continuing
readership.


# Publication and distribution –
# The Cockpit Gallery, Holborn

Our interest in having a gallery was strategic. Our major interest
wasn't, and still isn't, in running a public photographic gallery, but
we needed one in order to attract funding for work to be produced
and in order to attract interest in work completed. There were two
sources of work in exhibitable form in the early days: work produced
as campaigning and touring exhibitions which wouldn't normally get
seen by or used in schools, and our own work with students, where
making an exhibition was an important part of our approach. The
question of distribution came up sharply with both. By having a
gallery we were able to promote a range of work through publicity,
viewings and seminars specifically for educational use. We were also
able to guarantee a public outlet for students' work. In both cases,
showing the work in the Cockpit Gallery, Holborn, was a basis for
further interest in that work. Both work by outside producers and our
own productions continue to be shown in the gallery. It is now the
case that much more work of our own production with young people
takes up the concern of the gallery, which is how we intended it.*
(There is, however, a considerable amount of energy and time spent
on reproducing the gallery itself. Each year we have had to apply for
funding, which last year included a salary for a part-time gallery and
touring show administrator, as well as the salary of our photographer-
in-residence. Since April, 1984, we have been in receipt of a Greater
London Council grant to pay for three full-time workers for one year,
plus a production budget.)

---

* This is a considerable expansion in the gallery operation, through which we hope not
only to produce more, but also to look more closely at what happens to what has
already been produced.

# Publication and distribution –
# The touring exhibition system

The touring exhibition was part of the original conception of the
Cockpit Gallery... We often talked of the gallery in the image of a
shunting yard with exhibitions being turned round, sent out,
reviewed and inspected. This was much more important than
attracting an off-the-street audience for the gallery. The demand for
exhibitions for hire or loan took us by surprise, and it was clear that
we were not going to be able to administer it from the teaching staff.
For the last three years we have had a part-time administrator,
funded by the Greater London Arts Association. This enabled an
efficient system of booking out, invoicing and publicising to be done,
but it was insufficient to enable any follow-up work. Our choice of
subjects/themes was guided by our concern to provide material on a
range of contemporary culture and political issues and experiences
for educational use, material that otherwise wasn't available to
schools and colleges, work produced by young people which deserved
a wider audience. There was, in any case, good material that needed
outlets. Jo Spence's work in *Beyond the Family Album*, the work of the
Hackney Flashers in *Who's Still Holding the Baby*, were early
examples. After a while Jo came to work as the administrator for the
gallery. We took on laminated photo-text panels as one form for our
own work. The first exhibition we instigated and collaborated on was
*The Good Ones Have Their Top Buttons Done Up*, produced by second-
year photo-arts students at the Polytechnic of Central London, with
ourselves and students from two London schools. The material was
originally for an article in *Schooling and Culture*, which was censored
by the head teachers of the schools. Producing an exhibition was one
way of getting it seen. It was based on P. Willis's account of a counter
school book, in his book *Learning to Labour*. Since then our
experience has grown and we have produced exhibitions directly with
our students, as in *Our Way of Rocking*, or *Home, School, Work*, or
with outside producers, as in *Big Bang for the Bureaucrats*. What we
have not yet done, but are now in a position to do, is look more
closely at how the exhibitions are used.


# Short history of the department

1972                Visual Team established to work in relation to
                    performing Arts – 'Art Events'.

| | |
|---|---|
| 1974 | Art Department established. Major practice centred on developing secondary Art subject to include contemporary media as a school practice and to provide historical and theoretical components of study. |
| 1975 – 78 | *The Art Studies Courses* run in 16 schools as a pilot CSE option within the Art syllabus. |
| 1978 – 79 | We develop a critique of the severe limits of trying to reform the Fine Art basis of the secondary Art subject, of working within the exam structure, and of our own pedagogy. We mark out the limits of 'Radical Analysis'. |
| | Run a pilot project of the *Schools Photography Project.* |
| | Run a week block course for school leavers and sixth formers entitled *The Photograph.* |
| | Run lecture programme *Feminism and Photography* in conjunction with *Photography Workshop.* |
| | Establish our journal *Schooling and Culture* and produce the first three issues. First issue has a print run of 500. |
| 1978 – 79 | Establishment of the *Department of Cultural Studies.* The department moves out of the theatre building to the Drama and Tape Centre building at Holborn. |
| | *Cockpit Gallery, Holborn* established with grant aid from the Greater London Arts Association. |
| | *Photographer-in-Residence* scheme established with financial aid from the Greater London Arts Association. National *Touring Exhibition loan scheme* established, further assistance from GLAA for part-time workers to run the scheme. |
| 1981 | Cockpit Gallery exhibits the work of the Schools Photography Project as the *Work in Progress* exhibition. |
| Jan., 1982 | *Publishing Project* established to work with unemployed school leavers. Assistance is given through the ILEA special fund. |
| Sept., 1982 | Secondment scheme established with Northchurch Day Care Centre. |

1979 – 83    The *Schools Photography Project* runs in 14 schools as a 4th/5th year option.

March,    *No Kidding* publishing project established jointly
1983 – 84    between department and Post-16 Education Centre, Institute of Education. Produced first exhibition on themes of transition/leaving school. Project broadened to deal with a range of youth questions on transition. *No Kidding* exhibitions and publication – 'School leavers guide to the crisis'. Project joint ILEA/GLC funded.

1983 – 84    Department established *Southwark Project*, an initiative that locates department teaching resources in eight schools and off-site units in Southwark. Aim is to establish better cross-referencing framework for cultural studies work undertaken in school, with families and community.

1984    Department publishes issue 14, *Schooling and Culture*. Deals with ILEA initiatives on Race, Sex and Class.

1983 – 84    Second of summer *Looking Out* exhibitions staged at Cockpit Gallery. Drew together a number of community photography organizations and schools around the broad theme of young people and photography.

1984    *Cockpit Gallery development project* receives additional funding from GLC; three new staff are employed to develop gallery facilities/services for the production of exhibitions. New groups take up Gallery project: initiatives in peace studies, home working, women in history.

# The future of our practice

Much of our time has been spent on organizing and running the various projects and comparatively little time in making public our practices. As attacks on projects increase and as many workers feel a sense of the increasing inappropriateness of aims which were formulated over 10 years ago, it becomes more and more necessary to reformulate aims and argue for appropriate cultural practices. There is nothing fixed or sacred, for instance, about black and white still photography as far as the fluid currencies of our culture go, particularly as far as youth is concerned. In the coming period we intend to devote energy to publicise both our own and others' practice. The major means for doing this will be through a range of publications which are currently being negotiated. A book published in Macmillan's *Youth Questions* series, which describes much of our practice with young people and examples of their work, will be published early in 1985. A further essay on work with a young woman on representing her family is published in another book in the same series. An essay describing how we understand the photographs which young people take is to be published in *Photography Politics Two*. Other written work is being considered to cover the work of the photography residency, and we are in the process of considering how to produce a limited first publication of a youth novel.

We have long thought it important that there be a regular forum for London cultural workers concerned with photo-representation. Last year we held a London exhibition of young people's photography, entitled *Looking Out*. This was accompanied by seminars and workshops on themes and issues arising from the work. This is being repeated this year with a series of lectures for a wider audience. All in all, we do not intend significantly to change our course in the immediate future, but rather to develop, consolidate and extend our current work but, clearly, we do have to monitor and respond to attacks on youth and educational provision. We have to defend those we work with and for.

Simon Watney
# Photography — Education — Theory

## Notes on the curriculum

Although degrees and diplomas in photography are offered in Britain exclusively from polytechnics and Colleges of Further Education, this initial institutional uniformity guarantees nothing concerning the actual object of study. We may, however, distinguish between those courses which have been developed within the particular local traditions of *laissez-faire* art education, and those which set out to produce students whose work is geared towards the various commercial market-places of photography. Both types of course owe their existence to the complex institutional legacy of nineteenth-century education, with its careful hierarchical polarisation of 'art' from mere 'craft' and 'industry'. At the same time, both articulate their pedagogic intentions from the equally complex history of the ways in which photography has been theorised, since its invention, from the divergent perspectives of different areas of practice and employment – in other words from their specialized 'professional ideologies'.[1] To begin with, we should note that it has always been assumed that there exists a unitary 'thing', photography, which may be taught. But while it is evident that both types of course demand an equal degree of technical competence from students, it is also apparent that there is no consensus concerning what these students are supposed to do with their skills, or how they might move from any one area of practice to another. Quite the reverse. For deeply suppressed within the course outlines offered to the would-be student of photography, is the entire spectrum of uses to which the medium is put, the conflicting theoretical 'explanations' of these uses, and the specific acquired photographic identities which accompany them.

In this context 'theory' is almost invariably understood as a *technical* category, covering the study of sensitometry, photo-chemistry, and so on. In this dominant usage, theory is regarded as an aspect of 'practice', quite distinct from whatever course of studies has been devised to complement the acquisition of technical skills and know-how. For it is a fundamental requirement of all such courses that they provide the student with some kind of 'complementary' studies, since it is assumed that the photographer is a distinct type of person, fundamentally 'non-intellectual', whose manual and visual talents are in need of compensatory academic instruction. It is at this point that the two types of course begin to take on clearly definable and frequently incompatible characteristics.

The student on a 'non-vocational' course will thus be introduced to those historical and critical discourses which are to frame and make sense of his or her work. These are structured around the pivotal figure of the Fine Artist, and operate in such a way that the student will come to 'recognize' his or her work and identity in terms of the familiar aesthetic discourses of self-expression, innovation, creativity, and so on. These values are anchored in an historical model of The History Of Photography which endlessly privileges the isolated figure of the photo-pioneer, struggling against vague but determined odds to establish a unique 'vision' of the world, and to impose this on a necessarily abstracted and equally unspecified audience. The student is thus encouraged to aspire to membership of this same pantheon of epochal photographers, in such a way that the very sense of social isolation-cum-superiority which such an education engenders is read by tutors and students alike as further evidence of appropriately individual genius.

This framework of complementary studies is matched in 'practice' by a curriculum which sets students endlessly in competition with one another around the familiar circuit of photographic categories in which he or she is expected to shine – documentary, landscape, portraiture, and so on. It is in these terms, and through these seemingly discrete categories, that the student's work will finally be assessed. In each case a critical discourse of excellence, creativity and originality is ceaselessly projected across the field of technical competence, providing the student with a highly sophisticated sense of what is 'appropriate' to different situations, as if this stemmed from his or her 'self' as opposed to the complex mediation of market forces, which inform the photographer's work at every stage in the production of a photograph, from the choice of camera, film-stock and printing procedures, through to the actual selection of subjects, accompanying texts, and so on. Such choices are, however, understood as signs of immanent 'talent', rather than the result of contingent knowledge. And in this constant dialogue between history and criticism, tutor and pupil, image and 'reality', the student succeeds or fails. It is perhaps worth pointing out, should my irony not be sufficiently clear, that in educational terms examination success within such a system is unlikely to evidence much in the way of genuine intellectual achievement, and vice versa.

The situation of the student who opts for a 'vocational' course in this period of mass unemployment is no happier. He or she will be introduced to the same canonical roll-call of 'great' photographers, whose work, however, will be regarded with an inevitable eye towards commercial appropriation. Last year's history of photography option provides the material for next year's advertisement dummies. This is perhaps marginally more honest than the vanguardist model which obtains for the non-vocational student, who is subtly abjured to admire, envy, and then supposedly completely forget everything that has been held up as excellent, in order to demonstrate his or her 'uniqueness'. History and criticism are thus more frankly aligned within vocational courses, since it is assumed that the student has already decided which area of practice to pursue. For the student has been taken on to the course explicitly as an embryonic photo-journalist, fashion photographer, or whatever, whereas the non-vocational student is secure only in the confidence of 'artistic' merit. The vocational student is thus provided with a more frankly training-oriented education, and can expect at the least a course in business studies of some kind, while a non-vocational counterpart will be lucky if he or she learns anything about the gallery system. Both types of course tend to be surrounded by what Stuart Hall once described as 'the sociology of everything', while students are carefully nurtured by 'successful' figures from their chosen areas of professional practice. Such studio training is therefore unlikely to offer much in the way of oppositional analyses of, say, 'News' photography, or Page Three pin-ups, or Fine Art practices. For behind all the discussions of style, lightening, and so on, the student's work will ultimately be judged in relation to client satisfaction and sales returns, in markets whose own values and practices remain unquestioned.

If by any chance a lone voice from complementary studies is raised to problematize the criteria of professionalism which govern the studio and darkroom, it can only too easily be dismissed as 'merely' academic, or irrelevant because 'non-artistic'. In this way all interrogative intellectual work is automatically marginalized. And so, on both types of course, the pedagogy of the market is continually reproduced.

Both types of photographic education, however, converge around a core of key ideological issues. Central to these is the assumption that the photographer is, by his or her very nature, a purely visual individual. This point cannot be sufficiently stressed, and is the cruellest and crudest revenge of the professional and theoretical separation of writing from image-making in our culture. In photographic history and criticism its dominant formulation remains structured around Cartier-Bresson's notion of 'the decisive moment' – that moment which the 'true' photographer alone can recognize in any given situation, the one moment in which he or she is supposedly most closely in touch with that essential self to which photographic education endlessly addresses itself, the photographer's innate 'gift' to 'express' the 'truth'. What this system of thought can never ask is what we actually mean by a gift, what expression materially consists of, and whose truth it is that the photographer is constructing.

The dominant tendency to fetishize the 'seeing eye' of the 'great' photographer in the discourses of history, and to fetishize the moment of exposing film in the discourses of criticism, is unfortunately as common on the Left as it is in mainstream photographic education. This is nowhere more obvious than in the work of John Berger, for whom 'photography does not deal in constructs' since, he claims, 'there is no transformation in photography. There is only decision, only focus.'[2] And from a nearby eyrie, equally well-feathered with Left-humanist pretensions, Peter Fuller would also reduce photography to the level of 'mechanical process', arguing that the central and defining work of the photographer is 'arrangement', which he regards as 'a relatively slight aesthetic skill, comparable to that which we use when ordering the objects on a mantlepiece, or tidying the room.'[3] It is ironic that the formalist discourse of disinterested aesthetic values which such critics bring to bear on photography when they are unable to regard it as a direct political instrument, is widely shared within photographic education, which derives from much the same institutional and discursive backgrounds – Fine Art departments, state art-funding agencies, and so on. In this manner photojournalists, documentary and gallery photographers are equally taught to believe that their particular areas of practice represent some intrinsic and uniquely 'truthful' essence of the medium. But it is as absurd to claim that photography has a single, 'correct', essence as it would be to make the same banal demand of painting, or architecture, or film. It is one sign of the absolute poverty of mainstream photographic criticism in Britain that such preposterously reductive ontological assertions are incorporated wholesale into the curriculum of both vocational and non-vocational courses, as well as dominating the magazine literature for amateur and 'popular' photography.

As I have suggested, this is perhaps not so very surprising, given the historical institutional framework which positions photographic education in a passive relation, both to industry and the pedagogic tradition of the Fine Arts which relentlessly abstract and privilege the 'aesthetic' over and against all other areas of experience and aspects of signification. What should be noticed is that this entire pedagogy of the market, with its myopic emphasis on the individual print, and the individual photographer, rides over the fundamental economic distinction between professionalism and amateurism in such a way that these categories are rendered to all intents and purposes immutable. Walter Benjamin's optimistic prophecy of the 1930s that the non-photographer would be the illiterate of the future, has never looked less convincing.[4] For more than at any time in its history, photographic education is involved in sustaining the power and mystique of the professional, and resisting all attempts to redefine the nature of amateur photography, from the perspective of adult education, feminism, community politics, race relations, or whatever. This is a situation which is unlikely to disturb the sleep of photography lectures any more than photographic multinational executives or the owners of the ever-mushrooming photo-processing industry, all of whom depend in their different relations to one another on the preservation of the photographic *status quo*.

In this context we should recognize that photography has always presented certain structural problems to entrepreneurial capitalism, as a result of the intrinsic instability of the photograph as a commodity, given its infinite reproducibility. Thus photography continues to be marketed in two kinds. On the one hand the process as a whole can be sold, together with a range of professional identities. On the other hand film, simple cameras and processing services can  be marketed to 'the general public', who are systematically denied access to the relatively simple procedures of photographic technology by means of the wholesale bombardment of professional photographic ideology in the form of direct advertising, photographic monographs, and the whole culture of the medium. In between the two lies the vast, uneasy reserve army of 'amateurs', obediently printing up their sunsets, pets, and pin-ups in the good name of creative self-expression and technical excellence, as instructed by the copy-writers of the legion weekly and monthly photography magazines, which are themselves little more than adverts for the multinationals.

Thus photography remains what it has always been, a paradigmatic and exemplary model of capitalist production, as both a labour process and a system of valorization. It is equally clear that the divisions of labour within photography are also divisions of knowledge and identity, and it is at this point that photographic education begins to make more extended sense as a system which is continually involved in reproducing not simply a range of commodities in a patriarchal capitalist society, but also the dreams, fantasies and subjectivities which underpin it. Any amount of sociology, Marxist or otherwise, can be lined up behind the primary 'practical' curriculum of photographic education, as long as the basic opposing categories of vocational to non-vocational and amateur to professional are preserved intact. There is thus little point in trying to recover 'lost' or 'marginalized' areas of practice such as workers' or women's or gays' photography for the curriculum if that curriculum itself is perpetually doomed to be marginalized in the student's daily round from studio to seminar room, and thence, decked out with all the equipment which has survived the latest round of education cuts, to the 'real' world. For that world will inevitably be constructed by the photographer according to the categories and values which she or he has been taught to 'recognize' – the world as an endless scenario of potential assignments, each one of which only serves to confirm the authenticity and authority both of the student's 'vision' and of the institution which directs it. In effect this is rather as if film were to be taught and assessed exclusively by 'anti-realist' avant garde purists and television commercial executives.

It is against this backdrop that another tendency in photographic education has established itself in those few polytechnics where there is no strong Fine Art tradition, and where the concept of photographic theory is defended against the pressures of direct market forces. Principal among these is the degree in Film and Photographic Art at the Polytechnic of Central London. At the risk of seeming to blow my own trumpet, since I teach on this course, I think it remains necessary to note that whatever takes place at PCL proceeds from an initial refusal to prioritize 'practice' in relation to 'theory' or, for that matter, vice versa. It is worth pointing out that the 'theory' curriculum at PLC involving psychoanalysis, semiology, discourse analysis and so on, depends on the power, within the institution, to define the 'intellectual field'[5] which photographic studies might occupy in opposition to the pedagogy of the Fine Art and industrial markets. As I have suggested, this power does not reside in the vast majority of photographic courses. Nor, I should add, is it generally sought. In this respect photographic theory must necessarily be as sceptical concerning claims about the 'creative autonomy' of the individual photographer as it is of the working practices embodied in the pedagogic categories of documentary, Fine Art, photojournalism, and so on, as defined in advance by the moguls of Fleet Street, the Tate Gallery, or wherever.

For it is the task of 'theory' to raise precisely those questions which the aesthetics of 'the decisive moment' suppress. In place of 'the sociology of everything' we need to be able to account for the operations of the social and the psychic *in* the photograph. The curriculum must therefore be flexible enough to consider the historical emergence of those discourses which make up the basic organizing categories of photographic 'common sense', as well as providing an accessible alternative to the overlapping discourses of self-expression, direct perception, artistic integrity, and vulgar realism with which most students will be only too familiar. It goes without saying that this cannot necessarily be a painless process for students coming to the course from any background. For if 'theory' is problematizing those categories from which photographic identities are constituted, then it follows that lived identities themselves will be questioned. Hence the emphasis on collective work, at least in the early stages of the course, and continuing group criticism sessions which provide a support system in which problems or difficulties can be shared.

Photographic theory, as I have outlined it above, is therefore involved in a large-scale 'catching up' operation, especially in relation to film theory and education, which has already established an impressive curriculum around such concepts as suture, interpellation, sexual investment in representation, and audience-oriented aesthetics in general. Needless to say, the discussion of these concepts is of critical importance to any serious theoretical work on still images, work which remains simply inconceivable on most photography courses, with their continual displacements from representation to either 'the real' or the individual photographer. Photographic theory thus directs itself towards the establishment of a debate-based photographic culture, on a par with that which has been instituted in film studies by SEFT and other organizations. And since it remains the case that the dominant tendency in British photographic theory and criticism represents nothing less than a bizarre crossing of Bazin with Bloomsbury, peppered with more than a dash of Reaganomics, it is hardly surprising that there is still a long way to go. For the photo-theorist is up against the entire apparatus of reflection- and expression-based criticism, backed up by one of the most profitable and resourceful industries in the modern world. So if our work requires a certain degree of intellectual rigour on the part of students and photographic educationalists alike – concerning distinctions between political and ideological struggles, for example, which raise serious and even 'difficult' questions about the very nature of photographic signification – then I can only conclude that such work is long, long overdue.

This article is based on a seminar led by the author at the Department of Cultural Studies, the University of Trent, Ontario, in March, 1983.

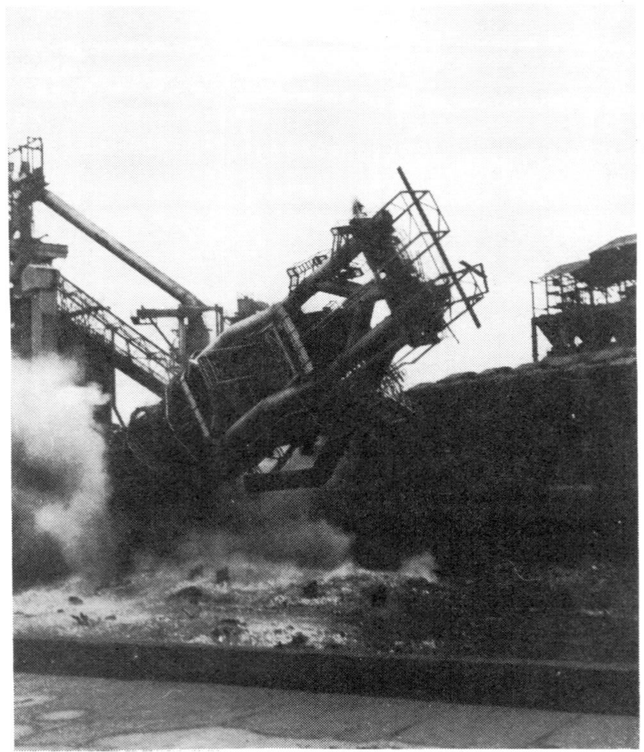

1. *Woman worker at Houndsgill Brickworks during Second World War*

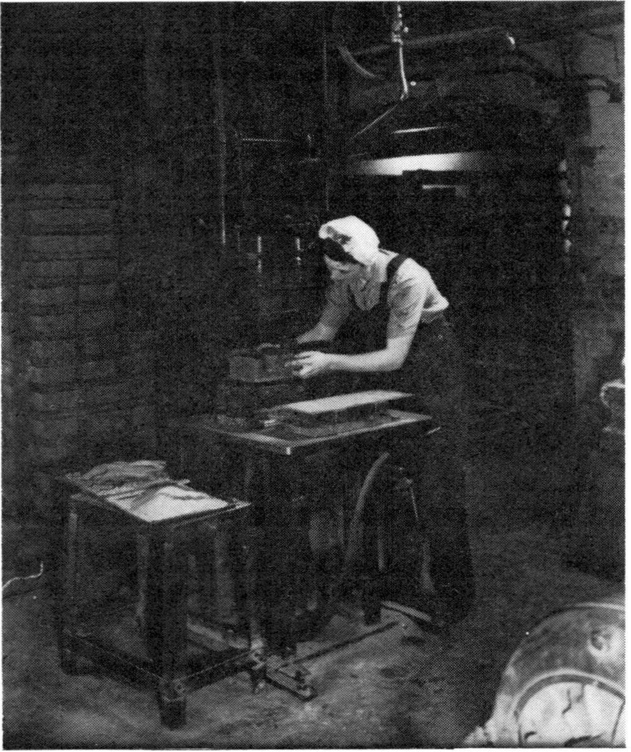

2. *Demolition of BSC Works, 1981*

Stevie Bezencenet and Haim Bresheeth
# Photographic archives

If we were to go searching for photographic images of our recent past which do not have the privileged status of symbols – images sanctioned by the establishment as illustrating facts and values – then, surprisingly, we would not have to look very far. Starting in our homes, we could explore outwards into the local press files, through the library records and the local authority departments, into the museum and elsewhere, in an ever widening scope. The problem is that this multiplicity of imagery is often not accorded any significance and consequently not 'mapped'. Such a process involves an attitude, before anything else – one which recognises the value of so many diverse images and how they can be made more meaningful, accessible and useful.

The feminist movement campaigned for recognition of the 'personal as political'; photography theorists have argued for acknowledgement of the family album as a key site of representation; and socialist historians have made the case for utilising apparently inconsequential and everyday subject matter in their researches. All this adds up to a case for the organised retrieval of the images of the past, together with a systematic documentation of the present. Apart from the records of libraries, museums, galleries, nationalised industries, commercial collections, private companies, state departments and private collections (many of which are not accessible to an ordinary member of the public), there are many institutions and projects which are actively gathering and cataloguing such images, as well as generating and commissioning new ones – the Labour History Museum and the Museum of London are two good examples. There are also many archives which concentrate specifically on photography, premised on the recognition of the private, domestic sphere (the home) as an endlessly rich source of material, which rarely receives attention in the public, institutional sphere.

The task of redressing the historical balance is not only one dealing with an elitist and distorted view of facts and events. It mainly has to deal with a much greater vice – that of omission, of an absence. As opposed to the privileged, mainstream historian, who is privy to the various research collections and institutes, government reports and documents, supported by a lavish academic back-up system – the socialist/feminist historian is faced with a job more akin to a social archeologist. The evidence and material have to be 'dug out' of numerous and diverse sources, ranging from the popular press, invitations to meetings, personal accounts in letters and interviews – the list is endless.

In this context, the use of photography offers both vast potential and enormous problems. The use of visual mass media like photography or film records of specific political events, debates and development (of the type not likely to be kept by the dominant media) is of crucial value to the continuation and furtherance of class/gender struggle. This type of evidence and analysis is a way in which the past is made real for a social grouping – history is made our own, and we are offered a place in it which we can understand and criticise. The use of photographic sources collected through research work from individuals and institutions can serve as a treasure for historians of the recent past, and aspects of liberation and oppression can be studied and examined across a wide range of visual expressions.

This raises, in turn, a serious problematic for the photographer/ activist in this area of ideological struggle and cultural confrontation. The dominant ideas about the nature of the image, its inherent truth value and its preference to so many words, are only too well-known. What is required from us is a different, critical approach towards the image as evidence – a process of interrogative 'reading', where the assumed 'facts' within the image are investigated in terms of our own knowledge and experience. We need to be critics at the level of the status of the individual image, as well as the whole process of constructing the past. Whether by amassing an alternative version of events with images, or whether we create strategies for 're-reading' existing ones – the role of photography in the retrieval of our pasts is a vital one.

The construction of History using a patchy and arbitrary collection of images as the basis for theorisation and analysis is clearly inadequate. What is necessary is the committed, long-term organisation of historical pictorial statements, through a process of consolidating and improving radical historical research/action archives. In this struggle, the options of the future depend on a well-documented and analysed past – this investigation and mapping of history is a form of socialist investment.

In this context, the pioneering work of the 'Photography Workshop' group is of a distinctive nature. Through years of committed and continuous work and concern with these areas, their practice has suggested a series of action models, which are quite unique. Activities ranging from postcard collection to sessions demystifying cameras, lectures and seminars, publications and exhibitions – all these have contributed to the building up of far more than just another archive, or a photographic picture library for activists to use. The combination of recording and analysing, teaching and theorising, has created a tradition of an alternative use of photography as history, and of the history of photography. (Their article here is made more pertinent due to their stand on grants and a refusal to rely on public funds, bearing in mind the problems facing similar activities in the near future.)

The use of many such resource centres is only beginning throughout the country, as the importance of the visual media becomes evident to various constituencies within the labour movement – a movement always wary of the dominant media and hence typically suspicious in this area. The urgent need for pooling efforts and resources emerges from Spence and Dennett's report of their activities – this raises the question of whether such work is best done within an institution or outside of them. Photography Workshop's answer is specific to the time/situation in which they find themselves – their varied strategies are evidence of the energy and inventiveness of a small, committed group and its potential. The argument for wider links, however, is one facing us all. For such a system to thrive and be continued, this individual effort has to be supplemented by a political system of links to the labour movement, so that the long term of the project is protected. This depends on many variables, not least the freedom afforded to such a group within a political context, and the priority allocated to cultural struggles within the labour movement and its institutions.

The Manchester Studies Archive began in 1974 and has amassed more than 65,000 images since then. It is a unit based at Manchester Polytechnic and is devoted to research into local history in general and working-class history in particular. As they researched into what documents of historical value were likely to be found in the home, they began to realise that most families do preserve a collection of photographs. This, in turn, led to the creation of an 'Archive of Family Photographs', which comprises copies and detailed information on the family and individual images. The collection is open to the public, but is also made accessible to the local community through an active programme of talks and exhibitions, whose aim was 'to stimulate or sustain an awareness of individual and class contribution to the life of the region in the past'. The major subject areas covered by the archive are: studio portraits, street portraits, interiors, school, work and leisure – a method of categorisation which is both an index of the material made available to the unit, as well as of their criteria of significance. However, within these broad categories are multiple sub-sections and these have formed the basis of some of the exhibitions, e.g. 'High Days and Holidays', 'The Life and Work of Manchester Jewry' and 'Early Days of Manchester Football'.

Recently, the Manchester unit has commissioned a contemporary photographer to document the locale as a juxtaposition to an historical exhibition on slums. This practice of combining the past and the present is seen as crucial by many of these archives and two examples are: the Consett Photo Archive in the North-East and the Beaford Archive in North Devon.

Consett was a steel town and it was decided to close the works down in 1982. The rationale for the town ceased to exist, the Steel Corporation had stood for everything and controlled most of the labour force – it had even controlled the history. With the demise of production, the corporate history slipped away, as did the possibility of work, and the town's population was left with a lack – an absence of social meaning in a society which measures it in terms of employment and production. Consett Photo Archive was started in 1982 by local people in an attempt to create a different social history, a different set of social meanings and possibly help to generate new attitudes to the current labour situation, together with alternative strategies for the future. 'We are very conscious of the fact that the most important time in Consett's history is now. If opinion and records survive, it would be a good idea if it were ours.' John Kierney, founder member.

Beaford Archive, based at Beaford Arts Centre, has been gathering material since 1971 and is concerned with Devon's own history and making it accessible to the local population (though some of their exhibitions do tour abroad). Like Consett and others, they also commission new work, so that the archive becomes a live and growing resource with the potential for investigating relationships between the past and the present and working through the implications of that.

Documentary imagery is the basis for most of these archives and it is not necessarily exciting, visual material. The strength and dynamic of this imagery is based upon its informational and revelatory function, rather than its aesthetic one. However, in order to survive, most of these archives rely partially or substantially on subsidy from the State, whose criteria is frequently measured in terms of 'creative photography'. In order for these projects to be protected, it is necessary to use them continually, thereby demonstrating their importance for *our* heritage.

# Distribution and publication

Owen Kelly and Charles Landry
## Distribution and publication

Radical and oppositional photographic practices which have been developing since the late 1960s have, of necessity, operated within the confines of the mainstream information industry.

This industry has disseminated photographic information in deliberately targetted forms, which relate on the one hand to the needs of those companies manufacturing photographic equipment and on the other hand to those galleries and publishers concerned to manufacture status. Thus photographic publications have traditionally concerned themselves with technical minutiae coupled with an uncritical acceptance of the individualistic (and almost mystic) genius of a limited number of highly paid professional photographers.

One of the main problems for oppositional photographers has been to find a space within which they could develop and make their work public without either being swallowed up by the mainstream or merely reacting negatively to its outpourings.

Broadly speaking, two parallel strategies have been pursued. The first to create a forum for discussion and debate, within which examples of radical practice could be shown. The second attempts to establish parallel agencies to those operating in the mainstream, and to infiltrate those markets while retaining their own political criteria.

*Camerawork* and *Ten.8* are examples of the first strategy. At the outset neither of these magazines set out to respond to prevailing market conditions but, instead, saw themselves as vehicles through which the political photographic practices could be developed. This meant that the criteria for success were not the attainment of economic self-sufficiency, but the perceived achievement of political impact. To assess their achievements by the degree to which they

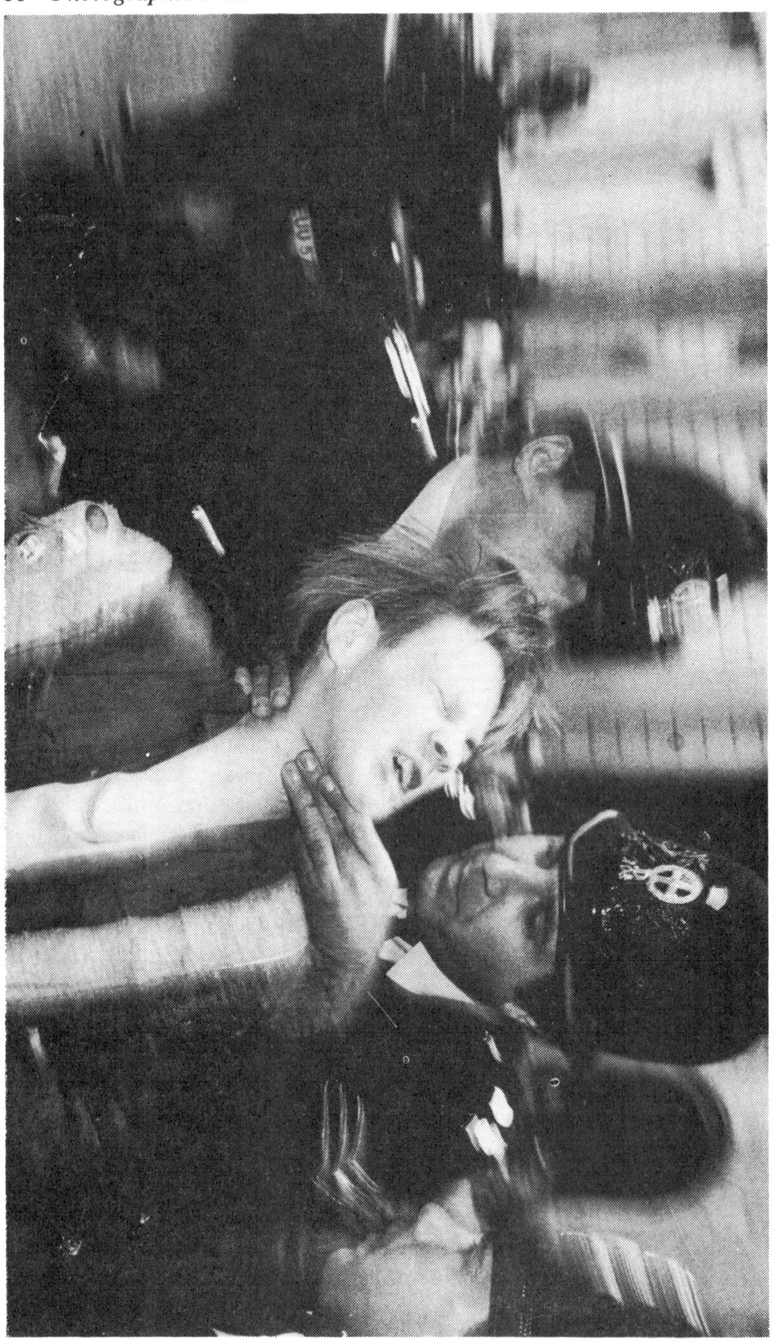

(David Hoffman)

successfully made roads into the markets of *Amateur Photographer*, the *British Journal of Photography*, etc., is to miss the point entirely.

The body of ideas that these two magazines represented was not conceived as being capable of being organised around the kind of fee-paying membership that could 'balance the books'; nor self-evidently were they the kind of magazine that would seek high circulations for its own sake and, thus, neither was willing or able to attract advertisers to pay for production. This method of subsidy would in any case have compromised their aims.

Their only possibility of finance was therefore grant aid. However, the period in which these practices were developed coincided with an economic decline and a consequent squeeze on the monies available for arts funding. Photographic publications with their particular need for high production values suffer disproportionately. Since publications have little room for compromise in terms of production, if costs are cut the object not only suffers but ceases to be what it set out to be. You cannot sensibly debate the value of an image which you can barely see because it is badly printed.

A further problem which these groups faced was that their relative success allowed the magazines they produced to become institutionalised. They existed because they had existed. Issue 31, for example, might seem to follow 'naturally' from Issue 30. In the case of *Camerawork* the weight of their own history produced at least two major crises and hindered the potential effectiveness of their attempts to deal with these crises by relaunching the magazine in different formats.

With any magazine-based initiative of these kinds, the questions remain 'How long can the ideas that spurred its creation be sustained in the magazine?', or 'Can we change our project?'.

Photography Workshop (see education section) whose members were part of the original *Camerawork* group, went on to develop a somewhat different strategy, by organising their publication so that it was produced, as journals are, by an editorial group, but is published, marketed and distributed like a book. This allows the branding advantage that magazine production inherently contains to be transferred to a book form. In this strategy they are not alone; within other cultural arenas, *Formations of...* series and *Granta* operate similarly.

This approach extends the notion of a thematic issue which both *Camerawork* and *Ten.8* have developed, in such a way as to remove the pressure of regular deadlines and guaranteed production, which makes magazines so costly, time-consuming and exhausting to produce.

If the organisation of ideas around a periodical is one strategy that has been pursued, another is the creation of counter-agencies designed to operate critically within and against dominant trade practices. Format – a feminist picture agency, and Rentasnap – a photolibrary, both do this by making explicit the criteria and limits by which they are willing to work. This affects the subject matter both are willing to use. For example, Format will always prefer to show a woman or a black person when asked to provide a photograph of a 'typical' situation. The core of Rentasnap's library consists of demonstrations, community and local action. The mainstream agencies also use criteria, of course, but these are predominantly market-orientated ones.

A problem of the counter-agency approach is that the balance between the aims of politicised photographers and their possible market-orientated clients may be difficult and, at times, impossible to negotiate.

Another problem counter-agencies face when they try to engage with dominant practices is that their work forms only a part of a larger whole over which they can have no direct control. Thus the use to which a picture is put when it is purchased from Rentasnap is outside the control of the library's workers and their ability to fix its meaning and context is incomplete. To overcome this means to go beyond distributing photographs and to work consciously and deliberately towards distributing the ideas and ideologies that inform their photographs.

The final example is Leeds Postcards, whose activities combine elements of both strategies outlined above. They have certainly infiltrated an existing market which is dominated by people like Athena, Medici and Camden Graphics – with their photographic images and cartoons. They have done this to such an extent that the mainstream postcard industry has come to accept political postcards as a given part of the postcard market.

As a result of this, postcards have assumed the role as key propagandising and organising tools for many pressure groups. Postcards have come to be seen as a natural way of getting the message across. Thus, CND regularly produces postcards that have sold in their tens of thousands, and when the GLC funded a series of peacemurals it naturally arranged for the images to appear as a set of postcards. The ground that Leeds Postcards was instrumental in capturing in this way has also allowed various unaligned political cartoonists like Biff and Joe Stalin to develop.

In some cases the political economy of photography may be regulated by the availability of grant aid, in other cases by the willingness of members to subscribe, and yet other cases by the ability of the project to align its work with the perceived needs of its audience. Richard Scott of Leeds Postcards made a conscious decision to seek out a method of production and distribution which would give maximum exposure to those photographic images he was interested in propagating.

Not only does the postcard have a low unit cost, it also has sufficient practical use-value in addition to the political statement it makes, to encourage people to buy several copies of each card. Also, postcards of this kind have two forms of distribution, one based on the internal network of the client commissioning the postcard in the first place and, secondly, a public distribution through bookshops and mail order. The disadvantage of the postcard as a means of disseminating radical messages is that what can be said on a card is severely limited, compared to what can be said in an issue of a magazine.

In this introduction we are not seeking to contrast any of these projects in order to draw conclusion to the effect that one embodies a 'better' strategy than another, rather we are seeking to demonstrate the particular advantages/disadvantages that any given approach has. All of these approaches operate (can only operate) as parts of an overall political economy and it is finally within that overall political economy that problems of distribution must be located. The successes and failures of individual projects can only point towards the need for developed links between those projects; this applies not only to the distribution issues outlined here but also to the examples in the other sectors.

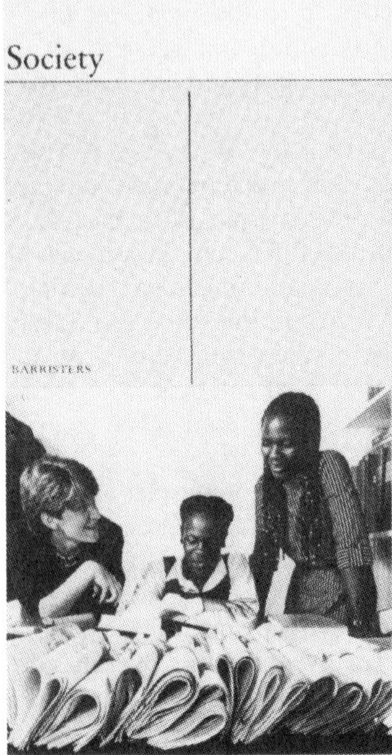



| | | | |
|---|---|---|---|
| Men | Police | Tennis | Women |
| Middle-age | *Police harassment* | *Weight training* | *Issues,* |
|  |  |  | *Politics* |
| Music | Public houses | Theatre |  |
| *Jazz, Blues* |  | *Fringe* | Women at work |
| *Musicians, Bands* | Religions |  | *Manual trades* |
| *1960 pop musicians* | Shops | Training schemes | *Office work* |
| *British & U.S.* | *Shopping* | Transport | *Professions* |
|  |  |  | *Services* |
| Occupations | Sport | Textiles | *Technical* |
| *Management* | *Badmington* |  |  |
| *Manual labour* | *Bowls* | Unemployment | Youth |
| *Office workers* | *Cricket* |  | *Sub-cultures* |
| *Professions* | *Cycling* | Welfare | *Unemployment* |
| *Services* | *Dog racing* | *Issues,* |  |
| *Skilled Manual* | *Football* | *Institutions,* |  |
| *Technical* | *Marathon* | *Personalities,* |  |
|  | *Netball* | *Policies* |  |
| Parks | *Squash* |  |  |

*Sample page from Format's catalogue. Format can be contacted at 25 Horsell Road, London N5, Tel. 609-3439.*

Stevie Bezencenet

# Photography, power and responsibility: the Format picture agency

Format is a picture-agency which started operating in May, 1983 – it stands for a new beginning in the coverage of social issues by photography.

The agency is a collective and comprizes 14 photographers, two administrators and one community worker who, between them, share the jobs of the production and circulation of visual information, working with a diverse range of clients from the traditional publisher, through to small groups in the community. This is an all-women collective and most members share feminist concerns for the place of women today and the biased manner in which we are represented. One of the aims of the agency is to help redress the ideological dominance of sexism and racism which characterize Fleet Street and picture agencies in general, themselves merely reflecting these tendencies in British society.

Agencies are established in response to market demands and adhere to those traditions of representation which usually deny the photographer any control over the use, context and final meanings of their images. Stereotypes are the stock-in-trade of this profession and when photographers are rewarded (financially and otherwise) for their ability to produce the 'strongest' examples of these visual conventions, it is not surprising that few have managed to produce alternatives, images which also have a 'currency' on the market. However diverse the subject area covered by these agencies, they do hold in common an attitude towards photography and the re-presentation of 'events' (an event being an occurrence, person or object). They operate in the interlocking realms of news, documentary and pictorialism, where the majority of the images are created and used out of an unproblematic belief in the empiricist base of photographic practice. Over and above this, the photographer who has the all-powerful gaze is denied in having a point of view; whilst, on the one hand, 'if it is not good enough, you are not close enough' (Capa), apparently, you also need to be invisible (Cartier-Bresson). The photographers in Format acknowledge both their literal/visual point-of-view and the corresponding ideological control this allows them – they understand the power and, wherever possible, take on board the resulting responsibility.

Photojournalism can be a solitary profession – creating work, doing research, covering administration and getting finance – all these come to dominate the actual making of pictures. The creation of the collective was partly in recognition of the value of combining resources and centralizing such necessary tasks. It was also in response to the patriarchal characteristics of existing agencies, which are male-dominated and often out of date in their visual strategies. Though some of the Format photographers had previously been asked to join other agencies, they declined, not wishing to be the token woman. The months of meetings which took place between a changing group of women (initially leading to eight photographers and two administrators), were an acknowledgement of a communal desire to create a working space which was not defined by men. This group wanted to investigate the advantages of a collective adminis-tration – as freelance photographers bound by similar concerns they were in a situation where the exchange of ideas, debate and access to new work were all made more easy.

Format was helped in its initial planning by other organizations (Network in particular), but their main problem was how to make themselves financially viable, whilst wanting to subsidize certain categories of their clients. It seemed that funding was the only answer and, after much soul-searching and hard work, they managed to get a grant from the GLC. This was to cover some of the basic administrative costs, allowing them to charge less to some groups and to operate in the community and educational sectors as a social resource. A grant from the GLC was by no means automatic; though current funding criteria would have favoured their applica-tion, their work is not local to London and a few of the photographers spend much of the year abroad. However, Format made the argument that they are concerned with a 'community of interests' and not a geographic one, and that the problem of certain sectors of the community in London obviously have their parallels and precedents in other parts of the world. One way of focusing on specific forms of oppression and control is to document a similar problem elsewhere, thus building up a comprehensive and more understandable 'map' of the issue.

State funding can become a way of life and some members are concerned about what one termed 'grant-funded mentality'. For organizations which are revenue clients of a Regional Arts Association or a Local Authority, it is not unusual to spend a substantial amount of time satisfying the demands of the funding body; indeed, they become the primary 'client' (see Owen Kelly's *Community Art and the State*). Format have seemed to avoid this pitfall by requesting a relatively small amount to cover that part of the market which is not commercially lucrative. If they were to charge proper NUJ rates for all who contact them, then they would be unable to reach a part of the public sector which they consider significant – this means the small groups, community work and education, rather than the established outlets of magazines, publishers and the mainstream media. This policy of subsidy allows access to their material and ideas for clients who are unable to afford standard market prices.

Whether or not funding continues after the initial two years, a time of consolidating the base and establishing working practices, Format would never be 100% commercial – it would be an impossibility – unless they removed the phone. The working of the collective is an organized, if sometimes chaotic business. The photographers all participate in the administration and the process of negotiating and discussing with clients as to the types of pictures that they might use, suggesting new and alternative images – alternative, that is, to the dominant view, both of the subject and of representation. The picture files are kept in the main office, whilst the workers have their darkrooms elsewhere. With the photographers sharing some of the office workload, it enables a coherent practice, policy and communication with clients; it also allows the weekly meeting to attempt the difficult task of resolving procedures, whilst also debating policy. The financial structure is complex. Each photographer pays a percentage into the agency, guaranteeing a minimum amount each month. (The three non-photographers are paid a fixed wage in recognition of their different function within the agency.) Each photographer subsidizes her own assignments, though the value of a trip may well be debated within the group. So, in order to participate in the agency, every member requires a reasonably high turnover of work to pay back the base rate into the collective. One of the most valuable lessons they have learnt during the first year is the need to make financial projections to help stabilize an erratic earning capacity.

Collective organization does not necessarily mean collective photography; indeed, they work in many different ways – usually individually. However, the chance of constant access to the new work of the rest of the group is considered to be a great advantage. Sometimes they will go on an assignment with a writer so that the research and ideas are pooled – the significance with which they consider the text is demonstrated by the extensive captions on the reverse of the images on file. When the occasion demands it they do work together covering an event which is too large or which will benefit from a variety of viewpoints, i.e., Greenham Common or a party conference. Format does not consider itself a news agency and so need not confront the problem of immediate delivery – their strategy allows a space for building a growing and changing picture of the events which they cover. Recently they have published a picture list, containing all the major categories of pictures on file: it is extraordinarily diverse considering that there were only eight photographers until recently, with three new members and two associates.

The scope of the file corresponds to the particular interests of the members, some of whom have been making a living in photography since the mid-60s, and the pictures are catalogued by country, political and social issues, with women and portraits as two major sections. There is a wealth of material under the following sub-headings: music, politics and industry, Central and South America, documenting welfare, trade unions, black society and political activities, Africa, children, disarmament, subcultures ... and, despite all this, some members feel that they can never have enough material under certain categories, i.e., housing, education and health, which are basic to our society and increasingly under attack. Format does not want to become known only as a feminist organization concerned with women's issues alone. Their interests are diverse: many of the categories are covered in South America, the West Indies, Africa and Asia, as well as Europe. Their main concern is to correct the usual gender and racial imbalance wherever possible – for example, they will try to send out strong and positive images, when a passive or stereotyped one might be the norm, and offer images of women doing a particular job, when traditionally an agency would supply a picture of a man, or a black person when an image of someone elderly is requested. The section on women in manual trades and the professions is substantial, for the group believes that circulating such images is very important for women's struggles. The images with which we are traditionally asked to identify (as women) are restricted and bear little relation to our potential. Positive images are necessary for new generations, so that they can establish a position in a society which acknowledges women as equal. Photographs have been part of the oppression and are here considered to be one of the ways of redressing the balance, of creating a strong external image with which women can identify, in order to create a strong 'self-image'.

There are some subjects which the collective have agreed not to cover, as the visual devices necessary to 'fix' the meanings of the picture are not sophisticated enough and the end result remains problematic. So they have a safeguard for other work as well and categorize certain images and subjects as having 'restricted use'. In such cases the photographer is contacted and asked if she agrees to a particular usage – the answer could well be 'No.' This policy recognizes the power that the visual image plays in determining attitudes to 'the social' and recognizes the relationship between ideology and the visual media. The group acts out its responsibility to the subjects in the pictures, otherwise they too would be replicating that same abuse which is all too common. Witness the recent coverage of the 'natural tragedy' in Ethiopia – the camera's function in colonising disaster for public consumption, under the guise of humanism, has never been as swift and extensive as here. The endless revelation of figure after figure delivered up by the myopic gaze of the lens is a form of voyeurism which is all the more powerful, operating as it does under the twin sanctions of charity and 'in-depth reporting'. The problem seems to be: how to make a strong and effective picture without degrading the subject.

One aspect of Format's work is to negotiate with clients about how a picture might be used, or how one might be 'set up' to meet their needs. This raises two points: the first is the extent to which a picture researcher or anyone requiring an image will be prepared to debate the significance of the 'how' of presentation, as well as the content of the image and the inflection of the caption. Format sees this role as crucial; it is no good creating alternative images if they are going to be used in restrictive and contradictory contexts. It is partly a matter of education. We are a literary society still and our ability to make sophisticated analysis of pictures is not especially well-tuned. We can recognize devices in spoken and written language, responding to them better than with images. We tend to be generally less imaginative in our use of images than words, more ready to accept conventionalized meanings in pictures. Format have discovered that many clients have conceptual ideas which are far in advance of their ability to visualise them; they use this 'space' to make suggestions which will create a more useful approach to the subject and a better 'ground' for their photographs. Time is spent discussing with callers what is being accepted and what is at stake by using standard (dominant) images – and what other representations there might be.

The second point concerns the tradition of photography for documentary purposes, with images couched in the 'realist' mode, using the alibi of the frame as *window*, whilst denying the mediating qualities of the whole process. Some of the group do work outside this form, using studio constructions and montage as invaluable pictorial devices, solving problems which 'straight photography' cannot deal with. However, there is the customer to convince – and this they are increasingly able to do.

Photography deals with surface, that is its nature, that is its dilemma. Format believes that it is important to show the issues underlying what is *only* visible, to investigate the conditions and causes of the phenomena at the surface. Certain members want a more integrated analysis, which they believe can only be achieved through exhibitions and books; this is where photography becomes a part of a broader work – that of dealing with social issues in all their complexity and contradictions. When photographers operate from a materialist point of view, the images will be an index of their political sensibilities, to some extent. The file is consistent in questioning the 'natural' and unravelling the 'mythic'. Many of the categories cut across continents and peoples, recognizing that crucial issues of racism and sexism, capitalism and colonialism have a history, a network of causes which, though serving powerful vested interests, can be queried, challenged and changed. Those who control language, control understanding; those who control the media are in a powerful position indeed – they are determining the form, the devices of rhetoric and, finally, the public's access to information. This is not to deny the audience's own power to refuse, to make fun, to make oppositional readings; however, the endless and consistent bias and stereotyping do clearly have an effect.

Format sees its role as a 'reflective' one, not in the traditional sense but with a different sense of 'realism' – one which seeks to investigate causes, to use representation for purposes of understanding and transformation, instead of its conventional function of documentary displacement, of 'dealing with' and then setting aside – to move on. There is an expectation by some who are interested in the progress of the agency, that they will be able to translate theory into practice, where others have failed – and to do it in a competitive and conservative market. But photography cannot change the world and there is only so much that can be done by this collective. Discussions are often at basic levels with clients and the public and need to be repeated time and time again – many have never heard the arguments before. To engage with the problematic of controlling a medium, which has traditionally been used in the service of the ruling class and the state, and to re-appropriate it to a more liberal and interventionist function . . . this is hard indeed. What is being contested is every site of information, every encyclopedia, schoolbook, manual, advert, illustration . . . Format are making an intervention into several spaces at once: the school system through talking and showing; the commercial sphere by example and persuasion; in community groups as a service; as a model for other women in many ways; by organizing debates and conferences; and, finally, by recording those aspects of society which they deem significant – the social and political issues which might otherwise remain 'invisible' or, if recorded, might be misrepresented.

For change to take place it is necessary to document the *why* and the diverse sites of its beginnings, so that others can identify with what is possible and not *only* what exists for the majority. It is this space that Format are attempting to open up.[1]

*Membership*
Joan Geoffroy, Sheila Gray, Pam Isherwood, Roshini Kempadoo, Jenny Mathews, Maggie Murray, Joanne O'Brien, Raisse Page, Brenda Prince, Suzanne Roden, Val Wilmer (Photographers), Sue Darlow, Sarita Sharma (Associates), Diana Ceresa, Jane Harper (Administrators), Amanda Hopkinson (Community).

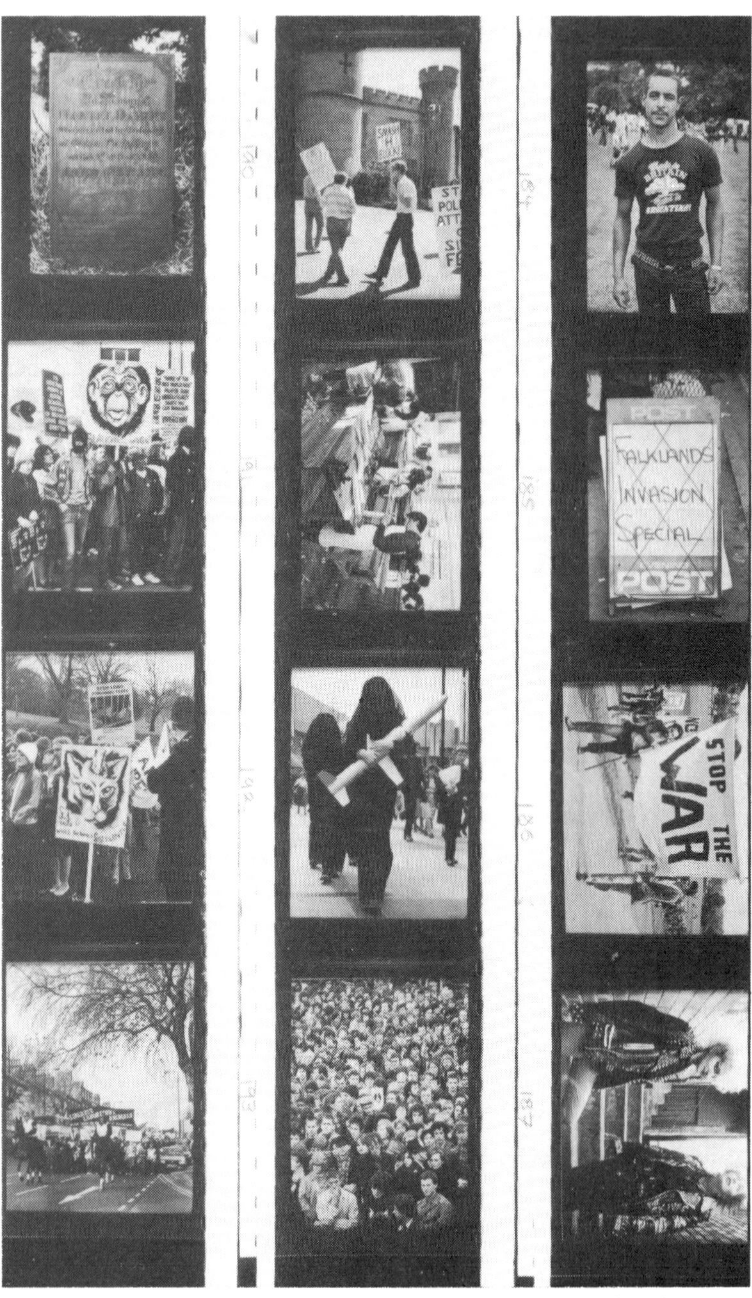


*Rentasnap: John Birdsall, Sharon Storer, A. R. Parkinson, Mark Salmon.*

Rentasnap Collective
# The Rentasnap Photo Library

Rentasnap has grown from two principal concerns: firstly, that many photographers and takers of photographs end up with large quantities of negatives and prints which lie unseen and unused, and which could probably be utilized in a number of ways, given a recognized point of contact and context. Secondly, that many grass roots political organizations are inhibited in the use of photographs, are unaware of the potential 'propaganda' value and don't really have access to relevant photo material. Rentasnap aims to bring these two elements together in a mutually stimulating and relevant way.

To date, user groups and contributors wishing to challenge the predominant media and visual stereotypes have, in the provinces at least, had to rely on a network of haphazard and largely personal contacts. Takers of photographs have become aware of organizations or publications who are likely to be interested in their work and, vice versa, groups requiring particular kinds of images have either relied on their own means or contacted a known photographer. This has not been particularly advantageous to anyone, due to its exclusiveness particularly, and has inhibited the development and growth of a pictorial record of local and regional events, campaigns and situations in the labour and community 'movements'. As with research and information facilities within the labour movement, photographic resources are too few and too often located in London, with the almost inevitable geographical and political divide that this creates. What we wanted to do was to develop a relevant and accessible facility based here in Nottingham, a city with plenty of print facilities but insufficient creative resources.

The sorts of groups and organizations we are aiming Rentasnap at are women's groups, environmental and anti-nuclear organizations, anti-racists, trade unions, socialist and community groups. The photographs are for use in newspapers, magazines, exhibitions, posters, tape-slide packs, etc. Consequently, we are attempting to ensure that the range of material included is likely to reflect the issues that these groups are working on. Equally, we are keen to build up a store of material of everyday events, situations and items which, while not being specifically relevant, do offer general design and artwork potential. Consequently, we are keen to enlarge our store of photos on transport, work, urban settings, people in social settings – shopping, in leisure, play, recreation, etc.

We are not concerned with working with specific arts or professional groups. Likewise, we suspect that there are many people who take photos that would be relevant but do not consider themselves as 'photographers'. We are trying to encourage all takers of photographs to include their material, professional and amateur, so to speak. We have found it difficult to encourage contributors who view their photos as too few or 'not good enough'. We hope that one of the values of Rentasnap will be that we can encourage confidence, not only in groups wanting to use images in new ways in their work, but also in contributors who can learn from the work of others, discuss their work, possibly work together, and see that their material can be of use and benefit to others. Hopefully, this will stimulate the taking of far more photos as well.

The photo library is located in two places – 118 Workshop, a resource centre for trade unions and community groups; and the Nottingham Community Arts and Crafts Centre (NCACC).

118 Workshop, presently with two workers funded jointly by Nottinghamshire County Council and Nottingham City Council, is an appropriate place for Rentasnap to be based. 118 offers an integrated resource facility for community groups and trade unions, campaigning, photographic, reprographic and technical resources; informational material and a library. Approximately 100 groups are affiliated to the project, ranging from trade union branches to tenants' associations; women's groups to cooperatives; ethnic minority organizations to solidarity groups; campaign groups to self-help groups.

Funded by Nottinghamshire County Council, the Inner Area Programme and the Community Programme, NCACC offers community arts and resource facilities for three inner city areas and, to a lesser extent, across the county. The facilities include photographic, offset and silkscreen printing, drama and craft.

Basing Rentasnap at the Workshop and at NCACC not only complements the facilities available, but also places the photo library at the focus of labour and community activity in the area, and we felt that this was vital to giving Rentasnap credibility and ensuring that contact was made and maintained with those most likely to want to use the library.

Both locations have a complete set of the 250-plus photos and a catalogue. Users can dot screen, photocopy, draw from the photos, reduce or enlarge via the process cameras, buy or borrow photos for exhibition, etc. We are aware of the possibility that photos can be used in ways contrary to the politics of Rentasnap/118/NCACC. Therefore, we have been asking users to give details of the uses and contexts of the photos. We have been aware, also, of the problems of being accountable responsibly to those people in the photos themselves. Hence, pictures of demonstrations, riots, campaigns or social/personal situations have contained known individuals in the area and, while it is impracticable to clear with them the use of any given photo, we want to safeguard individuals and groups as much as possible.

When we started Rentasnap we spent a lot of time evaluating the best way of displaying the photos, given that they were likely to be handled frequently and that they could be used not just for copying but also for exhibitions. We looked at unmounted prints, laminated prints, albums, different sizes, etc. In the end we have reached something of a compromise – 10″ × 8″ prints mounted on card and in plastic sleeves (at NCACC) and loose photos in albums (at 118). The drawback of this method is that it denies the user choice over photos used. We have begun to include contact sheets so that users can choose any number, but we are also aware that some users unfamiliar with looking at photos will not relate to the small size and will be unaware of the potential for cropping. Rentasnap does not carry negatives, other than some that have been donated and copy negs of two old photos included in the library. The taker of the photograph retains the negative and when we receive a request for a copy of a given photo, Rentasnap at 118 gives out the print and then gets a replacement from the photographer.

Other than that, the user makes the copy in whatever form appropriate, with or without the help of staff at 118 or NCACC.

For payment purposes, users are divided into two groups, reflecting the capacity to pay and the type of usage. Group A includes voluntary/community/neighbourhood groups and organizations with restricted financial means and limited circulations. Group B includes all others.

For Group A, if users simply screen and replace the photo, there is no charge. However, if they take away the photo the charge is £2. Group B pay NUJ rates, e.g. £12 for reproduction in a national paper, £8 for regional use.

If either group wishes to borrow for exhibition, then a small charge is payable, plus liability for any loss or damage. As a condition of use we ask that alongside each photo used, both the photographer and Rentasnap are credited and (for Group A) that a small advert as supplied by Rentasnap is inserted, and that two copies of the publication or printed item are given to Rentasnap for the records of Rentasnap and the photographer.

We are asking contributors to send us two black and white prints, 10" × 8" glossy, of each photo, with details of the photographer's name, address and telephone number, their reference number for the print, date taken (if possible) and brief description of the photo. Ideally, the prints should have had two-bath fixing and an extended wash to ensure print permanence. We have, at present, 12 contributors.

The library deals with invoicing, and income from a particular photo is split 30% to Rentasnap, 70% to the photographer. We are also interested in copying any material of historical or political interest.

We've tried to make the library as easy to use as possible, though the indexing of the collection has proved a problem. It seemed to us that the major difficulty lies in the language. We wanted to describe each photo as simply as possible, avoiding using language which required a certain degree of political awareness or sophistication. Equally, since all of us can look at and interpret photos in different ways, a plain description of the contents, such as 'anti-nuclear demo, women, Nottingham', creates a hierarchy of significance which others may not either perceive or agree with. In the end we have used a basic alphabetical index, not over-detailed, but with cross-referencing.

A community computer project, CODA, is also based at 118 Workshop and ready access to their word processing equipment makes it much easier to keep the index updated. The index has since been expanded to a fully-illustrated catalogue of the library. Each photo has been re-photographed onto 35mm film and the contacts of these films formed into a complete set of mini-prints of the collection. This, combined with the alphabetical index, plus a list giving full details of each photo in order, is proving to be a very valuable guide to the contents of the library.

The library has taken over two years to establish, with sporadic bursts of energy. Initially we, that is to say three or four of us (takers of photographs and resource workers), tried to develop a steering group to determine the growth of Rentasnap. That group collapsed due to lack of finance and momentum, until a new lease of life recently. Major difficulties have been lack of money, publicity and staff. Publicity is very important to encourage both users and contributors and to establish credibility. Money is needed to pay for this and to cover the necessary administration costs. Then, to round off the Catch-22, we need to ensure that there are enough people committed to making the library work in practice – in helping people take copies, in passing on orders, doing the books, publicity, invoicing, and so on.

At the same time, we are beginning to see Rentasnap in broader terms than simply as a library – partly out of necessity. For example, while trying to encourage people to use photos in their publicity at a local level, we realize that there is a considerable mystique around the reproduction of photos – how many people can do dot screening? To produce information about this would seem a worthwhile and integral part of our project. Similarly, to get involved in promoting courses and darkroom provision. One project we have recently completed is an exhibition, *See For Yourself*, which we hope will prove useful in giving information on community/left photography in its various forms and applications.

At present there are two people each putting in one day's work a week, running the library on a voluntary basis. This is supplemented by the paid staff at 118 and NCACC, who give some time to people calling with enquiries.

Most of the reproduction fees we earn are being ploughed back in to cover development costs; however, we are hoping that income will soon be sufficient to pay for a part-time worker of our own.

The library has been used by a range of local groups in their printed material and in display work. Photos from the library have been used in *Peace News*, *New Society* and a number of other national and regional publications. In the recent past, the bulk of the library contained photos from one person, but this situation is now changing. For the immediate future we hope Rentasnap will consolidate its position locally and also that we will be used regionally and nationally as a picture agency offering a wide range of material from 'something portraying anger' to campaign photos, by all those working directly or indirectly in the labour, women's and community movements.

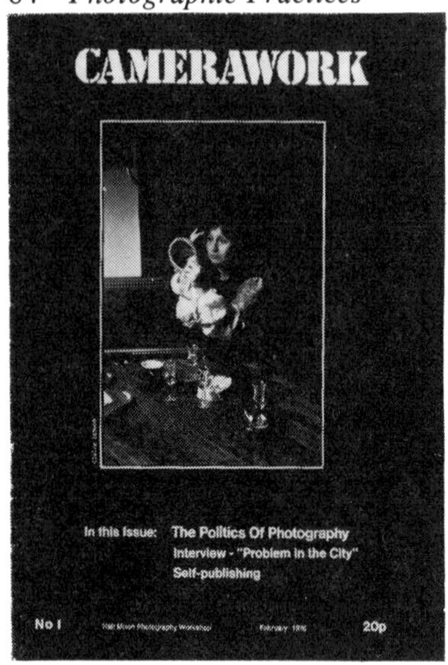
CAMERAWORK
In this Issue:   The Politics Of Photography
Interview - "Problem in the City"
Self-publishing
No 1   Half Moon Photography Workshop   February 1976   20p

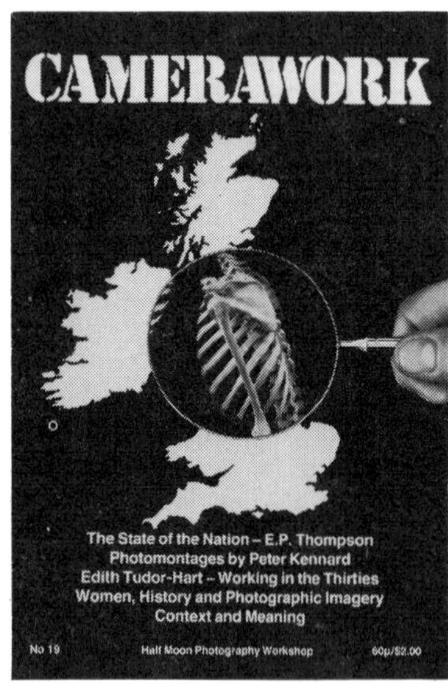
CAMERAWORK
The State of the Nation – E.P. Thompson
Photomontages by Peter Kennard
Edith Tudor-Hart – Working in the Thirties
Women, History and Photographic Imagery
Context and Meaning
No 19   Half Moon Photography Workshop   60p/$2.00

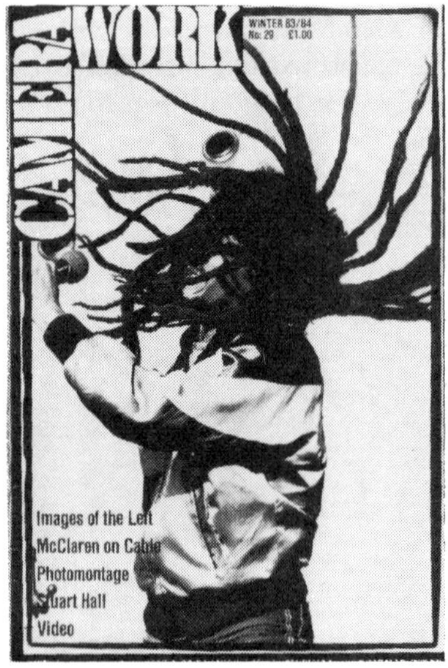
CAMERAWORK
WINTER 83/84
No. 29   £1.00
Images of the Left
McClaren on Cable
Photomontage
Stuart Hall
Video

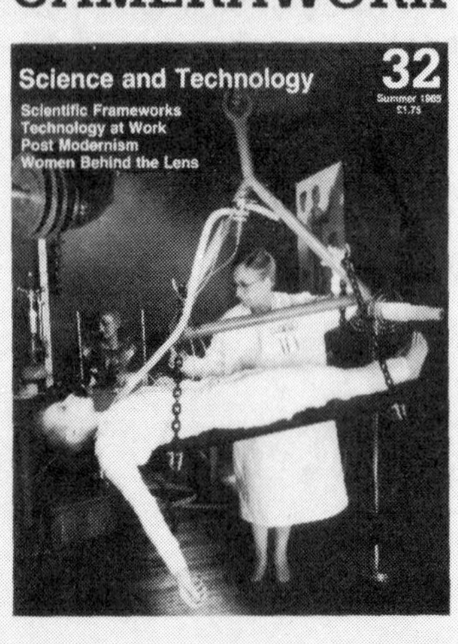
CAMERAWORK
Science and Technology   32
Summer 1985
£1.75
Scientific Frameworks
Technology at Work
Post Modernism
Women Behind the Lens

Kathy Myers
# Camerawork

*Camerawork* magazine is no longer in production. The last issue was published in June 1985. The magazine has ceased production with 10 years and 32 issues under its belt. This essay isn't intended so much as a wake or an obituary as an examination of the aims and ambitions of the photography magazine up to issue no. 30. An interesting case study because it raises much broader questions about the ways in which the political left and, more specifically, the image-making left, has attempted to engage with mainstream media culture and ideas of social change.

Back in 1976 the aims of *Camerawork* were quite clear. In Issue One, page one, Jo Spence outlined the magazine's intentions in 'The Politics of Photography'. Criticising the mainstream media's implicitly sexist and racist attitudes, she went on to point out the poverty of current photographic/media education and the photographic establishment's obsession with social realism and photojournalism: 'More often than not it is an unjustifiably voyeuristic and one-sided account of the stark situation in which many people are forced to live – or a superficial treatment of the joys and sorrows of celebrity life.' Spence pointed to the evolution of two 'alternative' practices during the 1970s: the establishment of alternative photo news agencies, such as Report, which concentrated on 'industrial and community action, showing solidarity among people, unlike the mass press which often depicts only the struggle of the individual', and secondly the development of community photography – 'The most recent break with traditional fields of photography as a TOOL by community activists ... The main objective here is to enable people to achieve some degree of autonomy in their own lives and to be able to express themselves more easily, thus gaining solidarity, with each other ... What long term results community activists can achieve with photography still remains to be seen.'

The world-weariness of community photography was not, however, to be tackled on a visual level. Instead, the *Camerawork* of the early 1980s effectively abandoned the cause of community photography, at that time lost in a documentary time-warp, in favour of a theoretical exploration of the nature, form and potential of the political image. A move which cut the magazine off from other corners of the *Camerawork* institution, notably the community darkrooms which at that time were battling with unreliable resources to keep an open access policy going, encouraging members of 'the local community' to come in, develop their pictures and learn rudimentary technical photography skills. Probably one of the last significant pieces to be written (*Camerawork* 20, 1980) on the subject of community photography within that period of *Camerawork*'s evolution, was by Don Slater, a long-standing and influential member of the magazine team. His article raised three points: the need for community photography to engage with the rhetoric and power of the dominant media; the need to establish a coherent alternative photographic culture and, finally, the importance of tackling head-on the criterion by which a 'good' photograph was judged. Implicitly his article warned of the dangerous complacency which existed within the community sector: an assumption that 'access', 'accessibility' and some wishy-washy notion of 'alternative' documentary practice was enough. He commented: 'The visual illiteracy and ignorance of the rudiments of creative propaganda, within the orthodox left, is dangerous. Good propaganda is sometimes produced, but the failure to engage seriously with the politics of representation as a whole, to carry out the struggle there, is potentially fatal.' (Ibid.)

Slater felt that 'good' community photography at that point in the 1980s should not be judged by traditional standards of the art establishment. He felt that it was more important to establish a comprehensive grass roots movement – he wrote: 'At the moment community photography is largely an advertisement for itself: it stands for and stands judged by a form of involvement; the real question is, "What is a good community photography project?"' He went on to argue against the photograph as purely a 'commercial object'. Slater suggested that the community photograph should be seen as a process, the outcome of a specific form of production and consumption which over-ruled the laws of the market-place by: 'Keeping the least possible distance between those who produce and those who consume images. This breaks through many ideas of what photography is and what photographs do. But the main question community photography asks is, who is the project for? Any judgement of the photo starts from the audience response.'

Looking back, this was to prove a crucial article in the genealogy of *Camerawork*'s photography debate, summing up many of the political contradictions and discrete traditions which ran through the pages of the magazine. The idea that community photography could only be judged by process and not by product, made a mockery of the idea of *Camerawork* as an institution which could 'showcase' the community's product. It also questioned the basis of the magazine's Arts Council funding which had traditionally been 'product' orientated. He continued:

'A community photograph is neither arty totem, personal snapshot nor political propaganda – though it involves the personal, the political and the visually stimulating. A community photograph cannot be damaged by technical or aesthetic criticism, the judgements of the art gallery.' (Slater, ibid.)

The idea of community photography as a social practice further hived it off from the other photographic traditions fostered by *Camerawork*. From the inception of the magazine it is possible to perceive a tension between four schools of thought.

## Photojournalism

Whilst Jo Spence's inaugural speech in *Camerawork* One had questioned the foundations of social realism and documentary photojournalism, the magazine continued to run 'picture spreads' which either let the image speak for itself – a window on the world – or were heavily captioned with political information. In the case of Nicaragua, Ireland, El Salvador, Clydeside, The People's March For Jobs and the Lewisham Riot issue, the magazine was overtly propagandist in its promotion of 'alternative' photojournalism, a move which many thought might jeopardise the magazine's 'arts' funded status. The propagandist use of the magazine was also criticised from the political left with photographers concerned that the magazine would become little more than a political vehicle for the latest crisis, event or picket and in that sense indistinguishable from other leftist organs like *The Leveller*, *New Statesman* or *Marxism Today*.

## Worker photography

Where worker photography stops and community photography starts is a matter of debate, but through the back issues it's possible to trace a consistent concern with the need to construct a visual history of the people. Firmly entrenched in the documentary tradition, articles on the Match Girl Strike, Labour History Museum or mass observation were underexploited: run as little more than evidence of the need for a contemporary community photography. Although it challenged the orthodox account of working-class history and forefronted class struggle, this kind of photography did little to advance the image debates which *Camerawork* was trying to encourage. Pictures of worker solidarity ran against vagrant images of the poor as disenfranchised or 'victims' of society.

As a historical form, this kind of representation played a crucial part in the recording and making of early twentieth-century history. Well-suited to the needs of the time, it appeared out of date and dangerously nostalgic when exploited as 'the' most appropriate form for contemporary community photography, which remained sceptical of more experimental types of image-making.


# Montage

Perhaps the most innovative visual tradition fostered by *Camerawork* was that on montage. Frequent retrospective pieces on artists such as Heartfield were run against exhibitions of contemporary work: Peter Kennard, Sylvia Gohl and David Evans, to name but a few. Exploited also by feminist image-makers such as Jo Spence, montage was the only photographic form encouraged by *Camerawork* which challenged the social realist foundation of photography and attempted to attach some political significance to the power of fiction. However, the form which montage took was always limited, firmly entrenched in Heartfield juxtaposition of opposites, on the one hand, and on the other, challenging a photograph's meaning through the assemblage of oppositional texts. In fact, text and image became almost a hallmark of *Camerawork*'s montage devices. Although montage is also one of the dominant languages of advertising, the magazine never challenged the thin dividing line between 'right on' political propaganda and 'offensive' consumerist advertising. This resistance to fighting over definitions or attempting to recuperate some of the rhetorical territory lost to the right (who in many ways had already appropriated the subversive language and style of punk, feminism, labourist democracy, anti-racism, etc.) meant that in the end modern montage tended to play safe.


# Theory

The inadequacies of the existing photographic forms, paralleled by the poverty of photographic theory, precipitated the need to establish a coherent theory of socialist/alternative photography. This academic trace element exists from the inception of the magazine, but is only fully realised after issue 18, which had witnessed yet another change in the editorial composition of the magazine. Over the eight years of *Camerawork*'s existence, writers such as Jo Spence, John Berger, John Walker, Jill Pack, Gen Doy and Rosetta Brookes contributed to the evolution of a theory of radical photography.

Against the two documentary traditions of worker/community photography and photojournalism ran a third discourse: the need to establish a coherent theory of socialist/alternative photography. This can be traced through the printing of articles by writers such as Jo Spence, John Berger, Don Slater, John Walker, Gen Doy and Rosetta Brookes. The need for such a theory became all the more poignant as the tension between so-called 'access' community photography and the product of the bourgeois media became more overt. *Camerawork* had to find a theoretical way of dealing with the fact that by the early 1980s images 'for the people' were by and large a sophisticated diet of floppy disks, pop videos, computer graphics and advertisements. Against such a visual onslaught, *Camerawork*'s position oscillated between a critique of the dominant media as a form of offensive, beguiling ideology and the need to establish an alternative, powerful and interventionist visual rhetoric for the left.

The solution was an academic one, and by 1980, issue 20, *Camerawork*'s editorial policy sought to replace the need to showcase 'alternative' community or photojournalistic work with a theory of representation: how images created and sustained meaning. Photography was at this point hallmarked by the absence of such a theory.

By issue 24 the mast head of *Camerawork* read as follows: *Camerawork* is a journal of the politics of photography. It is designed as a forum for analysis, critique, theory and information in order to provide the basis for using photography within socialist and feminist practices and to develop and encourage socialist strategies within the politics of representation.'

The political shift from 'access' community photography to the evolution of a forum for debate about the 'politics of representation' alienated a vast slice of the alternative photographic sector, who firmly believed that photographic strategy should exclusively concern itself with 'putting cameras into the hands of the people'. It was a time when the inheritance of the community sector firmly believed in the 'positive' image: the photograph which would correct the unsound bourgeois image culture through the presentation of an alternative point of view. *Camerawork*'s decision to divorce itself from the community sector went hand in hand with the creation of a new alliance with film theory.

Film magazines like *Jump Cut*, *Screen* and *Framework* were not so much concerned with access to the media (although groups like the IFA mounted consistent pressure to establish an alternative film-making culture) as with the politics of the image: how pictures created and sustained meanings in ideology. *Camerawork* met film theory half-way, adopting some of its rhetoric in parallel with a hard line Marxist critique of the politics of ownership and photographic production. *Camerawork* superseded the idea of photography as an access tool, with photography as an ideological weapon. The debate no longer centred around the creation of a safe alternative so much as the creation of opposition and intervention, hauling over the coals the existing visual rhetoric of both the political left and right.

The final stage in *Camerawork*'s evolution was born in issue 29, which adopted a new format and editorial line, although it must be seen as a continuity of the debates spawned by the magazine over the preceding few years.

The second term success of the Tory government in the spring of 1983 put the political left into a state of shock. The left was divided and in a state of disarray, and this dissension reproduced itself in the alternative photographic sector which had lost faith in its endeavours and was confused by the widening gulf between alternative community practices and the populistic rhetoric of the right. The community sector purported to represent the interests of the people, yet if the media victory won by Saatchi and Saatchi for Thatcher was anything to go by, 'the people' wanted gloss, sophistication and high production values. The left's propaganda had missed the mark: its ambition to be incisive, 'deconstructing' the right's rhetoric, had failed. By comparison left propaganda looked dated and out of touch. 'The people' just weren't interested.

The relaunched *Camerawork* arose out of this political hiatus. As a magazine it had previously provided an umbrella under which an 'alternative' photographic political culture could survive. It could not, however, tackle head on, contemporary image culture. Already on the defensive, the magazine failed to patronise a new image culture. The theoretical foundations were there, but still too academic in form and language, the magazine was in danger of languishing in a theoretical backwater. To compound these problems, the magazine lacked a co-ordinator and, subsisting on an itinerant hard-working voluntary team for over a year, was in danger of losing its funding. By the summer of 1983 when I was appointed as editor, the *Camerawork* staff and the Arts Council were both equally concerned that the next issue of the magazine should be more accessible and populist, although nobody seemed able to define either of the terms. Panic at the potential loss of revenue to the *Camerawork* institution resulted in a large watch-dog/editorial team being appointed to the new magazine. Memos flew with the speed of light and magazine advice came and went as a plethora of community photographers put their point of view into the melting pot. By the autumn, after three months of dissension, the editorial team was whittled down to nine people who had a similar vision of the new magazine.

The time had passed for *Camerawork* to act as a safe in-house journal for the left's community photographers. The magazine wanted to put into crisis all the commonsense assumptions which governed the rhetoric and complacency of the left. At the same time the potential of *Camerawork* was limited by its historical obsession with the still image which limited the meaning of photography. In accord with this, the editorial which introduced the relaunched magazine read:

'*Camerawork*'s interest in photography has expanded to include other aspects of the media. For example we have commissioned pieces on film, video, tape-slide and television. The editorial group felt this was necessary because photography is central to so many practices. The boundaries between the mediums are necessarily blurred. On the one hand many photographers now work within video and graphics and, on the other, debates originally fostered around film have proved relevant to the future of alternative photography.'

Pieces on the Rio Community Cinema, the Colin Roach video, cable and design were commissioned. An interview with media sociologist Stuart Hall and a piece on the Wright agency's handling of the 1983 Labour Party campaign investigated the poverty of left propaganda which arguably had progressed little from the halcyon days of the 30s, Russian Constructivism, Heartfield's photomontages and the 30s Worker photo documentary tradition. It also seemed ironical that a photography magazine should carry so little on the DIY of taking photographs. The magazine tried to close the gap between theory and practice by running short pieces over the next two issues on how to take certain kinds of photographs as well as, wherever possible, crediting photographs not only with names but also the method: film speed, aperture, timing, etc.

Apart from the desire for a new editorial direction, everybody felt that the magazine needed a new look. Ironically, whilst *Camerawork* purported to explore the visual image, design had never been top of the agenda. We decided to employ a professional designer to improve the look of the magazine and, in blatant marketing terms, make it easier for the magazine to compete on the open magazine market. We were keen to get the magazine out of the safe left ghetto and make it more attractive to people with a more general interest in photography and political culture. We also wanted the magazine to have a younger profile. A magazine and readership shouldn't grow older together.

I had a very strong idea of what I wanted the magazine to look like: half-way between a fanzine and a political paper. Something like the old *Temporary Hoardings*, the recently deceased *Kicks* or the still current *Face*. Andy Dark was an obvious choice: having worked on *Temporary Hoardings*, *Kicks* and *City Limits* as well as a number of *Camerawork* exhibitions, he had the right track record and was guaranteed to find favour within the *Camerawork* establishment. His design was fresh, fanzinish and modern with just a dash of the formal constructivist look which had become a hallmark of left design. He was effectively given an open brief, although the editorial group had decided on the smaller A3 format prior to this. We also worked out a more generous picture ratio of 50/50: the old A4 *Camerawork* had been dominated by text at the expense of images. Colour was too expensive, but we plumped for the most luxurious paper finish available, both to improve the quality of image reproduction and, we hoped, make the magazine attractive to potential advertisers. Although the editorial team was responsible for the production of the magazine's text and images, Andy Dark had a free hand with layout, typeface and picture location. On the first issue at least, editorial and design went hand in hand, making sure that the text fitted the space allocated, writing tight captions and headlines to fit the 'look' of the magazine and trying, as a point of principle, to make sure that the text didn't dominate the look or complexion of the magazine.

Hand in hand with the new editorial and design approach went a reassessment of *Camerawork*'s distribution and marketing. The magazine had traditionally enjoyed stable sales of approximately 5,000, of which roughly half were subscription. The magazine's future had been temporarily jeopardised by the collapse of PDC, the only existing 'alternative' distribution agency willing to handle small publications. Like the photo magazine *Ten.8*, *Camerawork* went to Theatre Dispatch, a small outfit in Covent Garden which had up till then only handled theatrical publications. At the same time a national distribution deal was negotiated with W. H. Smiths, using *The New Statesman* as a distributor. Unfortunately, this latter deal, which could have significantly increased *Camerawork*'s distribution and potential advertising revenue, was not finalised before the magazine's stoppage in the summer of 1984. Meanwhile, the Arts Council had commissioned a special report from Comedia to look into the marketing and distribution of the small magazines which it funded, and there was promise of an Arts Council supported distribution service.

As a package, both politically and financially, the new *Camerawork* seemed viable although, as subsequent events were to prove, the financial and managerial problems of *Camerawork* the institution – of which the magazine formed only a part – were to prove fatal for the life of the magazine.

*Camerawork* was internally in a mess. The place had experienced at least three previous political coups which resulted in staff leaving in droves. Often this was written off as 'personality clashes' but the real reason is that *Camerawork* was born out of misplaced idealism, the belief that different kinds of political endeavour could subsist under the same roof. *Camerawork* was being pulled apart by the gallery's investment in international photojournalism, the darkroom's commitment to the community sector and the magazine's ambition to intervene in political propaganda and create a new image industry. Add to those political contradictions overworked staff, years of bad administration and botched-up accounting, and you have a recipe for disaster. Ironically the *Camerawork* staff were almost unanimous in agreeing the reasons for *Camerawork*'s disastrous financial predicaments and political tensions. Instead of a coup, the staff agreed to try and establish the *Camerawork* dinosaur along the lines of the more progressive film workshops which had emerged out of the independent film culture's struggle for political, financial and union identity. Workshop principles would demand that *Camerawork* drop its photographic Jack-of-all-trades identity and unify the political practices of gallery, magazine and darkrooms. Although an attractive and expedient political plan, it foundered on the rocks of bureaucratic recalcitrance, not meeting with approval from *Camerawork*'s own management structure. The result of this political impasse over 'the right road forward' precipitated the resignation of most of the staff over the next few months. Salaries were unpaid, revenue thin on the ground and the magazine financially unviable. The funding authorities rightly held on to their money until *Camerawork* had sorted out its dirty washing.

Whether or not it starts up again is in a way irrelevant. Magazines come and go, and as a disposable form of political culture are by their very nature meant to be outmoded and superseded. What is important is that the aims of *Camerawork* to forge a new political vision for 'alternative', interventionist photography be taken seriously. Populism is often wrongly confused with a desire to oversimplify or reduce comment to the lowest common denominator. By comparison, *Camerawork* wanted to take a fresh look at populism, at the potential for producing powerful political images of and for the future which would represent the ambition of the left questioning the right's appropriation of the slick, the pleasurable and the stylish. As Stuart Hall commented in *Camerawork* 29:

'When you talk about Utopia, I think it's a real socialist struggle over language of the past. I think it's absolutely crucial that we have positive images of the future which meet people's rising expectations, and I think there's a lot about Labourist thinking on the left which is going to have to change ... Now we have to get down to the nitty gritty problem, which is – guess what – how to reach the people, so the ideological question about the left's rhetoric is not marginal at all. It's central.'

John Taylor

# *Ten.8* quarterly magazine

In 1979 it was easy to produce *Ten.8*. We turned out three issues in our first year and enjoyed ourselves. In our first editorial we stated 'our primary aim is simple: to get as many pictures as possible seen and to stimulate debates about the implications of photography'. In some respects nothing has changed. But none of us would now believe that such an aim could ever be simple, and when it seemed so to us then, we were mistaken.

We have had to deal with many problems, and one of the biggest has been to identify our audience. There was no money for market research, but probably it would have shown only that the prospective audience for our project was so tiny that it would be impossible for us to survive as a small business. Some of the tensions of the following years stemmed from the peculiar and contradictory assumptions which set up *Ten.8* like a small business that was making a product no-one wanted or which, at any rate, no-one had heard of.

In our enthusiasm for pictures and words we tended to downgrade the business side of things, and were overcome with inertia at the thought of distribution. We often bemoaned the fact that, unlike *Camerawork* and *Creative Camera*, whom we saw as our nearest relatives, we were not linked to some larger institution that might help us with the problems of cash flow – for instance, when two distributors went bust owing us money. And, since most of the alternative bookshops and photographic galleries were in London and we were based in Birmingham, it was much harder for us to push the distributors and to raise our visibility. At least distribution has been improved recently since we have been established with 'Theatre Dispatch'.

We started off with very local interests. We were funded by the Regional Arts Association, and part of the success of the application depended upon the fact that a lot of photographic work in the region was funded by the RAA – but at that time there was no Photographic Centre, and so no means of distributing information about photography. But once we had published a magazine full of regional interest, there was nowhere to sell it.

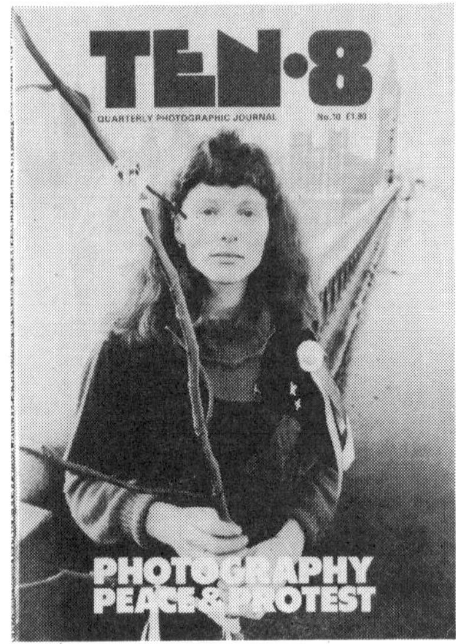
TEN·8
QUARTERLY PHOTOGRAPHIC JOURNAL   No.10 £1.80
PHOTOGRAPHY
PEACE & PROTEST

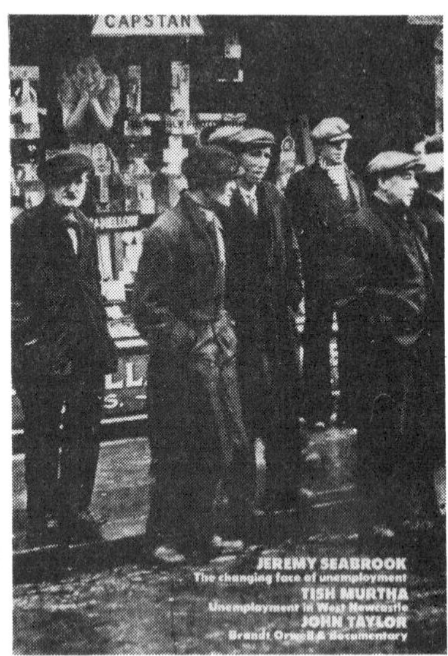
CAPSTAN
JEREMY SEABROOK
The changing face of unemployment
TISH MURTHA
Unemployment in West Newcastle
JOHN TAYLOR
Brandt Orwell & Documentary

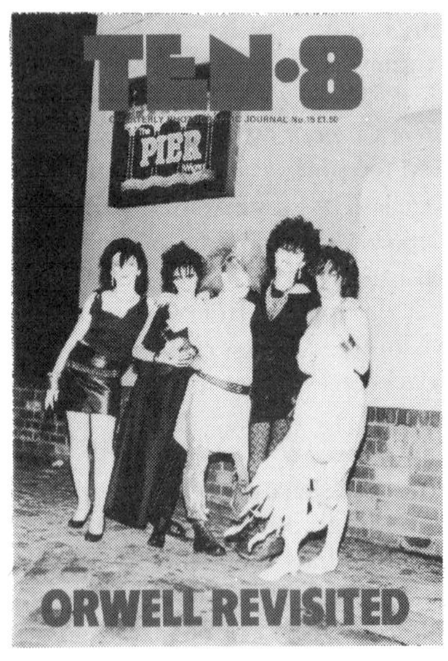
TEN·8
QUARTERLY PHOTOGRAPHIC JOURNAL No.15 £1.50
The PIER
ORWELL REVISITED

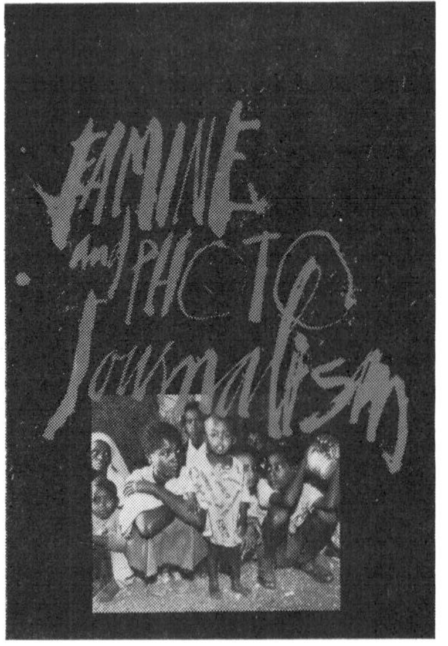
FAMINE
and PHOTO
Journalism

Our situation was exactly this: we were a small group of disparate people who were able to publish a magazine, but we had too little money to pay for work of a professional standard; too little money to pay anyone to do the huge amount of administrative work that is involved in setting up production and distribution; and too little knowledge of the identity that was needed for a new magazine in an uncertain market. We had the A3 format of *Camerawork*, but no conviction; we had *Creative Camera*'s approach to photographs, but without the glossy look. Although we were one year old, we were still invisible.

In 1980 we published *Self-Portraits* (No. 4). It looked the same as the others and was funded in the same way, but it was different. We included work of national significance, though we had still to rely upon the willingness of people to work for next to nothing. But, most important of all, was the piece called 'Handsworth Self-Portrait', one outcome of a grant awarded to the three of our group who were freelance photographers and in the process of setting up an agency. On one level it was a community-based project that enabled these three to draw closer to the local community, but it also signalled a new professionalization and commitment to journalism that in the long run benefited the magazine – though in the short term almost finished it. No more issues were published in 1980. This fact highlights how dependent the magazine was upon the input of the freelancers as designers and producers. Since there was no money to pay for this work, and none of the other editors had the professional skills that are needed to *produce* a magazine, it went into cold storage for the rest of that year.

In 1981 we started to receive our grant from the Arts Council of Great Britain, but as there was some uncertainty and delay in the change-over, we appeared later in the year with a double issue (No. 5/6). It was effectively a re-launch. It had a new look – A4 format, perfect bound – and was full of hard-hitting documentary photographs of the revolution in Iran, South America, Chris Steele-Perkins' reporting on starvation in the Horn of Africa, Mike Goldwater's pictures of the deforming effects of Agent Orange, and Nick Hedges' photographs of life in the inner cities. At last the magazine had found an identity. The provincial links were loosened; the *Camerawork* look-alike disappeared; the half-hearted commitment to art photography was abandoned; and photography that was not dependent upon grants was acknowledged. But still the issue was a flop. The underlying problems of production and visibility had still not been resolved.

We hit another low point, and it took another six months to produce the next double issue – 'Restricted Practices, Documentary

Photography in Britain Today' (No. 7/8). We aimed for a longer shelf-life and more synoptic and less ephemeral work than is usual in magazine journalism. All the work was shown in a touring exhibition which opened with a one-day conference at the ICA. Most important of all, we recognized that we needed a chief editor to take overall responsibility for the magazine, whilst still working closely with the rest of the group, who had finally to approve the content. This is still our preferred structure; and although the chief editor's role is now more definite, and in a sense more powerful, the role of the group has also become clearer: it now oversees everything, including the design. Furthermore, the group does not only discuss editorial matters, but also takes responsibility for business, promotion and many other unglamorous details of the organization. These structural definitions have helped professionalize the group, but none of it would have been possible without the success of our application to the ACGB for a grant to pay for a part-time coordinator who, once advised by the group, deals with all the administration.

It seems that the next logical step would be to apply for a salary for an editor. If this role was properly set up with sufficient pay and the right appointment, the last deficiencies of self-exploitation would disappear – the obvious being the uneven look of a set of issues that have been produced by editors with different ideas about the purpose of the journal. The usual oppositions in the debate are between popular journalism and academic respectability, and as long as we veer from one pole to the other, we can only confuse our prospective audience and ourselves. Neither pole is the best place to be, and to draw upon the best of each does not mean to sit on the fence or to suffer from a failure of nerve. We cannot hope to compete with the popular magazines as long as we are quarterly, are not advertising the technology, and print only in black and white. And it is not worthwhile to try to compete with the more academic journals that deal with visual representation, such as *Block* and *Screen*, because of our strong base in journalism and our recognition that photography has a wider constituency than intellectuals.

Still, it is the work of the intellectuals in fields of study far removed from photographic practice – in linguistics, sociology, literary and film studies and, belatedly in art – and photo-history – that meant it was no longer possible by 1982 to print photographs and to talk about them in the way of general appreciation. Our evolution over the last couple of years is a measure of the recognition of the significance of these other procedures and their relevance to our initial pledge to 'stimulate debate'. And so we have gradually moved away from appreciative pieces into asking awkward questions about photography, and towards building bridges between the work of photographers, critics and historians. It is the hardened categories of our education system, the powerful anti-intellectualism of much photographic practice and the elitism (as well as the difficulty) of the intellectual demands of the academic world, that has made our project so difficult; and, at the same time, so necessary.

One thing is clear. There is no discreet history of photography modelled upon orthodox art history – the star system of masters, of either the aesthetic or documentary modes. To understand photography we have to see it as a technology that reproduces reality, and to explicate it we have to write some new history, new criticism, new journalism; we need to reproduce old photographs as well as new ones, humble photographs as well as ones of professional competence or that offer aesthetic pleasures. It is a daunting project, and although difficult to sustain in a hostile climate, this is precisely the time when it is most needed. Six years on, and the times are very different – much harder, much sharper. Neither photography, nor *Ten.8* can escape their implications.

# Exhibition

## Stevie Bezencenet
## Exhibition

The existence of public spaces for viewing cultural artefacts has become sufficiently common to be taken for granted. However, it was not until the mid-1800s that the overlapping of debates around education, cultural heritage and the moral element of aesthetic values created the basis for legislation, which resulted in the national growth of public libraries and museums. This development and the rise of art galleries served to introduce the 'general' public to objects previously located in the private sphere, and the institutional spaces of the artistic elite. At last the arts of the past were being made accessible, whilst at the same time serving a double purpose – one acknowledged, the other not.

Cultural production in the nineteenth century arose out of the patronage of the ruling classes, the market-place of the bourgeoisie, and the cultural traditions of the working class. However, all practices were not equally reflected in the new public institutions. Those objects which had previously graced the interiors of palaces and churches, ancestral homes and private galleries became the 'raw material' for the museum process of amalgamation. Objects produced in a European tradition of imperialism, racism, oppressive religion and patriarchy – they were initially created and displayed in support of those values.

A great diversity of objects was displaced from their original function as conveyors of ideology and brought together into a new conceptual space, the museum, in order to undergo a process of being divested of their primary social meanings (as objects linked to a particular place and culture) and invested with another, unifying concept – art for art's sake. This co-option into the hallowed space of 'Culture' was aided by the development of a new critical vocabulary, which aimed to hide the social basis of the work, replacing it with an analysis based on subjectivity and aesthetic quality. This became the acknowledged function of the objects – to develop and improve the cultural life and values of a nation. The status of the works as ideological forms became denied and problematic for a spectator to 'uncover'.

The re-presentation of objects invested with one set of functions/ meanings in the guise of another is not *necessarily* disturbing, if the institution is sufficiently practised in the process of re-contextualisation and display. The 'dressing' of such value/able objects becomes a shroud, which serves to embalm the original meanings in favour of imposed ones. These secondary meanings may be sufficiently pleasurable to divert the audience from making other critical responses to the work. And so the museum and the gallery become precisely the opposite of the educational, historical and socially useful institutions they claim to be.

## Photography and exhibition

There are many photographic galleries throughout the country and many more art galleries, presenting photographic work as part of a general policy. There are also the less art-orientated spaces which make use of the touring shows (generated by the galleries and workshops, i.e. Impressions – York, Side – Newcastle, Camerawork – London) to present work whenever wall space can be found. However, only a few of these galleries/showing spaces have the combination of facilities and policy to integrate the visual material into a more comprehensive approach to photography.

The three spaces of the Watershed (Bristol), the Pavilion (Leeds) and the National Museum (Bradford) are all concerned with the 'showing' of the medium, but at a level which is concerned with far more than mere 'display'. They are interested in both informing and stimulating identified audiences (as well as the 'general' public), by employing a range of strategies to create the conditions for an active and critical relationship between the work and the audience. These three organisations have structural, economic and policy differences – but they share a concern for the inter-action of the participant, rather than the passive consumption of the spectator. In a variety of ways they take the basis of a general interest in the medium and try to develop it into a more substantial understanding of photographic culture.

Organisations where gallery policies are supported by other activites have the advantage of being able to engage with their public in a more complex/integrated manner. Programmes which include workshops, darkrooms, seminars, screenings, etc., on the same general theme as the 'exhibition' seem to have a more constructive social relationship with their participants, than those which rely on images to explain themselves. This structured framework of activities obviously does not automatically lead to a critical, progressive photographic understanding and practice. However, the mere 'showing' of photographs tends to collapse back into that process of containment and negation discussed in relation to museums.

During the 1970s and early 1980s there was a dramatic growth of photographic centres and workshops throughout  the country. Though the Photographers Gallery (London) was the first major 'space' to open in 1971, and receives the largest subsidy of any funded client, it does not fit into this category of 'progressive' centres. Despite its long history and the range of experience of its workers, the Gallery has never managed or wanted to act out a progressive role in the photographic community, with a sustained and coherent programme of photographic concerns. It seems to have become trapped between its own image of itself as a national 'Flagship' (Arts Council terminology) and new demands to become concerned with its local/regional constituency and their 'educational' needs. One lost chance should not be such a great problem; however, public funding is an increasingly problematic area for the arts and for one gallery to receive such a large proportion of the total subsidy for the country, this does affect the possibility of more radical ventures elsewhere – especially if the 'Flagship' is taken as the norm against which other practices are measured.

On the whole the Establishment's relation to photography has been an impoverished one – the major national institutions have only recently acknowledged the medium as a form worthy of their notice. However, when they do show work, it is from the traditional perspective of genre, masters, historical compilation or uncontentious modernism – attitudes which form the basis for much of the exhibition policy in this country. A good example is the policy of the Arts Council – it might claim to be interested in innovative and critical work, but if we examine what has appeared at its two premier sites of showing, the Serpentine and the Hayward, its policy is acted out rather differently. Apart from the 'Three Perspectives in Photography' show in 1979, which was 'disavowed' by the Arts Council in the catalogue introduction, and a few innovative shows at the Serpentine, the Council has not seen fit publicly to demonstrate its commitment to radical forms in its own showcases.

Exhibition spaces are social spaces. Or they should be. The experience of the silent, wall-hugging, progress around an exhibition is all too common – with the limited light relief of knowing that any display of an active relation to the objects will have a 'guard' at your side in an instant, protecting what is most valuable – the vacuum surrounding the quality and status of the art-object. Galleries are rarely *used* by the community and this is not surprising, considering that the fetishisation of the work, the structured presence of authority and the absence of social contextualisation all mitigate against making such places a pleasurable part of the everyday. Here we are faced with a contradiction: whilst the arts are considered as a repository of social values by the Establishment, they are becoming increasingly marginalised in terms of state funding and access. Whilst the values and perspectives of the dominant ideology can be disseminated through the electronic mass media, making the museums and galleries more clearly the shrines they always were – the cultural producers on the Left are unable to find sufficient funding or sites for their work.

# Photographic production
# and art management

The term 'exhibition' should be considered to relate to all those instances where a communicator has created a work to be seen by a public. This includes postcards, hoardings, posters and many other types of display. Such work usually has a limited life, due to the general lack of resources available for its production and the fact that the traditional structures of the Art Market – the galleries, auctions, dealers, critical writings, etc., are not able to re-work the images into a commodity for the market. If such images are re-presented within the conventions of the gallery system, they either appear crude or, worse, they stand in opposition to the fine-art values embodied by the institution. As a result, much of the most visually stimulating and radical photographic work of the last decade has only reached a limited audience – those who have access to the original sites of such work (e.g. the full-size hoardings of the Dockland Project, which combine a range of constructional and narrative devices, making arguments against the appropriation of the Docklands by property speculators).

   The philosophy of art-management is that anything can be 'managed' – all objects and practices can be absorbed into the ideology of Aesthetics and made safe against attempts to retrieve the work for other purposes. In practice this does not work, and certain safeguards have to be established to aid the process of appropriation. First of all there is that work which was/is made primarily for the gallery anyway – no problem there. Then there is the work which, when removed from its original context, still 'contains' enough interesting (art) elements to claim a place. After this any other type of work becomes problematic and it is only the more liberal institutions which are ready to show work which may have an unsettling effect on their own practices.

The safeguards which are created to control what is available for public viewing fall into two areas: 1) those which protect the values of the past and maintain them as natural and 2) those which resist contradictions, exploitations and resistances surfacing in the present. The processes of restricting visibility are various: censorship, editing, gallery policy, funding policy, a concern for 'good creative photography' and so on. Under these guises much of the more vital, immediate contemporary work which has been created by 'amateurs', children, women, collectives and minority groups has been dis-enfranchised. Instead, we are offered a continuation of the white, male, middle-class European and North American tradition; one which also colonises the area of publishing.

The artist/photographer is here faced with a dilemma: is the work strong enough to resist being 'anaesthetised' by the institution, is it too strong to be acceptable to the establishment? Institutions get round this in several ways, apart from straight rejection. Work can be displayed so as to enhance certain meanings, at the expense of others. Work is edited, so that problematic focusing points are removed, thereby diluting the power of the piece. A reactionary critical web can encompass the work so that its social/political voice is muffled. Or the institution can simply rely on the Art Market to re-invest the work with a commodity value, effectively draining it of the potential of a socially-transforming role, as its 'meaning' *becomes* its market value.

This is not a one-way process of absorption however; image-makers need an audience. Debates concerning the abolition of traditional galleries under socialism have never been resolved, and many practitioners believe it is possible to co-opt these spaces for their work, as much as they are being co-opted into them. Strategies have been developed to construct work which cannot be easily undermined by gallery management. Image-makers are experimenting with representational and presentational devices, which allow the audience a more complex relation to the imagery. At the same time, the work must not be so problematic that it is likely to be censored out of the public view. A difficult balance to achieve.


## Visual strategies

'It is easier to oppose and deconstruct than to construct alternatives and to capture the spectator's imagination while maintaining a radical approach to spectatorship and address. Riddles and enigmas offer the spectator the lures and pleasures of decipherment, while demanding active participation and work in creating the text's meaning.'   *(Laura Mulvey)*

Searching for new ways to construct meanings is not a simple matter – how do you go about it? If conventional forms are carriers of reactionary values, then is it possible to appropriate these to a progressive end? Some practitioners have done just this, by the use of irony and playing one convention off against another; through image-text pieces; with juxtaposition of images to cut across the 'frozen' moment of traditional photography and using analysis to tease out the absences in the work (absences which are indicators of a social system and ideology, and which sustain the work in its status as document or art-object).

Another strategy for creating a different relationship with the audience is to adopt the tradition of the 'classic realist text' (the standard 'factual' image) and to engage in a self-reflexive production. Here the control of materials and ideas in the production of meaning is apparent to the audience – they are able to participate in the process of 'making-sense'. Montage is a good example of this; the spectator is presented with a mixture of forms and cultural signs and herself creates the work – the audience *becomes* the producer. (It is interesting to consider whether there is ever an original moment of the creation of meaning in photograph – it is continually being re-made by everyone who perceives it.) The visual strategies and social concerns of progressive imagery allow the spectators to bring more of themselves into the process of 'reading', so that the work does not *impose* on us – instead, the spectators *collaborate* with it.

A third example of constructing differently is to create fictions in order to focus the attention of the viewer on particular ideas arising out of the work. The precise control offered by a combination of stylised photographic techniques and objects as symbols often draws on other signifying systems (advertising, film) in order to examine issues such as stereotyping, sexual politics of representation, labour/capital relations, etc. Such work may also use familiar forms (the snapshot), making it strange to us in order to make us look again, breaking down the habitual response to the familiar and creating the conditions of 'distance' between us and the image, so that we are no longer able to take these images 'for granted'.

There has been a long tradition of pictures operating in a wordless vacuum, denying both the need or use for contextualising them with words, *or* recognising that we articulate images through language – privately and publicly. Conventional photographs require this absence in order to maintain their position as revelatory texts. Their overlapping qualities of concealment (not 'speaking' what is not visible) and transparency (appearing to reveal all) give them a power to convey with authority, leaving the spectator in the position of being 'spoken to'. What is necessary today is a set of disruptive, dialectical modes of presentation, which do not alienate the viewer but delay that easy, painless consumption of the well-constructed classic photo.

Many sites and practitioners throughout the country are examining how this is possible, how to combat the 'deadly universalisation of meaning' and replace it with a critical response – a pleasurable process which releases the various perspectives by which the viewer can make sense of the text. The tendency of Modernism to generalised internationalism has been overturned in many corners in favour of work which acknowledges the specific in terms of geographic location, social concerns and likely audiences. The growth of regional centres for photography, such as the Side Gallery in Newcastle, the Triangle in Birmingham, Cambridge Darkrooms and Chapter Art Centre in Cardiff, has created a network of organisations which have become focal points for exhibition, debate and analysis in their areas. If these galleries and workshops are able to consolidate their futures through an imposed and necessary mixed-funding, then the basis of a more complex structure of work, practitioner and public interaction will become possible.

The showing spaces which are discussed here do not negotiate this matter of audience participation in the same ways. The difference of scale and concern between the multi-million business of the Bradford Museum and the Pavilion operating on a few thousand (plus volunteers) could hardly be more extreme. But the three share the concern with making photographic practices a more significant part of people's lives and with creating a new set of viewing relations. Exhibitions are not only concerned with the combination of spectacle and capital (Bradford), or the relation between feminism and representation (Leeds), or even the importance of acknowledging all readers as individuals, who need space to dream themselves in the images (Bristol). Exhibitions in these venues form part of a larger concern where 'showing' is not fetishised to the exclusion of explaining and questioning.

Stevie Bezencenet
# Photography at Bradford

In December 1980, the Arts Minister, Mr Norman St. John Stevas, announced the planning of The National Museum of Photography, Film and Television. This was a joint venture between Bradford Metropolitan Council and the Science Museum in London, who initially funded the project for £1.9 million and £0.5 million respectively. Now, the Science Museum finances the basic staff and running costs on an annual basis and the Council finances a special Educational Department.

The choice of Bradford seems to have been as a result of several factors: firstly, a willing council with funds and a suitable building; secondly, a government policy of devolution of cultural centres from the capital – there is a population of five million in and around Bradford; and, thirdly, perhaps the desire to establish a national institution of a type not yet in existence, but well away from competition –

'It seems to me that most of the existing state institutions – and that's what the word "National" means to most of us – are either art galleries which have collections of pictures, some of which include photographs, or they are museums of science and technology, some of which include collections devoted to the development of the technology of photography. I think that photography, film and television are art forms where you can never totally divorce the technology from the image.'[1]

Ever since the modern Museum was first discussed there has been opposition from existing institutions, those which already operate in the same areas of interest and which will not willingly give up a proportion of either their funds, their acquisitions or their audiences.[2] However, not everyone wants to trek to London and many will welcome the differing forms of presentation which the Bradford Museum has experimented with. The information pack states: 'This is a Museum about the art and science of photography' and that '. . . photography can be all things to all people: a likeness, a memory, a record, an adventure, a work of art. It is science, industry, news, history, self-expression.' In the planning there was a substantial questioning of what constitutes a museum and the designers and curators tried to create a museum which is 'fundamentally different'. This difference is embodied both in the general layout and the relationship of the public to the 'exhibits' in the breadth of work on offer. An essential part of the museum is the Educational Department, which ensures that the galleries and displays are widely utilised for their educational potential: this is considered central to the museum's policy and has been integral to planning since the beginning. Though the publicity continually stresses a concern for the 'general public', it also intends to serve the needs of 'historians, scholars, students and enthusiasts'.

There are already a number of organisations, galleries and museums presenting photography in a variety of ways: the National Photographic Centre at Bath, the Photography galleries and collection in the Henry Cole wing at the Victoria and Albert Museum, the Science Museum, the Arts Council collection at Sheffield Polytechnic, etc. . . . Most of these institutions have a history which determines their treatment of the medium. Bradford wanted to try something different, they 'want to recapture the sense of wonder' that early photography created in the audience. So – interaction with the medium – not only looking *at*, but looking *into* huge cameras and walking *through* others – so that the public will understand how it all works, from the first experiments to 'tomorrow's' technology.

Apart from its displays and exhibitions, the Museum has an informal collecting policy of images and artefacts and it is here that it is more likely to come into conflict with existing institutions. Sir Roy Strong, Director of the Victoria and Albert Museum, maintains that if Bradford collects photographs it will be going against an agreement reached by the museums about who collects what – and this did not include organisations outside London. As Bradford do not officially have a large budget for this activity, Strong is more annoyed than worried: '. . . but I have £1.2 million and I'll outbid them in any sales room.' Government policy is all very well, but when it cuts across the borders of cultural territorial imperative, obviously the contra-dictions in the system begin to surface.

The Museum has a combination of permanent (five to ten years) exhibitions and a range of constantly changing shows covering a variety of subjects and approaches. The 'permanent' galleries deal with a linear perspective on photography's development, utilising a range of set-ups to present the technology, the practice and the 'masters'; the temporary shows echo this with 'auteurs', genre shows and exhibitions where it is the technology which is the real 'subject'. There is a strength to this system, which is also supported by events and talks, because it makes the history self-evident, as if it developed as a result of its own impetus; the need for coherence for such a cultural institution is paramount, but it is at the expense of the audience and their broader understanding of how photography *was* and *is* used – not in technical or aesthetic terms, but in social ones.

The desire to 're-define photography' may have resulted in re-defining methods of presentation, rather than the subject itself. Indeed, several accounts of the Museum's 'success' specify how empty the 'quality' galleries are (the temporary shows) in relation to the crowded participation sections. Clearly, the success is substantial when over one million have passed through its doors since it opened, in June 1983, yet what have they learnt and what else might have been on offer?

Money is at the core of this. Not only government subsidy, for there is never any good guarantee of that, but sponsorship – industrial and commercial money, to the tune of hundreds of thousands. When the Keeper was appointed in 1982, Colin Ford was selected; when planning was underway and a policy for exhibition was created, choices were made; as expansion is in progress so must certain factors be taken into account – all of these are related – they concern the ability to attract money. Money is not 'innocent', it serves interests and so there must be a 'marrying' between the interests of the Museum and that of the relevant business community. All perfectly reasonable, but might it not lead to an institution which is trying to be too many things to too broad an audience – a leisure centre and tourist attraction as much as a museum? On the one hand there is the cinema with the screen 'five storeys high' and an Imax projection system unique in this country, which shows a limited range of films and tape-slides; on the other there is the acquisition of the valuable *Daily Herald* picture library of over one million photos, which will need to be carefully programmed to be useful.

Recently, Yorkshire Television has promised £100,000 towards the new television galleries, supported by another £25,000 from Lord Gowrie (former Arts Minister) under the Business Sponsorship Incentive Scheme Award. The plan for these two galleries seems rather more concerned with contextualising the social practice of the medium, as well as investigating its origins and how it works – though this 'how' will not necessarily be concerned with, say, ideology or finance. Perhaps it takes time for a new venture to come into its own, to make its identity – establishing a policy which serves the public in a proper sense; not as a distraction, but as an illumination of the everyday and the role of the lens media within it. However, with the increasing reliance of these 'national' institutions on 'private' money, it may well be that the interests being served are not those being presented in the substantial 'information pack', which the Museum has produced.

John Tagg
# The silent picture show

As northern city councils face the dire effects of depression and de-industrialisation, the political poor relations 'Arts and Leisure' have returned in new guise, as hoped for keys to revitalising tourist development programmes. Under new necessities, the traditional representation of the north in the south is being revised: out beyond the sunbelt lies not the wasteland but a bold landscape of picturesque industrial relics and dramatic townscapes – a Safari Park which almost hides the Bantustans. Now, in addition, there is the lure of culture. In West Yorkshire alone, Wakefield has its national Sculpture Park and Leeds its self-consciously prestigious Henry Moore Centre for the Study of Sculpture, but Bradford has the National Museum of Photography beside which the impact of the others pales away.

Commanding a panoramic view over the modernistic West Yorkshire Police Headquarters, the converted glass-fronted block of a failed civic theatre has been open as a museum of photography, film and television since June 1983. Within a year it will have welcomed over half-a-million visitors and its influence has already been felt on Bradford's active promotional policy. Hotels in the city are booked throughout the year and the ripple effects of tourism have spread to many other sectors of the local economy. Added to this, the Bradford region also benefits from the museum's unusually extensive and well-equipped educational service, which caters to local schools and offers a way in that is not just passive. Unlike so many art galleries, the museum projects the idea that people are welcome.

It is without question a high status, high profile project which gives photography a recognition it has not had before. But what sort of view of photography does it offer? As an outpost of London's Science Museum, the National Museum's displays are dominated by a popularised technologism presented in a suitably dramatic form. It is a kind of 'Wonders of the World' approach: from the camera obscura to the satellite picture, the story of photography unfolds seemingly of its own volition and always along an unquestionable line of technical progress. A gesture to social impact is made in the tableaux and exhibits of portraiture and newsphotography but here, too, meaning, purpose and context are equally hard to grasp; these complex institutions are made to seem like natural facts: in short, to have an evolution but no history. Photography as an Art, of course, occupies a level of its own. It has its special sanctum; a sheltered place, away from the amusement arcades of technology, as quiet and restrained as they are theatrical and brash, and as empty as they are full. A Victorian distinction is kept alive: photography may be the marriage of science and art, but separate bedrooms are still the order of the day. What visitors seem to find perplexing is the separation and connection beween what is exhibited in the art gallery and what is displayed on the other floors. But this, too, has a history which would have to be explained. It is the explanation which is wanting, however, and all the enthusiasm for visual revolutions, the conquest of time and space, scientific wonders, and new worlds of sight won't fill the gap. What keeps returning is the uncomfortable, repressed fact that photography owed its rapid and economically significant development and dispersal to an impetus that was not its own. It did not float in the air but was borne along by the very complex forces that were transforming the societies in which it was seized on and so eagerly exploited. To put it bluntly, what the museum will not speak about is the relation of photography to the growth of capitalism and the state.

From its beginnings, the history of photography was the history of an industry; a model of capitalist growth in the nineteenth century. Fired by a vast expansion of the market, first for pictures then for equipment, which mechanisation alone could satisfy, it offered at all levels an arena of enterprise ripe for entrepreneurial exploitation. At the same time, photography supplied a key technology to a number of emerging or reformed institutions in which the practices of social surveillance and discipline were being regularised. Police forces, prisons, hospitals, asylums, schools, sanitary and engineering departments, and sociological surveys all applied their techniques of examination and record to the camera. But there was nothing neutral about this technology. The representations it produced were highly coded and the power it wielded was never its own. Its power to arrest, picture and transform daily life was vested in it by the evolving apparatuses of the local state. These both put photography to use and guaranteed the authority of its images to stand as evidence or register a truth within a proliferating system of documentation of which photographic records were only a part.

Complex distinctions of practice were emerging in photography and different statuses were beginning to be accorded to the images it produced. By mid-century, the economics of the market-place already defined different levels of production from large-scale artistic prints to mass produced *cartes-de-visite*. The codes and protocols of an instrumental use of photography, including what was later called 'documentary', were being refined by scientific, administrative and social institutions which had the power to validate them. While, from another point of view, the question of whether photography fell into the domain of art or science, could not be separated from the regulation and control of a burgeoning photographic industry whose second technical revolution made possible the economic and limitless production of photo-mechanical images, and gave rise to a welter of chemical and industrial applications and processes. It was in the context of this economic expansion that legislators and legal experts began to call for copyright protection of those with 'artistic feeling'. The discourses of photographic art were mixed up with, and in effect subordinated to openly commercial considerations, and the dispute about the artistic status of photography was settled not in aesthetic debate but in the courts of law.

Following these interweaving histories would not mean being diverted by 'external' factors and led astray from photography itself. The problem is just this notion of photography in itself which the National Museum now enshrines. What has to be explained is not the workings of a 'medium' – a neutral technology or means of representation to which a general and unconditional definition can be given. The so-called medium has no existence outside its historical specifications. What alone unites the diversity of sites in which photography has operated is the social formation itself and the specific historical spaces for representation which it constitutes. Photography as such has no identity. Its status as a 'technology' varies with the power relations which invest it; its nature as a 'practice' depends on the institutions and agents which define it and set it to work; its function as a mode of cultural production is tied to definite conditions of existence; and its products are meaningful and legible only within the particular currencies they have. Its history has no unity. It is a flickering across a field of institutional spaces. And it is this field which needs to be made intelligible, not photography as such. A Museum of Photography makes as much and as little sense as a Museum of Writing. And if we could imagine such a museum – something far indeed from a library – it would be precisely to challenge the notion that writing is one thing, rather than a proliferation of small techniques which historians have till now ignored. If the idea has appeal, it is because it offers to displace the concept of Literature in a way that a Museum of Photography could have displaced the concepts of Art and Technology, instead of being assimilated to them.

Shirley Moreno

# The light writing on the wall: the Leeds Pavilion Project

This article will look at some of the issues that a feminist photography practice raises. It cannot be a survey of women's photography in this country, nor an analysis of all feminist photography – they would need books of their own. What I intend to concentrate on is the development of one project, the Pavilion in Leeds.

This project was initiated to draw together different feminist photographers with other women's art practices, within the context of the women's movement and as an intervention in/alternative to the mainstream art world. The project involved the setting up and running of a centre which would show women's photography, have a working darkroom and run various events: conferences, talks, films, video and performance. Its intention was to co-ordinate existing practices by showing them in a coherent programme, stimulate debate and encourage the production of new work – in general to look at representation from a feminist perspective. Many people have been involved in this project and what I have tried to do here is to pull together some of the common ideas in a brief history, but I am aware that I have done this in a personal way, as one woman who has been involved.

## The background

The ideas for the Pavilion project have developed out of the women's movement, which has, over the past 15 years, produced a very particular kind of arts practice in different spheres: the theatre, literature, the visual arts, music, etc. To some extent the impetus for these works has been common, in that they all assumed that if women described their own experiences to themselves and made that public, then this would radically alter our understanding of women. The dominant notion of 'woman', based on men's understanding of what women think, feel and need, would thus be criticized and alternatives, based on women's understanding, would be posited. Furthermore, it was assumed that if women were described differently, then they would act differently. These practical and effective strategies criticized prevailing notions of art in a number of ways. Firstly, the universal 'truth' of art and its apolitical nature were questioned. Women said this art reflects a white, male and middle-class view of the world, and its assumptions and politics are obscured by an analysis of it based on aesthetics.

Mainstream art world and its institutions: the galleries, colleges, publishing houses, etc., were all responsible for projecting this minority ruling-class view of the world, as if it was the view of everyman (sic). Alternative arts movements were few in number, owing to the classical left position, prioritizing work in economic struggles with the expectation that change in cultural forms will follow. Feminists argued that women stand in an unequal and ill-considered position in the economy and that this needs to be analysed. The problem in beginning this process was that:

(a)  the usual theoretical models were designed in such a way as to make them gender specific, and that

(b)  women's pictures of themselves and their position in society were so ideologically fixed that it was difficult to even get the problem on the agenda. In other words, the social and economic role of women had been so naturalized as to make it unreasonable to question it. This 'naturalization' was given a powerful validation through the mass communications media, art forms and culture in general.

It has seemed, therefore, that until this process is questioned, it will be difficult, nay impossible, to achieve changes in other social areas. For example, women are so persistently represented as sexually available to men that it is difficult to get legal changes in rape laws until this idea of natural availability is questioned and changed. Working within culture to intervene in those dominant representations must be seen as part of a broader movement to change women's roles in society. Within this context a feminist photography centre should be seen as:

(a)  logical in itself, in that it shows the view of an under-represented group – women;

(b)  a valuable contribution to the debates within cultural politics, as a feminist perspective sees these politics in a new way;

(c)  as relating to political struggles in other areas.

# The proposal

By 1980 it was clear that some kind of permanent feminist art centre should be established. Throughout the '70s, in the face of great suspicion and hostility, a number of women's art shows had been seen. They had attracted a lot of attention and a lot of criticism. But because the showings had been fragmented in place and time it had been difficult for the viewer to build up any kind of idea of a feminist art practice. In 1979 the Hayward Gallery exhibited *Three Perspectives on Photography*, in which it was posited that there were three main developments in contemporary British photography: individual expression, socialist practices and feminist work. This was followed in 1980 by four shows of the ICA of women's work: *Issues*, *About Time*, *Women's Own* and *Women's Images of Men*, the last of which broke all attendance figures.

It was in the early months of 1981 that a small group of women in Leeds started to press for a permanent exhibiting space for women's art work that could properly represent this perspective. It became apparent that funding was not available to set up a mixed-media centre, so it was decided to concentrate on photography. Within feminist photography work there are a multitude of approaches; the centre wished to represent all these in the context of thematic monthly shows that would relate to each other and be supported by talks, discussions, videos and films. It was also proposed that the centre should have a darkroom to promote photographic skills and the production of new work. Whilst it was considered essential to keep the ownership and running of the centre in the hands of women, it was necessary to call on the power and expertise of men when there were no women in that position to help us. The centre was projected as being open to the general public with certain events for women only. Leeds is historically an area of women's activities; the female labour force has been of major significance to local industry and has therefore played a crucial role in the development of the city. This has assisted the growth of a strong local women's movement. The Peter Sutcliffe murders and the resultant militant action against sexist imagery has encouraged debate and concern about the effects pictures have on women's lives. There is a large women's art movement, with nowhere to exhibit and also almost nothing significant to see, as the facilities for the visual arts in Leeds are appalling. All these factors made Leeds the perfect place for the centre. There were problems, though. The recession has hit the city badly and there is little money around. As culture is London-based, it is hard to get reviewers, viewers, funders and artists up the motorway. In spite of these problems the project went ahead.

# The waiting

By Autumn, 1981, the project had a beginning: a proposal, a little money, a couple of educational courses on the history of women artists and a group formed who were working on a show, *Anonymous: Notes Towards a Show on Self-Image*. The debate and the production side of the project had begun and were involving women and producing shows; this meant that the Leeds Women's Arts Programme (as we were called then) was at least active and visible. But we still felt very strongly that we needed a building, a centre.

Eventually we found one: the Pavilion on Woodhouse Moor, just north of the University and sited in a park. The local community was mainly residential, a few factories and mixed race, religion and class. The building was in urgent need of repair and during 1982–83 we obtained the lease and a grant from Leeds City Council to renovate it. The Arts Council of Great Britain gave us £4,500 to equip the centre and Yorkshire Arts Association gave us £4,000 to run it. We made countless applications for further money, all of which were unsuccessful due to shrinking assets of charitable bodies and their reluctance to fund a women's project. During this time we also became registered as a charity and a limited company.

This was more complicated than it sounds as we had three conflicting needs. Firstly, to run as a women's collective; secondly, to have a structure that would satisfy funding bodies of our economic reliability and, thirdly, to have a structure that would draw in the expertise that we needed to function. We developed a three-fold management structure, the first part of which was the Collective – women only – meeting once a week. This group undertook the day-to-day running of the centre and designed proposals for the future. This group was, at one point, represented on the Board of Management by an Executive. The second part of the structure was the Board of Management, which consisted of women and a few men who could give advice concerning the economic and legal side of the project. They were meant to delegate power to the Collective and be advised by it in matters outside the concerns of the Board. The third part of the structure was an advisory group consisting of people throughout the country involved in the arts who had access to publicity and who could give us artistic advice: this group has always been most helpful. The problems arose between the Management and the Collective, in particular around the issue of the rights of representatives of funding bodies to become members of the company, i.e., on the Collective, which wished to maintain its autonomy. The other problem was that the Board of Management wished to make decisions on the day-to-day running which the Collective felt were properly their concern, although they (the Board) were finally accountable. This led to further problems, which I shall outline later.

The building was renovated and ready for opening by 1st May, 1983, as an exhibition and discussion centre for feminist photography. We oversaw all the renovations ourselves and Leeds Building Collective, who did the work, were very adaptable to the particular problems of the project. We did not want a cold, impersonal place that alienated people. We did not want a row of unexplained and unapproachable pictures on the wall. We did not want the building to be inaccessible to people in wheel-chairs – and all this on a very small budget. We spent hours talking about all these and many other issues, e.g., how to light the walls efficiently and cheaply, without using fittings that looked as if they had come from an armoury or factory. The whole intention of the decoration was to attract people into the building and present the images in an accessible way.

## The Programme 1: The shows

Once the building work was underway, the programme of events had to be designed. The concern was to put on shows based on themes, e.g., child-care, health, romance, etc.... in which a variety of different approaches would be presented together with a text, expanding on the issue and putting it in both a historical and geographic context. The exhibition would be supported by other types of material, depending on what was available.

We wanted to use photography in an unusual way; big and expanding, full of possibilities, rather than small and neat and closed. We wanted to operate outside the fetishization of the single 'quality' image, using photographs with other media where relevant and not being constrained by traditional and restrictive notions of 'good photography'. We wanted to break with that tradition of personality-based artists' shows which forefront style and, instead, to concentrate on the content and methods of approaching the subject, where the 'form' does not become the primary 'meaning'. However, at the same time we wanted to establish a means of investigating the process of representation itself, through theoretical and practical courses, in order to stimulate a desire to understand the conventional methods of signification and work through to possible alternatives.

The programme wanted to use photography and show it in the following ways:

(1)   to show the work of women photographers, both past and present, which have previously been ignored or given scant attention;

(2)   to generate shows dealing with issues relevant to women in Leeds and, by implication to women elsewhere;

(3)   to develop an educational programme, so that the public may develop a growing understanding of the power of images in society and of cultural practices in general;

(4)   to help people become proficient in the practice of photography – the construction of arguments; combining image and text; experimenting with and controlling the process of representation;

(5)   to investigate the traditional role of photography as document/ truth/reality and to deconstruct the reductive images of women generally, whilst encouraging women to document the conditions of their own lives;

(6)   to use photography as a means of covering issues, which arise out of feminist concerns, for example:
  – the representation of women as workers,
  – as objects in pornography,
  – as portrayed in their domestic lives,
  – concerns of self-image,
  – stereotyping: mother, consumer, madonna, whore, etc. . . .,
  – patriarchy: race, gender, class,
  – women and health,
  – women and children, child-care, etc. . . .,
  – women's role in art practices, past and present
  – relationships between art/photography/new technologies;

(7)   to consider photography as an ideological practice, serving the specific interests of class and capital, and, therefore, men;

(8)   to use the medium as a means of acquainting the audience with similar work, constructed through other art/craft practices; thereby consolidating the broad constituency of feminist concerns;

(9)   to make the resources of the project, i.e., building, publicity outlets and so on, available to other groups.

# The Programme 2: Why photography?

We chose to concentrate on photography for several reasons. Firstly, it is a common and accessible process of representation – anyone can do it. Nevertheless, photography is usually presented as high technology and a male activity, so the many women who take pictures are not seen as 'photographers'. Secondly, photographs are common currency in our society and commonly received as 'real' and 'truthful'. Everyone has photos, sees them, takes them, keeps special ones, and in this process positions are described and values are given. These relationships have an effect on our lives in that they help shape our view of things. In certain areas a great deal of work has been done on analyzing this social effect of photography, especially in relation to advertising and pornography. In these and other practices the images do not only reflect a point of view, but also work in constructing one: they produce and promote certain values from the position of an (usually unacknowledged) author. This is not simply a one-way, unproblematic process, resulting in a precisely 'constructed' spectator. However, the presentation and location of images do incline the viewer towards a 'preferred reading' as we learn to make certain responses to images depending on their context, i.e., art gallery = expressiveness, file = documentary truth. The whole world of signs operates this way but photography has a particularly privileged role in this method of communication, because of the kinds of claims it holds concerning 'objectivity'. Much of women's work has challenged this concept of 'reality', staunchly held by mainstream applied photography, by showing another 'point of view'. This is one way to open up debates about the controlling and monocular vision of the camera and the uses to which it has been put in constructing certain types of world-view.

Looking at photographs in this way and exhibiting it in a centre, means that, to some extent, it becomes an art 'institution' that criticizes other art practices.

The word Art has a whole set of meanings and implications concerning who makes it and who sees it. It appears to stand in relation to photography as the gold standard did to currency; to pin value rather than to do with day-to-day exchange. Concerning the question of quality – the conventional attitude is that the 'artist' is a professional and much of the work we are dealing with is 'amateur'; namely, lacking in high-gloss aesthetic appeal, pomposity, market value and acceptable 'subjects'. We are not working within the art market and its concepts of exchange value. We believe that if an object has a use value, one you can identify with, then it is possible to assess the quality of the object in relation to that use value at any time.

We try to give the work we show a use value, rather than an exchange value, by the context in which we exhibit it. The work is used to open up an idea and to generate discussion and analysis, rather than merely 'showing'. By exhibiting outside of the commercial circuit, we limit and try to redefine the exchange value outside of the world of investment, so necessary to capitalism at this moment.

We would see 'aesthetic value' as being constructed within a social structure, where the division of labour is hierarchical: one kind of labour and its product is singled out as being of greater value than another, because of the 'author' and the effect of this 'authorship' on the market/exchange value. The value of the art-object is seen as intrinsic and ornamental, although this is backed up in our society by hard cash. The ornamental nature of art is considered to be beyond understanding, not accessible to everyone. The way that we show photographs completely breaks with this tradition – they have no 'market value' but are useful for understanding both the process itself and the social issues which the process (of photography) is making public. The work is produced by people who are not prestigious artists and it is shown in a context that is open and familiar. The open darkroom is very significant to the shows, because its availability makes every viewer/consumer a potential producer.

# The Programme 3: How we run

As we are trying to break with a valuation of the object that rests on the philosophy of elitism and the individual, we encourage collective work. A number of the shows have been collective and this is a reflection of the way in which the centre is run. We try and keep the decision-making power in the hands of the workers, who are all women. Each week the different jobs are allocated, as it is important that workers who have a prestigious skill teach others that skill, as well as doing their share of the more mundane tasks. So, our attitude towards the restrictive concept of amateur/professional is to refuse its implications of the insignificance of unsalaried labour, of the necessity of technical mastery and of an elitist activity producing a commodity. We question these values, both in the work produced and exhibited, as well as in the structure and running of the project.

The collective nature of the project does acknowledge the differences of its worker/members, in terms of class, race and training; these have to be understood and used as productively as possible. However, discussions and decision-making often take a long time and this is not always readily available. We lack, sometimes, that clear profile of intention that dictatorship gives you, but we are agreed on the necessity of operating as we do, with a talked-through series of aims and projects and with a consensus of opinion and an acceptance of difference.

The significance of running as a centre, rather than simply as a group, is that it enables us to present work that might not otherwise be made public, and show it in a context which is determined and controlled by us. The relationship of the photographic shows to the other programmed activities begins to make possible an understanding of feminist cultural practices, both to a particular/defined audience and to a broader constituency, as a result of the public character of the centre.

## Open/closed

The Pavilion opened in May, 1983, ironically at the very moment when political debates had moved so far right that, in the main, people were hanging on to what they had, rather than doing anything new: it opened at a moment of closure. The Right moved more right, what was left of the Left needed to turn to the immediate problems of survival; cultural practices seemed to float off to the empyrean. The Pavilion was seen by the Left as elitist, the art world saw us as propagandist and the Right simply withdrew funding.

We fear that, given the political climate, feminist issues and the critiques and debates that they have stimulated will be further marginalized in the future; this leaves us few options. Either you become silent, or you move your arena of debate into the mainstream, or you shout from the sidelines as an alternative voice. The Pavilion could well be seen as a slightly eccentric organization, operating as an alternative to mainstream culture, rather than an intervention in it; we would not choose to be in that position. It is necessary to be both interventionist and alternative at different moments, responding to specific needs as they arise. However, we feel that we are being forced into the latter role as other options close down. This is completely unsatisfactory, for it suggests that a feminist perspective is a marginal one: women are 53% of the population, the biggest 'minority' in this country! One of the roles of culture in our society is to project and protect the point of view of the ruling-class, of monopoly capital, of men. Or, rather, that class and capital is controlled by men. This point of view is presented as normal, which it is, and 'natural', which it is not. Now there are other views of the world that are in direct contradiction to this – feminism is one of them. Women are substantially outside of that power, that dominant perspective, yet so close to it. Being brought up alongside men, they have an informed contradiction at their fingertips. If this can be mobilized and turned into language, both verbal and visual, and acted on, then a feminist perspective should not be considered marginal. Instead, it would become the critique of society in all its manifestations; not narrow, but all-encompassing.

These shifts in the social and the political formations meant that many of the arguments and ideas that the Pavilion had been designed to articulate and develop, seemed suddenly to have been shelved. We opened, the public came, the project was successful in many ways; but, with funding bodies and the local authorities, we were called upon to justify our original proposals. The art world has decided that feminism was an 'ism' of the '70s and, thus, has largely ignored us. We have found ourselves working against a prevailing institutional indifference or hostility. However, among the community that the Pavilion serves, both locally and nationally, it has achieved many of its original aims, run by an unpaid collective on a small budget.

Now the Yorkshire Arts Association has stopped that funding, verbally giving two reasons for its action. Firstly, that the aesthetic quality of the work is not high enough and, secondly, that the company is separatist (women only) and the YAA is designed to fund art for the 'general' public. Both of these criticisms were anticipated and answered in our original proposal. To re-cap: aesthetic quality is a standard distilled from contemporary main-stream art. Any critical practice must contradict its aesthetic as well as its meaning, in order to evolve new aesthetics/meanings; so, of course, feminist art does not conform to prevailing aesthetic standards. Secondly, a feminist project must be run by women, yet the Pavilion *is* open to the general public 90% of the time across the range of its activities. It cannot be called separatist when it merely operates positive discrimination consistent with its policies for creating a space for women to communicate with each other. The official reason for the withdrawal of funding is lack of money. The Y.A.A. gives the Pavilion £4,000 per annum, for which it gets a unique centre; to cut it is a false economy and a betrayal of their original commitment to us. We are struggling to stay open, applying for further grants, pressurizing the YAA to reconsider their decision, and getting as much publicity as possible. However, running a centre with no wages and, now, no funds either, is finally impossible. The Pavilion is the only project of its kind in the country, promoting work not otherwise visible in a new kind of context, and stimulating the production of further work in this area. There are so many galleries devoted to mainstream photography that to close the one place devoted to women's work seems perverse and pointed. We hope that our lobbying and arguments will persuade the Arts Council and the Regional Arts Association to reconsider.

(My thanks to the many women who have helped me with the ideas for this article – the faults, however, are all my own.)

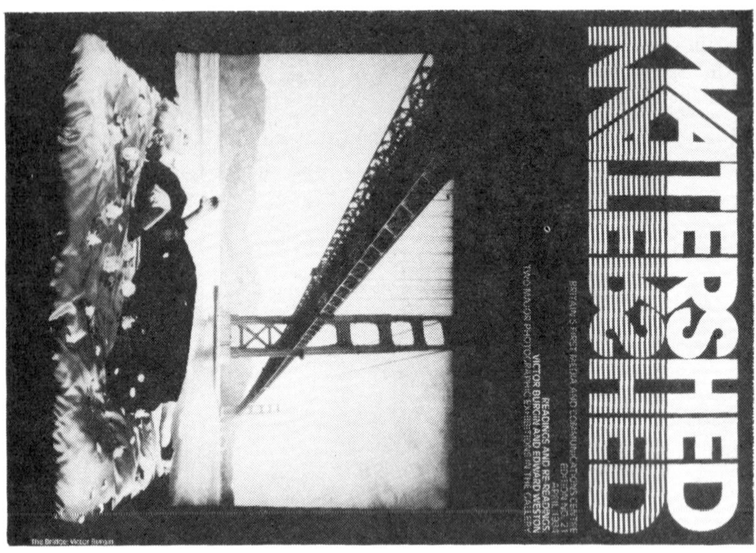
WATERSHED
WATERSHED
BRITAIN'S FIRST MEDIA AND COMMUNICATIONS CENTRE
EDITION NO. 21
APRIL 1981
READINGS AND RE-READINGS
VICTOR BURGIN AND EDWARD WESTON
TWO MAJOR PHOTOGRAPHIC EXHIBITIONS IN THE GALLERY
The Bridge: Victor Burgin

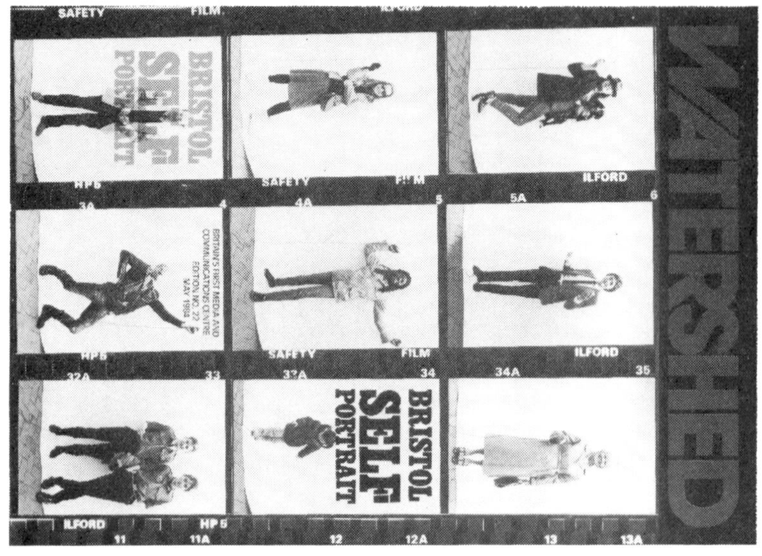
SAFETY   FILM   ILFORD
BRISTOL
SELF
PORTRAIT
SAFETY   FILM   ILFORD
BRITAIN'S FIRST MEDIA AND
COMMUNICATIONS CENTRE
EDITION NO. 22
MAY 1981
SAFETY   FILM   ILFORD
BRISTOL
SELF
PORTRAIT
ILFORD   HP5
WATERSHED

Deborah Ely
# Watershed Media and Communications Centre

Looking down the list of sponsors on the *Watershed* monthly brochure – and there are around 40 sponsors who regularly appear – you would be forgiven for thinking that the US model of big business supporting artistic enterprise had at last found ground in Britain. Everyone from Kleen-E-Ze to Sun Life Assurance, ICI Paints and Kodak have played some part in the birth of Britain's first Media and Communications Centre. Or enough of a role to get a mention. Yet the complexities of arts funding are such that those in the know will have already discovered the presence of the British Film Institute and South West Arts on the list and realized that this is an organization as financially dependent on state subsidy as any other arts institution in Britain. You might ask how such an organization came into being when funding for the arts has shifted from a period of no-growth to one of actual contraction over the last five years.

Much of the interest and controversy surrounding *Watershed* centres on the way it is funded. The 'mixed economy' of private sponsorship, central state funding and commercial self-help has raised the inevitable questions about artistic autonomy on the one hand and accountability to local and regional interests on the other. Neither a plaything for rich businessmen, nor simply as a showcase for the BFI, *Watershed*'s public profile and activities are nevertheless a reflection of its financial organization. The history of the project closely parallels the crises and solutions experienced by the arts and education sectors in the late '70s and early '80s. The necessity to circumvent complete financial and artistic dependence on the major state funding agencies, coupled with the genuine desire to expand the audiences for often marginalized yet expanding areas of cultural concern, produced an organization which often sits uncomfortably in the arts landscape. But, at the time of writing, *Watershed* finds itself thriving while other, broadly similar, organizations are having difficulty surviving.

# The building and its audiences

Housed in the converted interior of two Victorian dockside warehouses, *Watershed* occupies a key site in one of Britain's most rapidly developing cities. The quality and location of *Watershed*'s facilities have played an important part in its success. After only two years of operation it has achieved an annual visitor rate of 500,000 and established itself as Bristol's third largest visitor attraction.

*Watershed* has two cinemas, gallery and exhibition areas, darkrooms, video production and two post-production suites, bar and restaurant and high-grade conference spaces. Despite public and private sector revenue support, *Watershed*'s survival and growth have depended heavily on maximising square footage and installation. The two cinemas are used during the day for either educational events with schools and higher education, or as part of a conference package. In the evenings, Cinema One (200 seats) showcases recent new releases or high-profile retrospective material, while Cinema Two (55 seats) shows repertory programmes, frequently in collaboration with external agencies, or is used for extra-mural and other types of informal education courses. In addition, both cinemas are used for debates, speakers and special events.

The gallery forms part of a photographic department which incorporates three darkrooms, black and white and colour and a small studio area. Another production component of the centre is video. Initially based around a single post-production facility and camera kit, the video facility has expanded to include a highly sophisticated, three-machine editing suite, further production resources and a production team.

Perhaps the most visible example of *Watershed*'s 'mixed economy' is in its use as a conference venue. This usage promotes not only valuable income but also exhibitions from the media and communications industries. The most spectacular examples of this were the two wildlife film and television festivals, 'Wildscreen '82 and '84' and 'BBC Enterprises Showcase '84'. Both were international events which benefited from *Watershed*'s environment and flexibility. ('Wildscreen '84' achieved the signal honour of over two hours' prime time television 'on both sides'.)

The combination of commercial and cultural activities has had an overall effect on the style and 'feel' of *Watershed*. It is regarded locally as a facility which belongs to the city and not as space for those with marginal interests or concerns. Its bar and restaurant areas have been spectacularly successful, with the business community using them regularly during the day and Bristol's young taking over in the evenings. On Saturday, shoppers and families with young children dominate the Media Centre.

Recent market research carried out by Bristol Polytechnic, however, reveals that the percentage of visitors to the cinema, bar and restaurant and gallery are about equal, with cinema attendance being the highest at 58% of regular users, restaurant accounting for 53% and gallery 51%, demonstrating that the catering facilities do not dominate *Watershed* to the exclusion of all the other activities on offer. The same survey revealed that many people were unaware of *Watershed*'s photography and video production facilities and an appropriate marketing campaign is being launched locally.

## Policy

*Watershed* is a development of the Film Centre model operated for some years by the British Film Institute. Its primary function is, therefore, explicitly educational. Policy for photography at *Watershed* is set against a background of discourses around film and television, sharing the view that as a cultural practice they are embedded in the social and political fabric of our lives and, as such, operate across the areas of work and leisure, art and popular entertainment. This view of photography is increasingly shared by educational institutions and evidenced through various photography and film publications. It is a view which is rarely expressed through exhibitions of photography. The one-off nature of exhibitions and the inadequate support mechanisms for practitioners and independent exhibition organizers means that the development of a new exhibition practice is set against the traditional, authorial approach to photographic production and distribution. These exhibition conventions take their direction from mainstream art history, rather than seeking to examine the particularity of photography or to bring photography into a wider cultural context. Photography activity at *Watershed* aims to open up to the public debates around the role of photography as a reproduced image, a form of everyday visual currency. In addition to interrogating the still image, being located within a media centre enables the gallery and education programme also to address the concerns of cinema, video and television; the role of design and advertising; and the part played by the news media in the construction of our world view.

## Exhibition

An overview of the exhibition programme at *Watershed* reveals this working of policy in practice. In order to encourage a range of different readings of photographic/visual material, and to move away from the singular, fixed meanings generated by 'one-man' shows and other similar exhibition practices, many of *Watershed*'s shows rely on the juxtaposition of visual material. Exhibitions like *Survival Tactics*, about youth culture and unemployment in the 1980s, interspersed around six or seven different bodies of work, with no material being privileged above the other. The inclusion of sound, moving images and 'found' objects (largely clothing) offered a wider social and cultural context to the still photography in the exhibition, which in itself could only offer a partial view of a contradictory and complex subject.

A variety of strategies have been employed in the area of historical material. An exhibition on *Mass Observation*, generated by another gallery and in itself both critical and multi-textual in approach, was combined with an exhibition on the *Daily Herald* of the same period. Audiences were invited to view the role photography played in the most popular daily newspaper of the 1930s alongside the work of Mass Observation (which utilized film-makers, writers, visual artists, anthropologists and photographers), rather than being presented with 'outstanding' individual photographers isolated from their production contexts. An alternative method of dealing with historical figures in photography, often familiar to audiences through major retrospective exhibitions and glossy monographs, has been the re-interpretation of a body of work. The exhibition *Re-Reading Edward Weston* was selected and presented by art historian Robert McGrath, whose 're-reading' introduced into an exhibition format psycho-analysis and feminism, ideas usually reserved for theoretical journals, and consequently less available to a wide public.

Contemporary work presents specific problems for the gallery. In particular the tension between foregrounding the photographer and foregrounding the subject of the work. In an attempt to sidestep the tired formula of promoting the 'artist' there is a danger of engaging with the work purely at the level of explicit content. It is here that marketing strategies around exhibitions as product play a crucial role in the public's consumption of photography.

Work which addresses specific photographic conventions can often suggest methods of packaging an exhibition which will encourage audiences to read the material as more than just a display of 'excellence'. *Cindy Sherman* (May, 1983) and *Victor Burgin* (with Edward Weston, April, 1984), for example, both rely on audience recognition of cinema and advertising forms in order to explore our contradictory relationships with dominant culture. This area of photographic practice, which deliberately plagiarises media-generated imagery in order to investigate and extend our knowledge of the familiar, reproduced image, incorporates into its structure an awareness of the spectator's daily encounters with these all-pervasive photographic forms (via advertising, film, photojournalism, etc.). This work often also addresses the specific experience of viewing images in galleries through certain formal and didactic strategies. It is this area of photography which represents the largest body of 'new' work shown at *Watershed*.

In the same way that work which references our other experiences of viewing visual images can expand a public's awareness of photography so, too, can exhibitions which make reference to their own production. The technical aspects of production (cameras, lenses and the like) are only one part of the making of a photographic image. The social and economic conditions of production are equally determining. By placing these aspects of production at the centre of the exhibition, audiences can gain a broader understanding of how and why certain images have evolved. An occasional series of exhibitions entitled *Work In Progress* enables photographers (usually locally-based) to show and explain projects at various stages of development. Other exhibitions take as their starting point a particular economic, historical or material intervention to give an overview of the growth of a specific area of practice. South West Survey (September, 1984), for example, looked at financial support for photography from the Regional Arts Assocation (in this case South West Arts) over a five-year period. Commissions, bursaries or a residency might provide similar opportunities. Equally, exhibitions based on local archives, from the High Street photographer, to collections held by local industry, can demonstrate the development of a particular area of photographic practice.

An even greater level of engagement with audiences has been achieved by encouraging participation in the production and construction of exhibitions. Many of the exhibitions and projects we have set up at *Watershed* are based on well-tested models adapted from Community Photography. Work with oral-history groups, the training of local people in photographic skills, courses and workshops with young people, trade unionists or the local black community, are all examples of projects which involve the participants in the actual production of photographs. Other exhibitions, like *Survival Tactics* (November, 1982) and *Bristol Self-Portrait* (March, 1984), rely entirely on the involvement of people living in the city for the content and appearance of the exhibition, but do not require the acquisition of photographic skills in the conventional sense.

# Education

Galleries generally offer an interrogatory framework for the viewing of visual images. On entering such institutions, audiences bring with them not only expectations of 'pleasure' and 'entertainment', but of 'culture' and 'knowledge'. An *active* audience is created by fulfilling some of those expectations and disrupting others. In this sense, all *Watershed*'s exhibitions are self-consciously didactic. There is, nevertheless, a need to extend that educational aspect beyond the gallery walls. There are regular, open discussions around the exhibition programme, evening courses and occasional lecture series, which offer the opportunity of looking, in depth, at photography and the reproduced image. However, the primary thrust of the education work around photography at *Watershed* is centred around our production facilities.

Established to encourage group work of various kinds, and to offer 'hands on' access to photography, the darkrooms also offer a focus for discussion and for sustained contact with the full breadth of the education and community arts sectors. Courses for school teachers, community photographers, voluntary organizations, trades unions and youth training schemes, operate alongside courses and workshops for the general public. In addition to this, the production facilities also operate a membership scheme – open to anyone of proven competence. Introductory courses in basic darkroom skills offer the training necessary for confident use of the facilities by individuals. These facilities are fully used by 'amateurs' and 'professionals' alike – the scale of payment depending on whether the user is waged or unwaged, or if the work is grant-aided or commercial. Since there is currently no direct subsidy for the darkroom, it is inevitable that some users must subsidize the others and that all the education work should cover its costs.

After 12 months of operating the darkrooms we were able to identify gaps in the kind of users we were attracting and some revealing patterns of use. Some inventive carpentry has now given disabled photographers easier access to the darkrooms. A series of workshops run by local black photographer Eddie Chambers, has forged important links with black cultural and community organizations in Bristol which will hopefully make the facilities more accessible to potential black users. The greatest impact has been felt with the introduction of financial concessions for the unemployed, for students and pensioners. Large numbers of young people now use the facilities and there has also been a significant increase in the number of women users.

Although economics has an important bearing on women's

involvement with photography, this cannot provide a complete answer to the ways we found women were relating to our photography facilities. For example, we discovered that most of our introductory courses in photography had a very high take-up from women, yet our darkroom membership was 90% male. We adopted a number of strategies in order to encourage women to identify more strongly with the facilities and to sustain their involvement beyond an initial course. We employed a higher proportion of women as tutors on all courses and placed women in key technical roles within the darkroom. Women-only courses are also being introduced. These attempts to indicate to women that photography is an activity which they can legitimately pursue is obviously up against the massive photographic industry which only addresses women as the subjects of photography. Many key exhibitions at *Watershed* have taken up this issue but we have recently tried to increase the number of women participating in small-scale exhibitions in order to underline the connection between education and the production of exhibitions. *Work In Progress* exhibitions have been useful in this process.

## Exhibition/education – integration

In order to encourage darkroom users to come together more around their work, to discuss it and consider its wider implications, we established a space for the display of work produced from *Watershed*'s production facilities. We decided to use this space to encourage the kind of practice we would like to see coming out of the darkroom as well as to describe, to users and public alike, the range of practices taking place and thereby to establish a kind of dialogue between the producers of different kinds of photography. This was the initial brief for the *Work In Progress* exhibitions.

Although the space for the exhibitions remains the same – a small area adjacent to the darkrooms – the concept has grown since the shows started at the beginning of 1984. Initially an invitation to show work was seen by photographers as the opportunity for a mini, one-'man' show – with openings, press advertising and carefully matted prints. It was clear to us that there were two main reasons for this response. Firstly, the conventions of showing work are so strong that photographers were reluctant to describe their production *processes* through exhibition, or to exhibit work in an informal way. Secondly, there is a shortage of spaces to show portfolios of work. Having uncovered this local demand we have incorporated it into the function of the exhibitions, creating the space for the display of completed portfolios. But we are interventionist in how work is displayed, insisting on the inclusion of additional material – notebooks, test prints, contact sheets, examples of other visual sources and an informal commentary. Within this the finished prints have a different kind of importance. *Work In Progress* exhibitions are also the only place in *Watershed* where we actively encourage some focus on technical information. Participants are generally drawn from our darkroom users, although we do bring in photographers from elsewhere from time to time, in response to work that is going on in our own production facilities and thus using the space to introduce one form of practice to another.

Along the same lines of bringing together different approaches to photography the *Picture This...* series of presentations – where speakers are invited to talk about a single, reproduced image – draws together photography, film and television, suggesting shared theoretical concerns for all these areas of cultural production. Similarly, *Breaking The Codes*, an adult education course initiated by *Watershed*, looks at recent theory around photography, film and television, and discusses the ways that our ideas about art and culture are formed and put into circulation.

The motive behind much of this education work is to intervene in the process of passive consumption of exhibitions and, most optimistically, to encourage the public to consider themselves as potential producers. There is also a broader intention which is to extend our understanding of the ways we interact with visual images and to encourage audiences to bring that knowledge to bear on their other encounters with images – outside cultural institutions. Revealing the mechanisms of how meaning is produced in images is something which *Watershed*, as a whole, tackles at a number of different levels, addressing in turn specialist audiences and the occasional visitor.

## Regional and national profile

The South West contains institutions which represent the full range of British photographic culture, from permanent collections and media and arts centres, to collective and community work. The Beaford Archive is located in North Devon and the Fox Talbot Museum at Lacock Abbey, just outside Bristol. The move of the Royal Photographic Society from London to Bath has brought to the region a major photographic collection which complements *Watershed*'s exhibitions and also those taking place at Axiom in Cheltenham, and occasionally at Arnolfini in Bristol and at Plymouth Arts Centre.

The distinctive view of photography held by *Watershed* not only complements these varied regional resources, but also the other photographic institutions throughout Britain. There is a natural affinity between *Watershed* and the educational and community galleries dealing with photography, but recently opened centres, such as the National Museum of Photography, Film and Television, in Bradford, suggest many possibilities for this approach to photography in the future. The development of *Watershed* has coincided, and to some extent precipitated, the growth of Media Centres in Britain. All over the country there has been a move in cultural institutions towards film, video and photography and away from the more traditional plastic and performing arts, which are often more expensive to house and maintain.

*Watershed*'s importance on the local and regional landscape has already grown into a national identity of equal significance. The organization is continually experimenting with new formulas for programming and financing its activities. The touring of exhibitions, the production of publications and the presentation of work on video are all ways in which *Watershed*'s programme is beginning to circulate outside Bristol. By going to bed, economically, with several 'communities of interest', *Watershed* is attempting to intervene in the way we experience culture from a position of strength, but it will need the support of like minds to maintain its position in a period of deepening economic recession.

## Structure

Watershed Arts Trust is an educational charity with Trustees at its head and a Council of Management to which the appointed officers (employees) must report. The Trust's activities are largely grant-aided, from central and regional state funding agencies (primarily the British Film Institute, South West Arts and the City of Bristol). There are also a number of private trusts and commercial companies who make small, regular grants to the Trust as a whole. Two subsidiary companies also occupy *Watershed*, each feeding any profits back into the charity: Watershed Trading Company, which deals with conference hire of the Trust's premises and Watershed Video Limited, the video production and post-production facility which operates commercially, as well as servicing the grant-aided and education sectors offering those users preferential hiring charges.

This combination of funding sources has meant that *Watershed* is not totally dependent on annual grants, although they are a crucial component in the overall financing of the centre. Initial capital investments by private companies have in some instances been followed up with continuous revenue commitments. These 'no strings' funding agreements are not only financially beneficial but they have also introduced the business community to *Watershed* and to the advantages of using the centre for conferences, trade exhibitions, production of videos and the like.

# Photography and the community

Stevie Bezencenet
## Photography and the community

## A concept of community

There are many ideas of what constitutes a community. There are progressive ideas amongst politicians, intellectuals, activists and others, of what this concept entails in terms of geographic location, shared ideology, social interests, class base, or common experience. It is considered here as a combination of two factors, both of which are widely discussed in Kelly's *Community, Art and the State*. The traditional socialist belief that people should be free to group together to meet their collective needs, forms the basis of one idea about community. This is in opposition to the increasing tendency of a centralised, corporate state, which purports to satisfy our social needs, whilst removing the possibilities of our acting for ourselves.

'The state must never become a substitute for personal responsibility or private initiative. One of the hardest things in the world is to stand tall, to shoulder one's burden. One of the easiest is to succumb to the temptation of believing that a state – that imaginary mother figure of our age – will be able to provide, to protect us from harsh reality, to shoulder our burdens.'

The conservatism of Margaret Thatcher attempts to convince us that the way forward is to 'go it alone', thus making a notion of community/ies redundant – however, her government's policies make even this increasingly difficult.

The other factor necessary for the establishment of a community is the conscious understanding that we are participating in a set of shared meanings and goals with an identifiable group of other people. A community is an active process, constantly changing as the needs of its constituent members develop and as our relationship with each other and the world at large changes. Communities are comprised of individuals and this must not be ignored – each of us has our own particular set of interests and desires. However, this idea of the larger social grouping is premised on the belief in the productive potential of collective activity, activity which contains the seeds for social change, coming together and acting out shared beliefs. The characteristics of proximity, class and so on are significant, but they are not enough on their own to create a community of commitment.

## Who speaks?

The general subject of this chapter is 'Community photography' and one of the basic themes is, therefore, that of self-determination. If we accept that there is a relationship between our experience of the world and our ability to comprehend it and act within it, then we need to understand how the world is 'articulated' to us, and whose interests are served by controlling the various sites where meaning/value are produced – the law, education, media, religion, and so on. It is not until we are able to analyse how we are co-erced into identifying with an ideology (one which does not necessarily serve our interests), that we are able to generate activities which speak of a different experience and alternative aspirations. Community practices, cultural activities and photographic programmes all have a role in this respect.

Many of the cultural activities undertaken in the name of the 'community' do not assume a single, coherent community, or that a structure of interacting communities is actually in existence today. As Kelly argues, community is something to be aimed for, rather than a social structure with a current, material existence. What many workers active in this sphere advocate is that all members of a society should be able to participate in the process of determining the social order, and that no-one should be disenfranchised from this basic right. This might be termed democracy. However, with the rise of the corporate state, the possibilities of our achieving a 'voice' and of influencing our relationship to the social order are gradually becoming truncated. The recent legislation on rate-capping and the abolition of the Metropolitan counties is a good example. A socially equitable system would allow/encourage us to 'speak for ourselves' and to participate in activities, which would help us to become informed and creative citizens at an individual level, and identify ourselves as members of larger groups or communities, at the social level.

In 1981 the wealthiest 1% of the country owned 23% of all assets and the poorest 50% owned a mere 6% – this gap is widening all the time. In a system where those who control the means of production are encouraged to continue developing their wealth and political purchase at the expense of the workforce, it is difficult to imagine how any reformist ideas could make a qualitative difference to the social order. We exist in a situation where we need to *buy* the chance to 'speak', to be heard, and for the majority of the population there is only minimal access to a public arena.

So where does this 'speaking' take place, whose is the voice of authority?

We grow up in a society which has its various versions of history, truth and knowledge – generally presented as objective and value-free information. Implicit in this production and consumption of 'facts' is the basic neutrality of both the process and the product being consumed. We are rarely presented with a situation where the set of values, the ideological position of the 'authority' offering us information, declares its position. If this were the case, it would allow us to make an 'interpretation' of the information on offer and to keep its 'truth' open to question. However, our training-ground for the consumption of fragmented values is through our history books, geography classes, the encyclopedias, our laws and statutes, and the media – with its continuing 'update' on the state of the world. Imagine this scene:

- a teacher, who declares that her social ideas influence what and how she teaches;
- a newspaper proprietor, who speaks of ownership of the press and its related editorial power as a means of influencing public opinion and privileging vested interests;
- an editor of *News at Ten* who introduces the daily diet of items with an explanation of the selection criteria.

Marx wrote that: 'the class which controls material production controls mental production', which is not simply to say that the ruling class has direct control of our speech; rather, that the set of values which determines the *status quo* at a particular moment in our society, does influence how we relate to that society and how we 'speak' ourselves within it. In today's society, value is determined by the market-place, which reduces everything to the status of a commodity – goods, labour, activities, ideas . . . The market within a capitalist economy tends to reduce the measure of value to an economic one, privileging this standard over all others. Such a yardstick has a reciprocal effect on our cultural activities, for any freedom which we might have to express ourselves is substantially defined by the market and the ideological regime which operates through it. Some art forms have a greater currency than others in this respect; the traditional 'fine arts', for example – painting, sculpture, opera, literature and dance particularly. Other forms, such as street theatre, film, photography, poetry, the performance arts and others, are accorded a lesser status; especially if they do not generate a material end product, one which can be displaced from its original production (and possibly its social meanings) and exchanged in the market for money. The status accorded to art forms become synonymous with their market value, rather than their social value.

## Arts and the people

Today, there is a multiplicity of cultural forms and activities – some are national in their appeal, some are specifically aimed at local audiences. Many of these activities operate at a social level as well as an aesthetic one and the integration of these qualities is a fundamental part of the activity – people participating in the production of ideas, debates, events, products and the production of meanings – all in a way which does not segregate the arts into a rigidly defined and 'dead' space, where they have no relevance to the rest of their lives. These arts are often called the 'community arts' and ghettoised into a bureaucratically controlled box; this is labelled as separate and distinct from all the other forms, however much they may have in common in terms of forms and materials.

What constitutes the community arts movement is continually open to debate and it is generally considered as an approach, as much as a series of forms. This approach brings together cultural workers and the community 'to use appropriate art forms as a means of communication and expression, in a way that critically uses and develops traditional art forms'. The activity is often a collective one, involving the transferring of skills from worker to community, rather than a passive consumption of process and product. The intention of the work ranges from the development of personal expression and the acquisition of technical and aesthetic skills to the development of social and political sensibilities within the community. Many workers operate in the belief that social and political change is influenced by cultural change, or that there is a circular relation between them: we require new methods of articulating our experience, new ways of speaking the world, in order better to understand it – perhaps to participate in changing it.

Participation is a key concept. In terms of health, education, legislation, culture and so on, we are required to 'consume' centralised, autonomous and specialist services. They exist outside us, answering our specific, local and inter-related sets of needs with a displaced and fragmented system. Whilst we are in the position of non-participatory audience, we are locked into conceiving of the arts as a commodity; one which serves the needs of a 'leisured' society, requiring stimulation of the aesthetic and intellectual senses. However, this model is not appropriate for all of us – there are alternatives. Anyone who has been involved in a music festival, street carnival, video project, community publishing workshop, poetry reading or open exhibition will appreciate the difference between these types of activities and the conventional, subsidised art forms. Involvement by the people breaks down the barriers of artists and audience; this is no longer a relevant way of conceiving arts activities – instead they become social ones, fulfilling more complex functions and more likely to become an integral part of our everyday lives.

There are many processes and values within the fine arts which we should consider refusing. The stress on the 'appreciation' of arts and its implications of elitism and genius by the artist effectively removes the possibility of a majority of the population becoming creatively productive in this sphere. Traditionally, the eurocentric, patriarchal and commodity based philosophy of the arts in this country, which always privileges the product over the process, generates practices and objects which are elitist, racist and sexist. Standards have been set which are considered suitable for the fine arts, but have also been applied to the community arts, where they are not necessarily appropriate. Standards of 'excellence' are constantly being quoted at community artists when their practices have failed to measure up to the levels of quality and professionalism.

The arts establishment holds conflicting attitudes to these 'deviant' forms; attitudes which change according to the political climate of the times. The more liberal see them as a step towards an appreciation of the real arts, a learning procedure for those groups and classes as yet unable to understand the value of the traditional forms – community art as a kind of artistic 'kindergarten'. The less liberal consider them unsophisticated, tangential, disorganised and potentially damaging – both in terms of undermining the elite status of the fine arts and as a network for subversive activity. So, usually there is a compromise. It might be termed support, or appropriation or colonisation, with the state and certain statutory social agencies taking over the organisation and control of much of this work, in a gesture of acknowledgement, which is also one of containment.


# Community photography

The standard practice is based on workers and community in a collective activity, whether it be concerned with a tenant's campaign or a youth group project, or creating a show to examine stereotyping. The relations of the community to the workers will be one of access, in terms of equipment and resources, ideas, skills and development of work. Some projects function as a passive resource for the community, answering needs as and when they arise, providing a service. Other groups act out a more dynamic social role, organising structures and projects which may be taken over by the community itself in an active manner. Many people do not understand the idea of a community artist, artist/photographer... yes: community worker ... yes. But what, precisely, is a community photographer? To answer this question one could point to all the projects, organisations and workshops throughout the country, which engage with their communities in this spirit. The sum of all these is what constitutes this type of worker.

The development of community photography in this country has been a very uneven process, relying on the energies and enthusiasms of individuals, rather than on statutory authorities – they step onto the scene when the pressure groups become significant enough to warrant notice. Indeed, the general development of subsidised photography has been due to workers in the field painstakingly educating the authorities to recognise the need and the 'value' of these practices.

Community photography exists across many different social formations – the education sector, community arts, history workshops, youth projects and women's campaigning groups, amongst others. In the 1970s, Paul Carter undertook extensive research in the area and some of this information was analysed in Sue Braden's book *Committing Photography*. However, some general comments on these practices will be made here in order to contextualise the points which arise in the following articles.

In 1976, the Half Moon Photography Workshop published the first issue of *Camerawork* magazine and included a statement of aims: 'to promote alternative ways for photographers to use and develop their skill' and to develop strategies 'in terms of contributing through photography towards social change'. The workshop was primarily concerned with 'Who is it for?' and presented a co-ordinated programme of projects, which included the gallery, publishing, education workshop and information and advice. They advocated the value of the exchange of ideas in seminars, exhibitions, articles and workshops; of circulating material (in many forms) which arose out of these practices; in constructing archives of the past and the present – an alternative history, and one which had a real relation to the struggles of the working class; and in developing alternative photographic technology to begin a process of independence from the monopoly of the industry. At the same time, they collaborated with local groups in documentary projects and offered practical help to organisations and activists who wanted to structure their own programmes and facilities.

Many of these aims are held in common with other organisations today, but they become refined and qualified through a constant process of debate amongst the workers, the communities and, occasionally, the funding bodies.

Camerawork is probably the 'largest' project in this country in terms of the funding it receives and has become a major influence on the developments within this area of practice; both because of their example and their willingness to help newer projects become established. There have been changes during the ten years since Photography Workshop was started, and tracing these is amazingly informative; a history of the cultural and ideological battles in a microcosm. However, suffice it to say that though the venue, the personnel, the funding bodies, the programmes and the ideas have all suffered and benefited by varying degrees of change – it remains one of the initiators of the whole movement. Today, its work is divided into five areas of production: the darkrooms, the gallery, the touring shows, the magazine and the administration, and it is the relationship between these areas that partially determines the organisation's success – at different moments. The communities with which they work vary from the specifically local, through regional and national, to an international audience for its magazine. A darkroom project aimed at young Asian women and an article on the politics of representation can be productively related to each other, and this is one of the key concerns of Camerawork – to construct a coherent set of practices across a range of communities, whilst *enabling* those very different groups to work with and in photography in the ways that are most useful and accessible to them. For example – a gallery show might include images that have been generated by a darkroom group; this whole exhibition might become a touring show; and the magazine might cover the same issues. (There have been difficulties in the past, when the target audience or community of the varying production areas seemed too disparate – there seemed to be several small organisations operating under the umbrella and the security of the larger/nominal one.)

Today, when Camerawork is again beginning to concretise its philosophy and working practices after a period of reduced activity, due to internal disagreement and bureaucratic obfuscation, its future is in jeopardy. The abolition of the GLC has affected hundreds of cultural and social organisations and there is scant hope for many of them to achieve the same level of funding elsewhere. One can only hope that the Arts Council, for whom Camerawork is still a revenue client (August 1985), will be imaginative enough to compensate for this subsidy shortfall, rather than devastate the project by insisting that they raise the difference themselves – either privately or through other state and borough sources.

The photographer's relation to community activities frequently began in the late 1960s and early 1970s with the image being utilised for its documentary/recording function and its fund-raising potential. It was only gradually that the image was acknowledged as a site for creative, social and analytical production in these community ventures. Indeed, Paul Carter's role in the Blackfriars Settlement in the early 1970s was of this former nature, until he began to investigate how photography could be used in community development, over and above its basic function. It was not until 1976 that the first advertisement for a community photographer with a brief to set up workshops appeared; this was with the WELD project in Handsworth. Other projects have come into existence through a group activity and the creation of a working space, out of which a variety of practices is developed. Community photography does not necessarily mean *photographers* working in or with the community; it is equally applicable to the instigation of image-making, analysis and retrieval, which is a substantial feature of this kind of practice.

Working with a medium which has traditionally been valued for its 'realist' base and its documentary capacity to show 'the facts', image-makers have been faced with the problem of how to utilise the photograph in the service of a questioning practice; one which seeks to investigate beneath surface appearance. This dilemma has generated one of the key debates within community photography – that of the politics of representation. Many image-makers have had to rethink their commonsense acceptance of the image as a record, and consider using other visual, textual and presentational strategies to construct the kinds of work which will generate an understanding of how photography works, and how it has been used to represent in mainstream practices, reportage, portraiture, advertising, amateur photography, art images and so on, in a manner which excludes our understanding of its operations, and of what is being shown.

'A capitalist society requires a culture based on images. It needs to furnish vast amounts of entertainment in order to stimulate buying and anaesthetise the injuries of class, race and sex. And it needs to gather unlimited amounts of information, the better to exploit natural resources, increase productivity, keep order, make war, give jobs to bureaucrats.' *(Sontag)*

Philip Wolmuth wrote in *Camerawork* no.18 that '. . . there is a rich language of visual imagery well understood by the propagandists of our capitalist institutions', and he goes on to argue that it is time that we on the Left become more sophisticated in our own forms of visual rhetoric. Roland Barthes writes of the difference between 'showing' and 'telling': we urgently need to continue our critique of the forms of communication and persuasion controlled by the establishment and its reluctance to 'tell' us anything, whilst continuing to explore alternative uses of photography and other language forms, to enable us to 'tell' our world ourselves.

Obviously, it is not only in 'community' photography that these concerns are acted out. Similar ideas are expressed in every section of this book. What is valuable about presenting these ideas to an individual or group working with a community-concerned organisation, is that those who may not previously have had the opportunity or desire to think through alternative methods of constructing meanings with images/words/design/sound/graphics, etc., are presented with a choice. This choice can be acted out, with access to the means of production, guided by a technically competent and committed workforce, and the results discussed in relation to the intention and an audience's role in 'reading'. This is an ideal situation and one which is nowhere common enough, but it is one of the several ways in which members of a community are encouraged to work *with* images and to develop a visual literacy – one which is not part of the standard educational process – which will help in perceiving that photography (and the media in general) is not the neutral/transparent process we are led to believe.

The process of decoding or deconstruction is a complex one and requires an openness to questioning that which we 'take-for-granted', which is not unproblematic. The community sector faces a difficulty also experienced in photography courses in education – how to escape that oppressive process of 'co-ercion', which is one of the subjects under discussion: co-ercion in terms of a cultural hegemony, where the ruling class generally fixes the cultural agenda for all classes, seemingly with our consent. As long as those engaged in this process are clear from what position the critique is being presented, then there is an opportunity for critical analysis and understanding.

The sites of community photography are visible in many ways, from the work of the Docklands Photography Project and its use of local hoardings to inform the public, to exhibitions in supermarkets and alternative family 'albums'. There are many poster workshops which apply the photographic image imaginatively in different contexts, and the campaigning aspects of community concerns have developed the use of the placard, audio-visual presentation, and text/image work. The skills which are necessary to community projects using photography are not only visual ones – the production of the image may be only part of a process, which may involve collective debate and authorship (not easy), research and writing, design and layout processes, organisation and campaigning, and always, a consideration of the audience and how they will be able to inter-relate with the work.

Access has been one of the keywords for community work, and this presents another problem. Projects are usually clear what type of community they wish to work with, whether it be simply a geographically local one, or those communities often disenfranchised from the means to work with images, i.e., ethnic groups, pensioners, kids, women, the unemployed . . . Alternatively, there may be a group which requires specific skills to help it realise a project.

But what of the individual or group who wishes to use the facilities to print sexist or racist images, or to further a commercial practice? This is always a delicate area, especially if the implications of the pictures are not self-evident. This is just one of the instances where policy gets created and adapted during the working procedures and opens up a space for learning and teaching at the same time. Whilst darkrooms offer an opportunity for people to learn for themselves, to learn from others, collectively to take pleasure in 'playing' with images and experimenting with their potential; and whilst many projects and organisations operate from a feminist/socialist/anti-racist position, this does not constrain the membership from working in a much more basic and unresolved manner.

One of the continuing problems faced by photographers working with community groups has been the question of 'quality', as defined by establishment aesthetic standards. Frequently the funding bodies have criticised this type of work for failing to conform to their artistic requirements and reduced or stopped the funding. This problem is compounded by the political characteristic of much community work, which does not necessarily require an elaborate 'artistic' coding, but which may escape the scrutiny of a nervous funding agency, if it *does* exhibit fine art values. Unfortunately, in order to sidestep a problematic confrontation on this issue, many projects have persuaded themselves that it is essential to achieve a certain (established?) 'quality' in order for those producing the work to feel it is significant. This does seem to be falling into the trap of conformism, in the name of reformist or radical activity.

The funding bodies may publicly speak of their 'arm's length' policy of non-interference, but to some groups it feels like a stranglehold – but a slow and sometimes even delicate one. It becomes necessary to adopt strategies which maximise the work of the project, whilst reducing its capacity to be controlled and curtailed by financial restrictions. This leads to the matter of accountability and to whom. Few organisations working within the community sector are answerable to their membership, which might have a minimal voice in determining its running. Unfortunately, accountability seems to work one way and is directed towards the money, rather than the community/ies. A large proportion of the working time of these projects is spent in satisfying the agencies, rather than the consumer, and awareness of this problem has not led to its diminution. Some projects are increasing the membership element of control, in the hope that this will lead to a working with, rather than for, the community. The major difficulty is that of effectively being employed by the state whilst working to question or undermine it.

There have been traditions of work in photography which have variously been termed 'concerned', 'committed', 'humanist', 'socialist' and 'radical'. All of these labels have a place in community activity, but 'committed' and 'socialist' may be the most applicable. The commitment comes from the conditions of work. Many in this sector are volunteers, often 'unemployed' and working for no wage, whilst others are working under youth and MSC schemes and are exploited differently. Despite the lack of any or sufficient financial reward, workers in community projects do commit themselves to their aims and programmes, so it becomes a sector which wields little economic power, and those working within it have only a marginal status. Some projects are funded by agencies which insist on a reasonable wage (the GLC) and others are becoming unionised. But the majority of workers are badly paid and overworked in this area, and at the same time are often working to assuage a common sense of frustration and alienation. The irony of this situation need not be counter-produtive. If enough communities are stimulated to demand local projects and are prepared to support those projects, then there is the potential for growth in this area.

In 1984 the Federation for Community Photography was established: it grew out of a seminar held at Camerawork, attended by groups from all over the country. It has published its initial aims:

–   to provide a forum for national dialogue and a framework for the support of workers and users of community photography organisations throughout Britain

–   to organise regional training initiatives for workers and users of workshops/projects as well as representatives of outside agencies sympathetic to the aims of the federation

–   to implement a network of advice/information and distribution and to support the initiatives of traditional venues, as well as the promotion and co-ordination of alternative touring circuits

–   to pursue new and alternative funding initiatives with a regional and national perspective.

The Federation has organised a membership structure with regional co-ordinators to ensure a representative management body. It has already held seminars in several parts of the country in order to engage with local projects and expertise. Though much of this organising and communicating had already begun in certain parts of Britain, particularly the North East, it should be extremely valuable in co-ordinating production, distribution, funding possibilities and general debate.

If we ask the question: 'To what service has photography been put – in the construction of the past, the sanctioning of the present and the promise of the future?', then the photographic practices which fall under the heading of 'community photography' create one of the sites of a collective and democratic cultural process – one which can help achieve the goal of self-determination and social emancipation for the communities of the present and of the future.

Pete Bullock
# The Tondu Photo Workshop

'Scargill's stormtroopers' and 'fascist bully-boys', these are just two of the many attacks levelled at the leaders and rank-and-file members of the NUM by the majority of the national press over the duration of the current dispute. The media have, from day one, stated that it is merely the intransigence of Arthur Scargill and, to a lesser extent, Ian MacGregor that has prolonged the strike. What the media rarely report and the government underestimated is the resolve of not only the miners and their families, but also whole communities affected by the proposed pit closures.

In the Maesteg area (one of the valleys Tondu Photo Workshop works in) the St John's colliery and the washeries employ a total of over 1,000 people. During the last three years St John's has been starved of capital investment and therefore conditioned for closure. There are 30 years of coal in the 6ft seam, with new development, and four years in short-term in the Bute and the 9ft seams.

The Union has detailed information on the Margam Project, proving that the deepest seam in the Margam Reserves is two-and-a-half miles from the shaft of St John's colliery and would be accessible by two underground tunnels at a gradient of 1 in 6. The development of the Margam Reserves from Maesteg would be a quarter of the cost of that of the 'super pit' which is planned to be sited at Margam itself. It would cost approximately £50m over six years to develop it from St John's, but it would cost £300m over the same period to sink new shafts.

The union agreed to the closure of Caerau Colliery in 1977 on the promise of the construction of the new mine at Margam. Coegnant Colliery, which is now closed, was promised eight years of life in 1979, after which the men would be transferred to the 'super pit' at Margam. These promises have all proved false. What remains true is the argument, based on sound mining engineering, that St John's would, with investment, secure a long-term future for the mining industry in the Llynfi Valley.

If St John's and the washeries close, there will be 50% unemployment in Maesteg. The town would become a dormitory with only a few small engineering industries remaining, and the whole

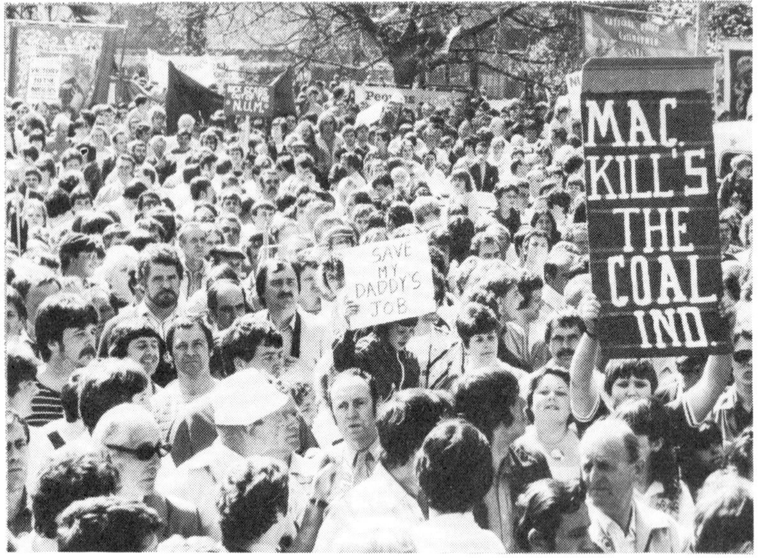


*1. Rally at Sophia Gardens, 28th April, 1984.*

*2. "One of the most welcome things about the strike is that the women have not just been there as back-up but they've been on the front line of the struggle." Ken Smith, Chairman, Maesteg Miners' Support Group, Port Talbot Steelworks, 15th May, 1984.*

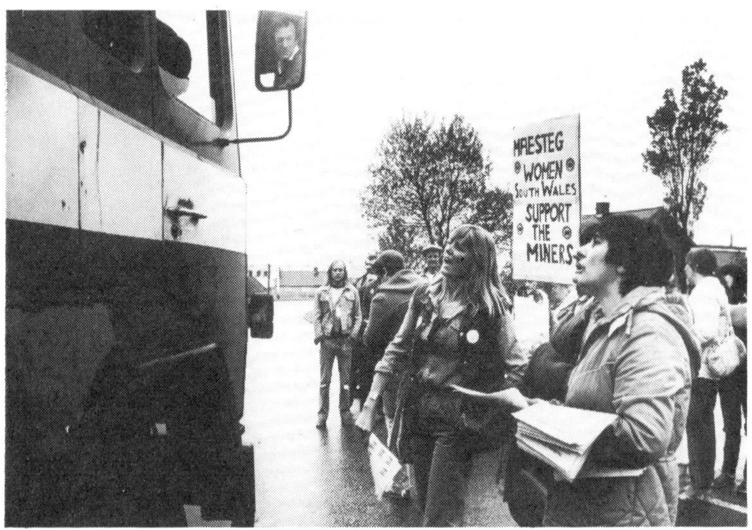

social and cultural fabric destroyed within a very few years.

The St John's colliery, which seven years ago was classified as a long-life pit, has now been told that, because of geological difficulties, it has less than three months left. The threatened closures are seen as the start of the MacGregor Plan to get the industry to produce 100m tonnes per year in 100 pits with 100,000 miners. At present there are 180,000 miners in 176 pits. All the promised investment didn't materialize after 1981 and was directed to the central coalfields of Yorkshire and Nottinghamshire. There has been a policy of starving the peripheral areas (Scotland, Durham, Kent and South Wales) and the planned closures are only the tip of the iceberg.

People have realized that the strike is not just against pit closures, but covers the wider aspect of retaining the social and cultural life of communities and the right of the children to employment. It is within this context that the Tondu Photo Workshop was set up in June, 1983, by Valley and Vale Community Arts. We work in the three valleys of the Ogwr area and our base is an old junior school in Tondu, which is a junction where these valleys meet. The group is made up of mainly unemployed people who have come together for the purpose of learning about photography and its uses in a community context. It is also involved in doing workshops for Mid-Glamorgan Social Services and producing a number of other exhibitions. The Workshop has explored the present strike and its implications for the Llynfi valley in an exhibition of photographs and text called ' ... A Few Hotheads' (the name came from a quote from MacGregor in which he showed that he thought the strikers were just a small percentage of agitators). We tried to put over an alternative point of view to the media by showing all aspects – fund raising, marches, rallies, morale boosting carnivals, as well as picket lines. The exhibition is based around the activities of the members of the St John's Lodge of the NUM and the very active members of the support group. It takes the form of 30 laminated panels and, obviously, cannot be completed until the end of the strike, even though the first part has toured extensively throughout the country.

The exhibition grew out of our involvement with the St John's Lodge, which we approached at the beginning of the strike with an offer of help with the day-to-day running of the operation, i.e., driving, producing news-sheets and posters for benefits. The Lodge Secretary gave us a letter sanctioning our photographic work on the picket lines, which helped us gain the trust of pickets from other areas who have been misrepresented so often by the right-wing press. We feel that the theme of the exhibition echoes the solidarity not only of the NUM, but also other trade unions, and so on. In fact, the solidarity of the majority of the working class in this country, not just the 'few hotheads' that Ian MacGregor singled out.

The Lodge realized the value of the images in our exhibition, i.e., large amounts of people in other areas could see what was happening in South Wales and not rely on the media propaganda. The Lodge also saw that an exhibition of photographs and text could put over certain points much better than an individual speaker could. So far the exhibition has been in *Camerawork*, Wembley Conference Centre and Newcastle Side Gallery, as well as various public meetings and miners' galas in our area.

Just before Christmas the Workshop and the Lodge discussed the possibility of the production of posters to be distributed throughout the area. At the beginning they came with ideas and wanted us to get on with it, but we decided on working collectively throughout the process, from deciding on location, to which photograph would be used, to text and design. One poster was a direct appeal for children's toys for Christmas. The image used on this poster was in many ways a throwback to the 'helpless' appeal of the Oxfam and Shelter campaigns of the '60s and early '70s. We realize that we should have been working with unions in times of 'peace' and developing a new visual language. This would compete with the glossy and positive images seen daily in the press, on hoardings and on the television. It is too late to experiment with this new language during this dispute, as results have to be immediate. The toy appeal poster had directly increased the amount of donations to the Lodge.

In the future we want to develop our links, not only with the NUM, but with all trade unions within our community. We are, at the time of writing, involved with organizing a conference between community artists and unions to further this aim. We are interested in involving not only officials and officers, but grass roots members, in appreciating the power of imagery and understanding how the media use this power to distort facts and misrepresent issues.

Ultimately, we would like to see the unions produce and develop their own imagery and even challenge existing networks of distribution by means of posters, union-produced daily newspapers and by extending into other mediums, such as video and cable TV systems.

Photographs produced by: Gary Bevan, Paul Davies and Hazel Gillings of the Tondu Photo Workshop.

We would like to thank the St John's Lodge of the NUM for all their help.

Stevie Bezencenet
# Bootle Arts and Action

Bootle is the northern limit to the city of Liverpool, although a politically separate entity governed from the genteel seaside resort of Southport, having little in common with the suburbs and green belt to the north, and everything in common with the inner-city areas of its larger neighbour. The Tory dominated local authority, Sefton Metropolitan District Council, has little history of urban aid; Art in Action is one of the very few independent community projects in the Sefton area.

In just over a decade, cultural, social and psychological deserts have been produced in Bootle. People have no voice. To avoid complete social decay urgent help is needed for our area. The number of people whose talents are suppressed in areas like Bootle is phenomenal. With all the experts pondering and trying to show why working-class families do not take up education, we would ask, 'Can this environment foster a love of learning, thinking and awareness of the human condition?' It is no coincidence that here live the people who consume the least of society's resources. Manual workers form the majority of the workforce and in general they earn less than non-manual workers, have less autonomy in their work, are less influential in politics and their children have less opportunity for educational advancement. In these potentially explosive circumstances people live and work and help produce the wealth this country needs. The wonder is, not that crime is increasing, but that so many people are law-abiding.

In the early days of 1977, Margaret Pinnington, Allan Parry and Les Edge, who are now active members of Arts and Action, were all involved with the Church Street Community Association. One activity that involved all three was the production of the community newspaper. In March 1977 Church Street submitted an application to the Merseyside Arts Association for community arts funds. 'We asked for a full-time worker and money for equipment and materials. We were very naive then and if we had been given all that we had asked for, we wouldn't have known what to do with it! We got our first community arts grant of £3,000.'

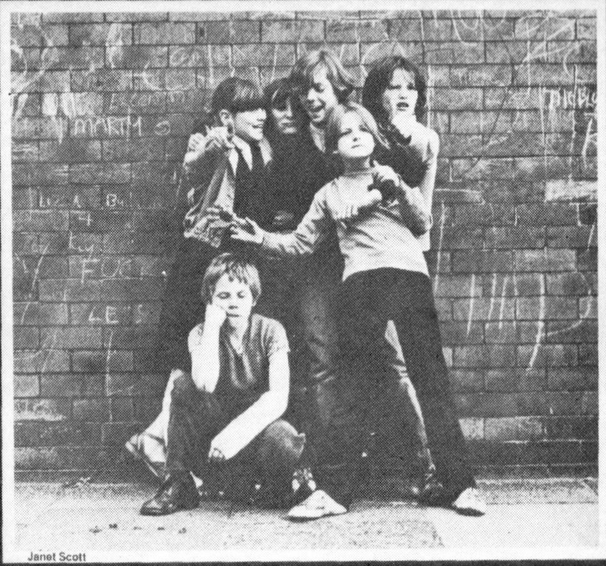

ART
IN
ACTION
Janet Scott
A COMMUNITY PHOTOGRAPHIC PROJECT ON MERSEYSIDE
AN ARTS & ACTION PUBLICATION

This grant was used to employ Bill Dolce, a local guy who had learnt photography and other artistic skills.

'. . . it was general art in community art terms, it wasn't a specialist thing like we do at Arts and Action. I had to cope with demands from local people and kids for all kinds of different activities. I didn't mind this and just got on with it. I did manage to concentrate a bit on photography doing a lot of workshops after buying a camera. We did some social documentation as well as the normal recording of community activities. We had taken a lot of photographs of the area. The power of this form of expression came home to us after the introduction of photographs in the newspaper. In issue number six we showed people living in desperate housing conditions, they were rehoused shortly afterwards. We didn't think in terms of community art – no jargon. Our interpretation seemed to differ from others but we had seen the power of the visual media in the hands of our community. The idea of a photographic booklet was born.'

Due to a division of interests with Church Street, Bill, Allan, Les and Margaret decided to set up a new group in the summer of 1978, which came to be called Bootle Arts and Action; this name combined the two main interests of community art and community action and received its first grant of £900 from the MAA later in the summer. Everyone worked on a voluntary basis, with new workers joining from the local community. The focus of the group towards photography and its social potential resulted in one of their most significant projects so far.

'We had accumulated an amazing amount of material and our two cameras were in constant use. Photography had really taken off, kids, adults, everyone was photo mad. We were thinking of producing a bumper edition of *Communitywise* with lots of photographs of Bootle or perhaps of making a film, however we eventually decided to undertake production of a book of photographs: it became very important to us. Through the photographic media we would show that local people could have their say. We also wanted to show that working-class people could produce a book that was of the highest standard. We were aiming to produce a work of art as well as a political document.'

This book, *Bootle – a Pictorial Study of the Dockland Community –* came out in October 1978 and was distributed to all Local Authority Departments with a covering letter asking them to join with all local groups in setting up a working party to 'look in depth at the environmental and social problems of Bootle' to seek to bring about improvement. The response of Sefton's Chief Planning Officer was to send a directive to all his staff, stating that under no circumstances should any officer reply to or acknowledge this letter or in any way offer co-operation or information to this 'organisation'. Since then the booklet has been accepted by others as an important artistic document and has been used as a model by other organisations.

Soon the project moved and moved again, always searching for cheap, local and suitable premises. A darkroom, gallery and offices were established and the local response continually increased, so that it became difficult to respond to all the demands. It was agreed to concentrate on those kids who were genuinely interested in the visual media, at the cost of those who wanted a much-needed place to hang out and feel welcome; it was a necessary decision in order to make their minimal resources effective. But the fight for money went on – as always:

'I want good photographic equipment for the community and myself, because I am part of this community. It is no good having a good enlarger costing hundreds of pounds with a lousy enlarging lens. People were beginning to say that they wanted equipment of better quality to work with. They know when something is good and they appreciate it. We make it clear to them when they come into this place and pick up a camera, that this equipment belongs to them, the community, and the project is a resource for them to use. It is their responsibility to help look after it. If it is mistreated or stolen it will affect them and their mates, and other members of the community who use it. In fact I can't remember anything being damaged belonging to the project and we have never had anything stolen.'

In March 1980 the Merseyside Arts Association agreed an 'A' priority rating for the project and recommended a 100% increase on the previous year's grant aid. However, arts funding and local politics are never that simple and soon the project discovered that their grant had been frozen. Sefton Council had made an allegation that they had indulged in '... activities of an extreme political and/or antisocial nature, which rendered them an undesirable body to assist financially out of public funds'. Rather than take time defending the project, the workers decided to compile a comprehensive study of the project's work, which was published as a substantial booklet, *Art in Action*, in late 1980. This became one of their most creative periods as they re-assessed their work to date and considered their future. In common with other projects the work has a clear class base; though it produces artistic work of the highest standard which satisfies the Arts Council's criteria, it adheres to a particular philosophy, which is totally  justified by the attitudes of residents of Bootle.

Community art is a particular process that can relate to all forms of creative expression, provided that such activity is relevant to a general process of community and individual development. The activities involved should help people perceive, understand and control their relationships to their environment, with the ultimate aim of controlling that environment. Community arts techniques are obviously attractive in themselves (murals, theatre, music, printing, photography, video, festivals, etc.) because they are concerned with the re-integration of creativity into everyday life. They are able to get to the roots of, and express, real community need in a given situation, certainly lively and full of energy, and which often results in developments far beyond the field of creative activity.

Community arts enables people to take an active rather than a passive role in the arts and to participate fully in the creative and decision-making processes involved. They help create a recognisable and valuable function for cultural activities within a local context. People are encouraged to leave their homes, to meet others, to express themselves and explore the potential of new skills and ideas. Barriers caused by isolation and the inability to communicate are broken down. Community arts are not concerned with a new role for the arts as a leisure-time activity in a working-class environment. They are concerned with exploring and giving voice to the consequences of urban decay, the inequalities of our distribution of wealth and the divisive class structure of our society; the effect on large sections of our population of the lack of opportunity available to others and the effect on the individual of having a complete lack of self-confidence, self-respect and faith in his/her own abilities. Community art is therefore not a neutral process but is actively orientated towards social reform. At the same time it is concerned with personal expression – the techniques used are a means of enabling people to develop a vision and they offer ways of at least beginning to do something about that vision. The art of the community therefore becomes a primary expression of the issues of common concern that otherwise would not find an outlet.

'The work of Arts and Action has inspired art work and community activity that accurately reflects the social conditions in the area in which they are active. This is inevitable and in the tradition of all great art.'   (*Allan Roberts, Member of Parliament for Bootle*)

The *Art in Action* booklet demonstrates the type and quality of the work being initiated by the project; when it was published in 1980, Bill Dolce commented:

'The photographic work being produced is of excellent quality. I was concerned that when one person is doing most of the workshops, that person's style, techniques and methods might show through in a lot of the work. I am glad to say that this has not happened. The individuals using the project are exploring their own methods of self-expression and I look at some of the work and wish that I had done it, it's that good. We have not done full justice to their work in publishing and distributing it. We do not have the "manpower" or resources to do an effective and widespread publicity campaign about the work.'

An independent investigation ascertained that the project was not the social threat feared by the Sefton Council and their funding was restored; however, Arts and Action has never been allowed to exhibit in any of the Council's properties – an unfortunate and curious loss.

Since their recognition by MAA there have been many developments, some of which are briefly outlined here:

–   in 1981 they made an *Open Door* television programme with the BBC Community Programme Unit entitled 'It's Bootle but is it Art?' This created an extensive response from other community arts groups and individuals around the country, whilst giving members of the project useful experience in programme-making, which is invaluable when making their own videos with equipment borrowed from Open Eye Video Unit, another Merseyside organisation;

–   a group of unemployed people from Halewood in Merseyside decided to photograph their involvement in the People's March for Jobs and the exhibition was photographed, written and laid out with the help of the project;

–   after the riots in Toxteth during the summer of 1981, the Liverpool 8 Defence Committee was formed to put forward the viewpoint of the local people. An exhibition, 'Toxteth '81' was produced during this period, in association with the L8 Committee;

–   in 1982 Arts and Action moved again to larger premises, creating a bigger gallery space and more darkrooms; they were still being funded by MAA on an annual basis and also received a capital grant from the Arts Council of Great Britain to assist in the transfer and refurbishment;

–   volunteers from the project worked with the Merseyside Workers Writers on their book of poetry and prose *Pass the Valium Martha*, by producing the photographic layout;

–   in April 1983, a small MSC project was set up employing 14 part-time workers to assist the full-time volunteers in providing photographic, video, silkscreen and layout and design work-

shops for the local community and organisations in the
Merseyside area;

–   in 1984 the MSC continued to fund the 14 part-time posts.
    However, the project is still based on the policy of local people
    running the activities for themselves and their community;

–   two project photographers went to Dublin at the invitation of the
    National College of Art and Design, in order to give workshops
    to the South Inner City Development Association, a group from
    the old-established Working Class Community of the Liberties
    South of the Liffey.

# 1984/1985

One of the major problems for the project today is production and
exhibition of that production. Though the project might seem to be
'funding wealthy', it is money for wages and overheads, with only a
small proportion (approximately 8%) going towards materials. This
is usual for this type of organisation, but some others attempt to
generate their own income to supplement their state funding; but this
supposes a community and users who have money to buy services. It
is a problem to consider oneself a service for the community in the
first instance, and then expect them to pay for what has been argued
already belongs to them. The darkrooms are a good example – given
that the level of unemployment amongst the youth in the estates
around Merseyside can be almost 100%, there is not much
'disposable income' around. At one point, Arts and Action did
consider charging for this facility on a sliding scale, then they
discovered that not a single user was employed: they abandoned the
idea.
   Currently, one of the 14 MSC workers is full-time and acts
as the Project Manager. Unfortunately, the MSC policy is to curtail
this full-time position after 52 weeks, on the basis that there are many
others who should benefit from the scheme; there can be extensions
for 'key personnel', but they are hard to get. This means that Dave
Swindlehurst, the current Manager, might have to vacate his post at
the point when he was best suited to continue, namely after a year's
experience. He would then have the privilege either of becoming part-
time or returning to the position of volunteer, which had been his
involvement in the past, off and on, since 1978. There are volunteers
who prefer to remain with that status and the relative freedom of
working that it allows – Bill Dolce, one of the originators of the
project, is a good example.

There are many years of effort, commitment and production vested in Arts and Action and they have much to teach others who hold similar interests. Yet without an appropriate publicity and distribution system for their exhibitions and other material, a valuable community resource is being under-utilised. An exhibition about to open (April 1985) is a historically based show of one Edward Rushton, seaman turned educator. He supported many social causes, including the abolition of slavery (he tried to help them during sea transports) and the French Revolution and, having contracted a disease at sea and becoming blind, he started the first school for the blind in Liverpool. The exhibition is as much textual as visual and is being shown at the Merseyside Trade Union Community and Resource Centre, with other local venues to follow. This type of work could have a substantial use for all types of institutions, but time and money are needed to organise such activity. One hope is that various recent formations of community groups around the country are coming together to benefit from different experiences and exchange ideas concerning mutual planning and events for the future.

The Arts Council stated in 1974 in their Report of the Community Arts Working Party that it was appropriate to support this general area of practice; however, they did not recommend that a separate Department be established to administer funding, as '. . . throughout its investigations the Working Party has been conscious of discussing a development with an uncertain future, which only time and experience will reveal', and '. . . if community arts is not a growth point for the arts, it will wither away, or be seen to be irrelevant to the development of the arts. But if it is a growth point it must be allowed and, indeed, encouraged to grow with the help of public support, whether from the Arts Council, the Regional Arts Associations, or the local authorities.' Unfortunately, there is always the subtext, will the practice lead '. . . to a product that can be judged by normally accepted standards'? When those standards are vested in the ruling class then it is all to the good that current developments, particularly the new Federation of Community Photography, organise a strong power base for future negotiations with those to whom it is still necessary to go 'cap in hand'.

Apart from the last section, 1984/1985, this article has been compiled from two existing sources: *Art in Action* – a community photographic project on Merseyside, published by Arts and Action, 1980; and 'Art in Action', Rob Murray in *BEE*, July 1984 (*Bulletin of Environmental Education*). Thanks to Dave Swindlehurst for information and co-operation.

Chris Boot and Gina Glover
# The South London Photo Co-Op

The Photo Co-op began in the late 1970s, defining itself as 'an informal working group of photographers, amateur and professional, part-time and full-time', differing from photographic societies and clubs by an 'engagement in local and broader issues affecting the community'. The term 'community' in its common usage at the time was used uncritically to refer to the working-class movement and a relationship to it based on social action. Membership of the group, then known as the Wandsworth Photo Co-op with very much a local identity, was drawn from local community workers, political activists and non-aligned amateur and professional photographers who concentrated on producing campaign materials around housing, welfare, unemployment, health and privatization issues at a critical time. A new Tory administration was busy gaining a reputation for pioneering Thatcher's schemes for local government, selling off public assets, closing hospitals, privatizing local services and constructing a new Wandsworth – now the 'Brighter Borough'.

We have since grown to be a major independent photography group, in part through substantial funding from the Greater London Council, London's city-wide local authority. Created in 1964 by a Conservative government as a successor to the London County Council, it was hardly intended to be a radical or popular body, but the Labour administration which came to power in 1981 under Ken Livingstone used it as a vehicle for radical departures in local government. One of its commitments was to re-evaluate its arts policies and this was to have a profound effect on how arts activities were conceived and funded. The Co-op was one organisation directly to benefit from this new approach, and assessment of our response in turn contributed to this general reassessment of roles.

The GLC had inherited an Arts and Recreation panel with responsibility, and a multi-million pound budget for national institutions on the South Bank, the Royal Ballet and the Opera. A community art sub-committee was swiftly created in its first year with a comparatively small, £1 million, budget. In setting it up, Tony Banks, chair of Arts and Recreation, seconded Alan Tomkins of the Cockpit Photography Project, to work as Arts Policy Officer – a powerful position, being a member's appointment – with a brief to expand the currently conceived concepts of culture used by officers and, by implication, the type of projects which were funded. Existing understandings about community arts, and the dominant position of theatre, were to be challenged, with photography, film, video and publishing projects gaining higher priority. Behind the planning of this shift lay a theory of photography's broad appeal, and a general awareness that its popular and critical potential was yet to be realized.

Tomkins personally recruited community arts advisors from 'grassroots' arts organisations able to perform a number of important functions central to change. As individuals who understood their particular arts field, they were chosen to provide 'expert' opinion to counterbalance the priorities of the existing officers, which favoured the tradition of 'fine arts', and who had little or no experience of dealing with community groups. They were also opposed to the then current assumptions of the 1972 Local Government Act, which defined culture in safe, conservative terms and outlined the legitimate activities of local authorities in this area. Specific provision was made for theatre and the gallery system, while there was no mention of television, radio, video, photography, or record and book distribution. Such 'expert' advice was used in legal challenges to establish whether a woman-only group could legitimately be funded, whether a café could be considered a gallery space and whether comics, murals and photocopying could be termed 'art'. It was a breakthrough to realize that the agenda was theirs – that the politicians only needed to state that they felt such-and-such a legitimate cultural activity and the lawyers had no choice but to tag along.

At the outset, the Co-op had chosen an informal strucure; some members were in full-time work, others were unemployed, and commitments varied. The essential shared premise was that individuals should bring photography to bear on issues they were already involved in. One benefit was that all kinds of skills were exchanged within the group. But, after an active period of campaign, calendar and exhibition work (with workshops channelled through a separate body, the Moving Picture Project), the lack of a formal constitution and irregular commitments eventually drained initiative. In 1982 three remaining women members saw the only way to consolidate the work of the past and to develop the potential of the picture archive was to formalize aims and obtain funding, thereby permitting regular involvement and continuity. With support from the local resource centre and Community Health Council with whom the Co-op had worked extensively in the past (and who knew the minutiae of the GLC's concerns and the application process), an application was submitted in 1983. This was for a single salary to be shared with materials money to undertake work with women's groups and to develop the Co-op's role as a photography resource centre.

We were aware that the term 'community' was coming to mean community-of-interest rather than the 'dispossessed working class', or any other catch-all concept. And as a women's self-representation group, knew we were suitable recipients for funds. What we did not know about then were the disputes within County Hall itself. Besides the opposition of existing arts officers, there were three members of the community arts panel who termed themselves 'community artists' and who saw their function as promoting the needs of local working-class people, resisting the change of emphasis towards pluralism and self-representation. Their particular concerns about democratic management were taken on board, but the differences were otherwise unresolved. Part of the problem involved the terminology; by referring to alternative arts activities under the heading 'community arts', and allocating them a budget accordingly, they had been defined in terms of a practice the Arts Policy Officer meant to challenge. Had budgets been separately allocated to women's arts and black arts for these activities, some of the obstacles to new policies would have been circumvented, though this would have caused problems for other groups.

The committee meeting at which our application was heard was confusing to say the least. At the first open meeting of its kind (Greater London Arts, the Arts Council's regional arts association, thought this was mad and refused to send one of their own officers). lawyers, politicians, officers and advisors scrambled for their own priorities, and it was not apparent who was who. Co-op members were left bewildered as to what was going on. Half an hour was spent arguing over whether a theatre group merited a minibus, while our application passed instantly. This 'radical democratic style' certainly had its far-reaching effects, but it did not engender clarity.

In our first year of funding, the picture library was established. This we consciously made available to local pressure and community groups, while project work included a major involvement in attempts to save the South London Women's Hospital. At this stage it was recognized that the Co-op had the potential for further growth. Individual Co-op members had had time to consider the overall project; the front room in which we were based was simply unsuitable for its needs; the library needed daily administration, and all sorts of new difficulties and opportunities were arising. A much more substantial application was submitted for 1984, this time for two workers' salaries to be shared by six photographers, as well as for premises, equipment and a half-time co-ordinator. It was at this stage that the Co-op fully formalized its constitutional status, opting for registration as its name had always implied a workers' co-op.

While the grant was awarded smoothly, the next year represented a period of anxiety about money. The letter confirming our financial position, due in December, wasn't received until the end of March, the first point at which we were able to borrow anything on the grounds of committed funds. The first quarter's cheque was five months later, the second three months later, and so on. Our work was crippled, and dealing with the bureaucracy of the finance department became our main preoccupation. They were an old guard actively resistant to change, no doubt overworked, too, but seemingly determined not to part with money as a matter of principle. The only way round them was to get the politicians hot on their heels. In theory the GLC was about providing space and access for groups which were traditionally excluded and, although anyone could barge into any office and challenge officers and politicians, it was only those groups with developed political nous who were in a position to do so.

Another problem stemmed from the fact that little interest was taken in our actual work. In all our assessments, no-one specifically looked at the work we were doing, so even an informal dialogue wasn't established. The first assessment had been by a Ballet-expert, who didn't begin to understand our community-of-interest and issue-based approach, and though this was understood by subsequent assessors, emphasis built up on the number of workshops we were doing. We felt pressured to work along the familiar lines of what a community arts group existed to do – conduct oper access workshops, operating with the backing of some imagined community consensus – and while we had always wanted to teach skills in the context of our other work, we were never particularly interested in straightforward, basic skills sessions. Without dialogue or any theoretical discussion around an alternative workshop agenda, we were left struggling to find an appropriate form. This was compounded by the finance department's separate assessment requirements along familiar lines. They produced subsidy ratios based on headcounts of people through the door, appropriate means for assessing the achievements of a theatre group or a photography group exclusively doing workshops, but not for a group such as ours involved in so many other fields. For the time being we were left confused, attempting to satisfy a number of different and conflicting criteria.

In the course of the year we began to resolve these tensions about what, precisely, our workshop role should be, developing an education policy which incorporated a number of existing streams of work. At one end of the scale basic skills workshops with existing women's, black, family and unwaged groups in the neighbourhood continued, which already had their own support structure and work context. Meanwhile, 'drop in' sessions, a talk series, workshops with educators on teaching and visual language and the development of resource work directed at the education sector were all introduced as means of efficiently stimulating debates about the use and meaning of photography, behind which remained our particular concerns about photographic representation.

This process all began when we first established ourselves in premises with a darkroom in mid-1984, and resource work (providing advice, library pictures, workshop sessions, photography and publicity production assistance) expanded to meet the needs of 120 local and special needs groups. An ambitious exhibition programme included self-initiated work on women in the unions, domestic labour and local elderly welfare rights and facilities, and 'enabling' work where, for instance, we assisted a Derbyshire miner to put together an exhibition of his pictures and a family workshop to produce a tape/slide show about their aims and activities. We were also increasingly being commissioned to produce publicity and campaign materials for housing associations, unions and voluntary agencies, so that production work in these areas became our speciality.

The development of the library was critical. It had already been recognised that it presented commercial opportunities in so far as a range of organisations, publications and institutions were discovering this source of images encompassing themes such as housing and homelessness, privatisation, domestic labour and other women-and-work issues. The pictures themselves were products of collaboration with local groups, their emphasis being on particular needs. The demand for these provided us with some leverage within the marketplace. We found we could argue points about representation with clients who had not considered such issues before. The demand for our 'products' from fee-paying clients – the GLC among them – besides providing an important source of revenue, was critical to the *individual* needs of Co-op members. We had already taken the decision to become professionals when funds were first applied for, with the corresponding change in the nature of our relationship with clients, and it was crucial for members now earning their living through photography to develop individual skills and security.

How the development of commercially orientated work related to our status as a funded arts project remained unclear, despite emerging hopes for the establishment of a 'vital cultural industry intervening in the market place'. This should have been crystal clear in the face of GLC abolition, and without any sign of another body interested or able to continue initiatives, as happened with arts enterprises in other sectors. Support and distribution networks were established for literature, publishing and film and video groups, encouraging new working methods and a lasting place in the market – all crucial to their future survival without a benevolent local authority.

A central difference for us was that the GLC had issued policy guidelines for each of these other sectors. The same was meant to happen for the socially based photography sector, but despite good intentions, photography, in the tradition of its marginalisation, was bottom of the list. The one initiative which could have established a centralized distribution network and permanent links was a one-day conference. The meeting was hastily arranged, no minutes were taken and, though groups had met each other in many cases for the first time, there was no follow-up of any kind. The lack of an existing independent photography lobby meant that no-one was organized to pressure the officers to make setting one up a priority – a vicious circle that the political will of the Arts Policy Officer could have broken.

It was then, however, that the Federation for Community Photography emerged, which may yet become the body able to lobby on behalf of the independent photography sector's needs. But it is the first of its kind, and the failure until now of the sector to be able to make collective representations has contributed to its own neglect, with no theoretical or political consensus, and groups working in isolation, never themselves realizing what it is possible to achieve. Why this movement has not even begun to happen until now has been for a number of reasons, not least of which is the interrupted history of the notion of collective, socially based photography. There has been very little critical work to turn to; Sue Braden's *Committing Photography*, the collection of essays *Photography Politics One* and issues of *Camerawork* magazine. Before 1985, no other arts-funding body had any published funding criteria, and prior to the GLC the Labour Party had neither shown itself serious about, nor to have any understanding of, the arts in general. Crucial to the development of the funded film and video sector has been the workshop agreement of ACTT, the cinema technicians' union, facilitating dialogue through union representation. The National Union of Journalists have so far resisted comparable moves, and would-be members still need to satisfy criteria that prohibit entry to most photography project workers.

It is possible in retrospect to see that a community arts support unit was necessary to handle all the work that the committee was processing. Such a unit could have co-ordinated initiatives on the sharing of resources and the use of new technology, pioneered publishing ventures and created other new platforms. And, most importantly, a dialogue would have taken place through which groups would have been able to contextualize their own work, saving so much duplicated effort. What happened in practice was that responsibility was concentrated in the post of Arts Policy Officer who, though capable of inspiring imaginative developments in all areas of community arts, depended on extensive members' involvement for the execution of day-to-day decisions. And while Tomkins was always personally approachable, five minutes in the corridor with him was usually as much time as he could ever afford.

In developing our project and identity as a broad, socially based production and education photography group, we now realize the potential the GLC represented for the sector. Its legacy will be judged by whether the few groups nurtured with GLC funds are able to survive its untimely demise, and to sustain our hard-won sense of direction.

# Directory of Resources

The following information is divided into geographical areas under these headings: East, East Midlands, Greater London; Lincolnshire and Humberside, Merseyside, North, North West, Scotland, South, South East, South West, Wales, West Midlands, Yorkshire.

It is further labelled under general categories, as follows:
G/Photography Gallery, Exhibition space
g/space where some photography is shown
W/Workshop or Lecture programme
D/Darkrooms
A/Archives
B/Bookshop
E/Exhibition for hire
PL/Picture Library (commercial)
L/Library (study).

The information is intended to act as a general guide to resources available in each area. Unfortunately there will be some omissions and inaccuracies, and some of the information may be slightly out of date. Where a name is given, it is the last known contact for that organisation. The categories do not cover all the activities of the various sites, especially in relation to film and video resources, tape-slide, laminating, copywork, silkscreen, etc.

The first entry for each area is that of the Regional Arts Association, which should be of help in providing further or more up-to-date information. The name of the appropriate 'officer' is given.

The following publications are useful in acquiring details of resources:
*Arts Express* – a monthly journal available from the Regional Arts Association.
*Community Arts Information File*, by Stuart Rawnsley, Art & Design Resource Centre, Bradford and Ilkley Community College, Great Horton Road, West Yorkshire.
*Directory of Community Projects in England*, June 1985, ACGB (reg. updated).
*Directory of Arts and Disability/Organisations & Projects*, July 1985, ACGB.
*Artists' Newsletter* – monthly journal available from *Artic Publications*.
*Photographic Information Sources*, M. Hallett, British Journal of Photography, May 1977 (out of date, but still useful international directory).
*Photography Education Courses* – a booklet listing courses across the whole spectrum is available from: BJP (as above), Henry Greenwood, 28 Great James Street, London WC1.
*Wedge* (Women's Education & Resource Centre), Princeton Street, London WC1.

This list of resources has been partly compiled from the following sources:

*Listing of Print, Photography, Film and Video Facilities 1982, Artic Publications.*

*Photography in the Arts: Organisations and Projects in Great Britain, October 1985,* Arts Council Directories, Information and Research Section, ACGB.

*Photography North* – a guide to photographers, exhibitions and resources in the Northern Arts Region, produced by John Bradshaw (see Northern Arts).

*Photography Skills for Women* – selection of resources – a draft compiled by Maggie Murray for the 1985 Women's Photography Day at Battersea, London.

*NOTE:* The entries are not listed alphabetically, neither in any order of preference or significance.

## EAST

Eastern Arts, 8–9 Bridge Street, Cambridge/Martin Ayres (0223-357596).

Burwell House Residential Centre, Burwell, Cambridge/Tim Iliffe. (0638-741256) W/D.

Cambridge Darkroom, Dales Brewery, Gwydir Street, Cambridge/ Mark Lumley (0223-350725) G/ W/D/L.

Luton Community Arts Trust, Refleks Gallery, 33 Guildford Street Luton, Bedfordshire/Tim Powell, Paul Jolly (0582-419584) G/D.

Norwich Arts Centre, Reeves Yard, St. Benedict's Street, Norwich/ Pam Reekie (0603-60352) G.

St. Mary's Art Centre, Church Street, Colchester, Essex/Michael Prochak (0206-77301) G.

The Minories, 74 High Street, Colchester, Essex/Diana Pain (0206-577067) G.

The Fermoy Centre, King Street, King's Lynn, Norfolk/Alan Wilkinson (0553-4725) G.

Cinema City, St. Andrew's Street, Norwich/Kingsley Canham (0603-22047) G.

Wisbech and Fenland Museum, Museum Square, Wisbech, Cambridgeshire (0945-583817) G.

East Anglian Film-makers, 22–24 Colegate, Norwich, Norfolk/ David Hilton (0603-22313) W/ D.

Mostly Photographic Gallery and Workshop, 10/11 Market Place, Southend-on-Sea, Essex/Peter Fredericks (0702-352784) G/D.

Community Arts Bedford, 36 Mill Street, Bedford/Ken Heanes (0234-504159) D.

Stevenage Community Arts, Mossbury Centre, Webb Rise, Stevenage, Herts/Gerri Moriarty (0438-314959) D.

Stevenage Leisure Centre, Lytton Way, Stevenage, Herts (0438-66291) W/D.

Centre 33, 33 Guildford Street, Luton, Bedfordshire (0582-419584) G/D.

## EAST MIDLANDS

East Midland Arts, Mountfields House, Forest Road, Loughborough/David Manley (0509-218292

Metro Cinema, Green Lane, Derby/ Laurie Hayward (0332-40170) G.

Picture House, Photography at Lansdowne House, 113 Princes Road East, Leicester/Roger Bradley (0533-549083/551130) G.

Phoenix Arts, Hyson Green, Leicester/Graham Watkins (0533-555627) G.

The Midland Group Gallery, 24–32 Carlton Street, Nottingham/ Chris Ledger (0602-582636) G/W/B.

Photographer's Place, Bradbourne, Ashbourne, Derbyshire/Paul Hill (033525-392) W/D.

The Fleet Arts Project, The Old School, The Fleet, Belper, Derbyshire/Chris Timms (0773-820484) D.

Corby Community Arts, Lincoln Square, Corby, Northants (0536-743731) D.

Derby Community Photography, Woods Lane Centre, 31 Wood Lane, Derby/Richard Sharland (0509-385601) G/D.

Fosse Audio Visual Unit, Fosse Neighbourhood Centre, Mantle Road, Leicester/Steve Bradley (0533-21973) D.

Rosebery Arts, St. Peter's Social Centre, Storer Road, Loughborough/Kevin Ryan, Sarah Laman (0509-268554/216682) D.

Community Photography Archive, Great Linford Community Workshop, St. Leger Court, St. Leger Drive, Great Linford, Milton Keynes (0908-605986) W/D/A.

Arts Development Northampton, Cliftonville House, Bedford Road, Northampton/Ken Heanes (0604-27158) D.

Nottingham Community Arts Centre, Gregory Boulevard, Hyson Green, Nottingham/Helen Bridges (0602-782463) W/D.

Rentasnap Photo Library, 118 Mansfield Road, Nottingham/ Pete Bullock (0602-582369) PL

Junction 38, New Street Centre, South Normanton, Derbyshire (0773-811142).


GREATER LONDON

Greater London Arts, 25–31 Tavistock Place, London WC1/Alan Haydon (01-388-2211).

Blackfriars Photography Project, Blackfriars Settlement, 44 Nelson Square, London SE1/Neil Martenson, Judith Crow (01-928-9521) G/W/D/E.

Camerawork, 121 Roman Road, Bethnal Green, London E2/Co-Ordinator (01-980-6256) G/W/D/E.

Docklands Community Poster Project, Unit 167 Cannon Workshops, West India Dock, London E14/Peter Dunn, Lorraine Leeson (01-515-6099) E.

North Paddington Community Darkroom, 510 Harrow Road, London W9/Brenda Agard (01-969-7437) W/D/G.

The Photographers' Gallery, 5 & 8 Great Newport Street, London WC2/Sue Davies (01-240-5511) G/L/B/E/W.

Photo Co-op, 61 Webbs Road, London SW11/Chris Boot (01-228-8949) G/W/PL/E/D.

Cockpit Gallery, Department of Cultural Studies, ILEA Cockpit Arts Department, Princeton Street, London WC1/Judith Rayner (01-405-5334) G/W/D/E.

Battersea Arts Centre, Old Town Hall, Lavender Hill, London SW11/Jude Kelly (01-223-6557) G/W/D/PL/B.

Black Art Gallery, 225 Seven Sisters Road, London N4/Shakka Dedi (01-263-1918) G.

Camden Arts Centre, Arkwright Road, London NW3/Zuleika Dobson (01-435-2642) G/B.

Centre 181, 181 King Street, London W6 (01-741-3696) G.

Interim Art, 21 Beck Road, London E8/Maureen Paley (01-254-9607) G.

Pentonville Gallery, 7/9 Ferdinand Street, Chalk Farm, London NW1/Geoff Evans (01-482-2948) G.

Coracle Press Gallery, 233 Camberwell New Road, London SE5 /Simon Cutts (01-701-5762) G.

Peoples Gallery, 73 Prince of Wales Road, London NW5/Margo Reid (01-267-0433) G.

Riverside Studios Gallery, Riverside Studios, Crisp Road, London W6/Milena Kalinowska (01 -748-3354) G/B.

South London Art Gallery, Peckham Road, London SE5/Kenneth Sharpe (01-703-6120) G.

Café Gallery, Southwark Park, London SE16/Ron Henocq (01-237-4397) G.

Photography Galleries, Victoria and Albert Museum, South Kensington, London SW7/Mark Haworth-Booth (01-589-6371) G/L /A/B.

Institute of Contemporary Arts, The Mall, London W1/Exhibition Organiser G/B/W.

Acton Community Arts Workshop, 1a Gunnersbury Lane, London W3 (01-993-3665) W/D.

Basement Community Arts Project, St. George's Town Hall, Cable Street, London E1 (01-790-4026) W/D.

Chatts Palace, 42/44 Brooksby's Walk, London E9 (01-986-6714)

W/D.

Greenwich Mural Workshop, The Macbean Centre, LEB Yard, Macbean Street, London E8 (01-854-9266) W/D.

Moonshine Community Arts, Victor Road, London NW10 (01-969-7959) W/D.

Barnet Borough Arts Council Workshop (BBAC), Avenue House, East End Road, Finchley, London (01-346-7120) W/D.

Paddington Printshop, 1 Elgin Avenue, London W9 (01-286-1123) W/D.

South Island Workshop/Mediumwave, 444 Brixton Road, London SW9 8EJ.

West London Media Workshop, 118 Talbot Road, London W11 (01-221-1859) W/D.

Walworth and Aylesbury Community Arts Trust (WACAT), 1a Wendover Road, Thurlow Street, London SE17 (01-708-1288/ 703-0415) W/D.

Poster-Film Collective, 20 Lithos Road, London NW3 (01-794-6675) E.

The National Monuments Record, Fortress House, Savile Row, London W1. A.

Lentham Road Workshop, Lentham Road, Hackney, London E8 (01-254-3082) W/D.

Centreprise, 136 Kingsland High Street, London E8 (01-254-9632) W/D.

Independent Photography Project, The Clock House, Greenwich (01-855-7188) W/D.

Monocrome (women's photography group), c/o Blackfriars Photography Project. W/D/E.

Format Photographers, 25 Horsell Road, London N5/Amanda Hopkinson (01-609-3439) PL/ W.

Photography Workshop, 152 Upper Street, London N1/Jo Spence, Terry Dennett (01-359-9064) A/E/W.

Black Women's Photo-Visual Collective, c/o 25 Bayham Street, London NW17 (01-387-7450) W/D.

Action Space, 16 Chenies Street, London WC1 (01-631-1353) D.

Network, 271 Kentish Town Road, London NW5 (01-267-9065) PL.

Museum of London, London Wall, London EC2/Mike Seaborne, Colin Sorenson A/L.

Royal Society for Asian Affairs, 42 Devonshire Street, London W1. A.

Island Art Centre, Tiller Road, London E14 (01-987-7925) W/D.

Shape (organisation for disabled and the arts), 9 Fitzroy Square, London W1 (01-388-9622).

Interaction, 15 Wilkin Street, London NW5 (01-485-0881) W/D.

National Museum of Labour History, Limehouse Town Hall, Commercial Road, London E14 (01-515-3229) A/G.

Greater London Council (GLC) Photographic Library/Greater London Record Office, 40 Northampton Road, London EC1. A.

Arts Council of Great Britain, 105 Piccadilly, London W1/Barry Lane (01-629-9495).

## LINCOLNSHIRE AND HUMBERSIDE

Lincolnshire and Humberside Arts, St. Hughs, Newport, Lincoln/Alan Humberstone (0522-335555).

Blackfriars Arts Centre, Spain Lane, Boston, Lincolnshire (0205-63108) G.

Ferens Art Gallery (Posterngate) Queen Victoria Square, Kingston-upon-Hull, Humberside (0482-222750) G/W/D.

Usher Gallery, Lindum Road, Lincoln (0522-27980) G.

Outreach Community Centre, Northumberland Avenue, Hull (0482-226420) W/D.

Scunthorpe Museum and Art Gallery (0724-843533) G.

## MERSEYSIDE

Merseyside Arts, Bluecoat Chambers, School Lane, Liverpool 1/Roman Piechocinski.

Bootle Photography Gallery, Art in Action, 482 Stanley Road, Bootle, Liverpool 20/Dave Swindlehurst (051933-5168) G/W/D/E.

Open Eye Gallery and Photography Workshop, 90/92 Whitechapel, Liverpool 1/Derek Massey, Neil Burgess (051709-9460) G/W/D.

Walker Art Gallery, William Brown Street, Liverpool 3/Timothy Stevens (051227-5234) G.

Aware (Merseyside) Trust, 4 Sefton Grove, Lark Lane, Liverpool 17/Colin Thomas (051727-7421) W/D.

Merseyside Trade Union, Community and Unemployed Resource Centre, 24 Hartman Street, Liverpool 1/Bill Dolce (051709-3995) W/D.

Disablement Resource Unit, Inner Temple, Temple Lane, Liverpool 2/Stuart Eglin (051236-6086).

Williamson Art Gallery and Museum, Slatey Road, Birkenhead, Wirral, Merseyside/David Hillhouse (051652-4177) G.

Atkinson Art Gallery, Lord Street, Southport/Sheila McGregor (0704-33133) G.

Sudley Art Gallery and Museum, Mossley Hill Road, Liverpool 18 (051227-5234) G.


NORTH

Northern Arts, 10 Osborne Terrace, Newcastle - upon - Tyne / John Bradshaw (0632-816334).

Castle Chare Community Arts Centre, Castle Chare, Durham City/ Duncan Brown (0385-46251) W/ D/G.

Brewery Arts Centre, 122a Highgate, Kendal, Cumbria/Graham Evans (0539-25133) G/W/D/E.

Newcastle Media Workshop, Room 9, 1st Floor, 5 Saville Place, Newcastle - upon - Tyne / Peter Fryer (0632-322410) Temporary address. W/D/E.

Side Gallery, 9 Side, Newcastle-upon-Tyne/Ian Tinwell (0632-322208) G/W/E/A/B/L.

Carnegie Theatre and Arts Centre, Carnegie Photography Workshop, Carnegie Unemployment Centre, Finkle Street, Workington, Cumbria (0900-61874) G/W/D.

Midnag (Leisure and Publicity Dept.) Town Hall, Station Road, Ashington, Northumberland (0670-814444) G/D.

Carlisle Museum and Art Gallery, Tullie House, Castle Street, Carlisle/Laura Hamilton (0228-34781) G.

Myles Meechan Gallery/Darlington Media Group, Darlington Arts Centre, Vane Terrace, Darlington, County. Durham/Anna Pepperall (0325-483271) G/W/D.

Gray Art Gallery and Museum, Glarence Road, Hartlepool, Cleveland/Liz Shaw (0429-66522) G.

Bede Gallery, Springwell Park, Butchersbridge Road, Jarrow (0632-891807) G.

Newcastle Polytechnic Gallery, Library Building, Sandyford Road, Newcastle - upon - Tyne / Maria-Helen Wood (0632-326002) G.

Hatton Gallery, The University, Newcastle-upon-Tyne/S. Selwood (0632-328511) G.

Buddle Arts Centre, 258b Station Road, Wallsend, Tyne and Wear/Carol Alevroyianni (0632-624276) G/W/D.

Washington Arts Centre/Washington Photography Project, Biddick Farm, Fatfield, Washington 7, Tyne and Wear (091-466440) G/W/D.

Alnwick Playhouse Darkroom, Alnwick, Northumberland/Martin Western (0665-603069) W/D.

Wansbeck Community Initiatives Centre, Station Villa, Kennilworth Road, Ashington, Northumberland/Derek Railston (0670-853619) W/D.

Consett Photo Archive, Old Miners Hall, Delves Lane, Consett, County Durham/John Kierney (0207-507310) W/D/E/A.

Queen's Hall Art Centre, Beaumont Street, Hexham, Northumberland /Dorothy Latham (0434-606787) G/W/D.

Photography Workshop, Maryport Unemployment Centre, John Street, Maryport, Cumbria/John Rigby (0900-4283) W/D.

North Ormesby Photography Group, c/o Pavilion Community Arts, The Pavilion, Esk Streer North Ormesby, Middlesbrough, Cleveland/Pete Roberts (0642-225290) W/D.

Byker Photography Workshop, Adjacent 26 Raby Way, Byker, Newcastle -upon - Tyne / Tony Keating (0632-2650649) W/D.

Walker Photography Project, Back 495a Wellbeck Road, Newcastle-upon-Tyne (0632-2652729) W/D.

Hendon Photography Group, c/o 4 St. Ignatius Close, Hendon, Sunderland, Tyne and Wear/Mick Catmull (0783-654948) W/D.

Sunderland Arts Centre, 17 Grange Terrace, Sunderland, Tyne and Wear (0783-41214) W/D.

Wrexham Photographic Workshop, Wrexham Library Arts Centre, Rhosddu Road, Wrexham, Clwyd/Lynne Morgan (0978-261932) G/W/D.

North Skelton Village Hall, Vaughan Street, North Skelton, Saltburn, Cleveland (0287-52392) D.

NORTH WEST

North West Arts, 12 Harter Street, Manchester/Sally Medlyn (061-2283062).

Scott Gallery, Pendle College, University of Lancaster, Lancashire /Helen Brown (0524-65201) G.

Greater Manchester Arts Centre/ Greater Manchester Film and Exhibition Centre, Cornerhouse, Oxford Road, Manchester/Sue Grayson (061228-6255) G.

Manchester Studies Unit, Manchester Polytechnic, Cavendish House, All Saints, Manchester/Audrey Linkman (061228-6171) G/A/E.

Oldham Art Gallery, Central Library and Art Gallery, Union Street, Oldham (061624-0505) G.

Rochdale Art Gallery, The Esplanade, Rochdale (0706-47474) G.

Salford Art Gallery, Peel Park, Salford (061736-2649) G.

Drumcroon Education Art Centre, 2 Parson's Walk, Wigan (0942-32184) G.

Counter Image Limited, 19 Whitworth Street West, Manchester (061228-3551) W/D.

Action Factory, Mill Hill Community Centre, New Chapel Street, Blackburn (0254-661292) W.

Split Image, The Old Post Office, Union Street, Oldham, Lancashire (061620-4063) W/D.

The Northern Picture Library, 14 Newton Street, Manchester. A.

Workers' Film Association, 9 Lucy Street, Manchester (061848-9782) G/W/D.

Documentary Photo Archive, Cavendish House, Manchester Polytechnic, Grosvenor Street, Manchester. A/E.


SCOTLAND

Scottish Arts Council, 19 Charlotte Square, Edinburgh/Lindsay Gordon.

Scottish National Gallery of Modern Art, Belford Road, Edinburgh/Douglas Hall (031356-8921) G.

The Scottish Photography Group/ Stills Gallery, 105 High Street, Edinburgh (031557-1140) G/W/E.

Corridor Gallery, Fife Institute, Viewfield, Glenrothes (0592-771700) G.

Fruitmarket Gallery, 29 Market Square, Edinburgh/Mark Francis (031225-2383) G.

Glasgow Arts Centre, 12 Washington Street, Glasgow/Graeme McKinnon (041221-4526) G.

Third Eye Centre, 350 Sauchiehall Street, Glasgow/Chris Carrell (041332-7521) G.

Peacock Printmakers' Workshop, 21 Castle Street, Aberdeen/ Arthur Watson (0224-639539) W/D.

Glasgow Arts Centre, The Island House, Alva Films Ltd., 16 Brook Street, Alva, Clackmannanshire/Bill Borrows, Russell Fenton (0259-60936) W/D.

Dundee Printmakers' Workshop, Dudhope Arts Centre, St. Mary's Place, Dundee/Keith Fraser (0382-26331) W/D.

Edinburgh Photographic Society, 68 Great King Street, Edinburgh/Grace Alison (031552-3415) W/D.

Edinburgh Printmakers' Workshop, Washhouse, 23 Union Street, Edinburgh / Kenneth Duffy (031557-2479) W/D.

Glasgow Print Studio, 128 Ingram Street, Glasgow/John McKechnie (041552-0704) W/D.

Cranhill Arts Project, 33 Lamlash Crescent, Cranhill, Glasgow/ Alistair McCallum (041774-8595) D.

Arts Live, 4 Muirton House, Charleston (Place, Inverness/Jo Heavenstone (0463-231370) D.


SOUTH

Southern Arts, 19 Southgate Street, Winchester, Hampshire/Hugh Adams (0962-55099).

South Hill Park Arts Centre, Bracknell, Berkshire/Josie Henderson (0344-427272) G/W/D.

Quay Hill Arts Centre, Sea Street, Newport, Isle of Wight/Phillippa Ecobichon (0983-528825) G.

Museum of Modern Art, 30 Pembroke Street, Oxford/David Elliott (0865-722733) G/W/B.

Photographer's Workshop, 103/104 St. Mary's Street, Oxford/Keith Barnes (0865-254321) G/W/D.

Salisbury Arts Centre, St. Edmunds, Bedwin Street, Salisbury, Wiltshire/Jonathan Hyams (0722-21744) G/W/D.

John Hansard Gallery, The University, East Street, Southampton, Hampshire/Barry Barker (0703-559122) G/W.

Winchester Gallery, Park Avenue, Winchester, Hampshire/John Gillett (0962-61891) G.

Havant Arts Centre, East Street, Havant, Hampshire/Paul Sadler (0705-472700) W/D.

Old Fire Station Arts Centre, George Street, Oxford/Adrian Litvinoff (0865-722648) G/W/D.

Portsmouth Film and Video Workshop, John Pound Centre, St. James Street, Portsmouth, Hampshire/Dave Baker (0705-753366) W/D.

Artspace Portsmouth Ltd., 27 Brougham Road, Southsea, Hampshire/Les Buckingham (0705-352784) W/D.

Media Arts Lab., The Arts Centre, Devizes Road, Swindon, Wiltshire/Martin Parry (0793-26161) W/D.

Pelican Resource Centre, Link Road, Newbury, Berkshire/Keith Prichard (0635-47277) D.

Bloomin Arts, c/o East Oxford Community Centre, Princes Street, Oxford (0865-245735) D.

Reading Centre for the Unemployed, 4–6 East Street, Reading, Berkshire (0734-596639) D.

Mount Pleasant Photography Workshop, Mount Pleasant Middle School, Mount Pleasant Road, Southampton, Hampshire/Judy Harrison (0703-23634) W/D/E.

St. Edmunds Art Centre, Bedwin Street, Salisbury, Wiltshire/Reg Bolton (0722-4299) W/D.

Fox Talbot Museum, Lacock, Near Chippenham, Wiltshire (024973-459) A/E.

Oxfam, 274 Banbury Road, Oxford. A.

## SOUTH EAST

South East Arts, 9–10 Crescent Road, Tunbridge Wells, Kent/ Frances Smith, Tim Cornish (0892-41666).

Photogallery, The Foresters' Arms, 2 Shepherd Street, St. Leonards-on-Sea, East Sussex/Morris Newcombe, Pauline Cavey (0424-440140) G/W.

Brighton Polytechnic Gallery, Grand Parade, Brighton, Sussex/Julian Freeman (0273-604141) G.

Gardner Centre, University of Sussex, Falmer, Brighton, Sussex/ Nicholas Sinclair (0273-685447) G/A.

Photography at the Metropole, The Leas, Folkestone, Kent/Jim Bryne, William Cummings (0303-55070) G/W.

North Star Studios, 65 Ditchling Road, Brighton, Sussex/Nicholas Sinclair (0273-601041) W/D.

Arts in Medway, Leisure Services, Park Lodge, Canterbury Street, Gillingham, Kent/Tina Glover (0634-50021) W/D.

Open Frame Community Photography Group, Adult Education Centre, Green Street, Gillingham, Kent/Pam Gill (0634-576830) W/D.

Brighton Community Arts Project, St. Anne's Hall, St. George's Road, Kemptown, Brighton, Sussex (0273-697493) W/D.

## SOUTH WEST

South West Arts, Bradninch Place, Gandy Street, Exeter/Christine Ross (0392-38924).

Watershed (Media Centre), 1 Cannon's Road, Bristol/Deborah Ely (0272-276444) G/W/D/E.

Axiom Centre for the Arts, 57/59 Winchcombe Street, Cheltenham, Gloucestershire/Stephen Foster (0242-527168) G.

The Royal Photographic Society Centre of Photography, The Octagon, 46 Milsom Street, Bath /Amanda Nevill (0225-62841) G /A/B/L/W.

Spacex Gallery, 45 Preston Street, Exeter, Devon/Robin Dobson. G.

Plymouth Arts Centre, 38 Looe Street, Plymouth, Devon/ Bernard Samnet. G/W.

F. Stop Photography Workshop, 2 Longacre, London Road, Bath, Avon/Dawn Langley (0225-316922) W/D.

Photographers above the Rainbow, 10 Waterloo Street, Clifton, Bristol/Andrew Grant. G/W/ D.

Exeter and Devon Arts Centre, Gandy Street, Exeter/Marilyn Floyde (0392-219741) W/D.

Bristol Media Workshop, c/o University Settlement, 43 Ducie Road, Barton Hill, Bristol/ Carrie Hitchcock (0272-559219) D.

Penwith Print Workshop, Back Road West, St. Ives, Cornwall (0736-795579) D.

Beaford Centre, Beaford, Winkleigh, Devon/James Ravilious. G/W/A/E.

Arnolfini, Narrow Quay, Bristol (0272-299191) G/B.

Newlyn Orion Galleries, Newlyn, Penzance, Cornwall (0736-3715) G.

Dorset County Museum, High West Street, Dorchester, Dorset (0305-62735) G.

## WALES

Welsh Arts Council, Museum Place, Cardiff/Peter Jones.

Aberystwyth Arts Centre Gallery, Penglais, Aberystwyth, Dyfed/ Alan Hewson (0970-4277) G.

the ffotogallery (the Association for Photography in Wales), 41 Charles Street, Cardiff/Sue Beardmore (0222-41667) G.

Chapter Arts Centre (plus U-Print/ Sol Jorgensen), Market Road, Canton, Cardiff/Gerald Deslandes (0222-396061) G/W (W/ D).

Oriel, 31 High Street, Welshpool, Powys/Michael Nixon (0938-2990) G.

Rhondda Community Arts Parc and Dare Theatre, Station Road, Treorchy, Mid Glamorgan (0443-776090) G/W/D.

Vale Activity Centre Photography Workshop, Harbour Road, Barry, South Glamorgan/Mark Pluciennit (91-747717) W/D.

Valley and Vale Community Arts, Blaengarw Workingmen's Hall and Institute, Blaengarw Road, Blaengarw, Mid Glamorgan/ Mike West (0656-871911) W/D.

Tondu Photo Workshop, The Old Junior School, Maesteg Road, Tondu, Maesteg, Near Bridgend /Ted Gibson (0656-724799) W/ D/E.

Crumlin Community Centre, Photo Workshop, Institute Buildings, Hillside, Crumlin, Gwent/Barry Cooper (08494-244064) W/D.

Deeside Community Arts Project, Deeside High School, Queensferry, Deeside, Clwyd/Mike McCarthy (0244-821003) W/D.

Holyhead Photography Workshop, Unemployed Workers' Centre, Townrow House, Hill Street, Holyhead, Anglesey/Andre Collett (0407-5028) W/D.

Watershed, Parc Pendre, Kidwelly, Dyfed/Neil Goddard (0554-891127) W/D.

Merthyr District Activity Centre, Bethesda Street, Merthyr Tydfil, Mid Glamorgan/Martin Thomas (0685-6877).

Valley Photoworkshop, Treorchy Youth and Community, Horeb Street, Treorchy, Mid Glamorgan/Mel Morris (940-77363) W/D.


WEST MIDLANDS

West Midlands Arts, Brunswick Terrace, Stafford/Frank Challenger, Geoff Sims (0785-59231).

The Triangle, Media and Performance Centre, Gosta Green, Birmingham/Derek Bishton (021359-3979) G/W/D.

Hereford City Museum and Art Gallery, Broad Street, Hereford/ Anne Sandford (0432-268121) G.

Ikon Gallery, 58–72 John Bright Street, Birmingham/Antonia Payne (021643-0708) G.

Lichfield City Art Gallery and Museum, Bird Street, Lichfield, Staffordshire (915-22177) G.

Stafford Museum and Art Gallery, The Green, Stafford/John Rhodes (0785-57303) G.

Walsall Museum and E. M. Flint Gallery, Lichfield Street, Walsall, West Midlands/Lindsey Brooks (0922-21255) G.

Wolverhampton Art Gallery, Lichfield Street, Wolverhampton, West Midlands/Peter Vigurs (0902-24549).

National Playing Fields Association, Playtrain Resource Centre, Ward End Park, Washwood Heath Road, Birmingham/Harry Shier (021328-5557) W/D.

Picture Box, c/o Word, Birmingham (021449-4024) W/D.

Saltley Print and Media Workshop, 9–11 Washwood Heath Road,

Saltley, Birmingham/Rob Boyle (021328-1954) W/D.

St. Paul's Project, 120 St. Paul's Road, Balsall Heath, Birmingham/Dick Atkinson (021440-4376) W/D.

WELD, New Trinity, Wilson Road, Handsworth, Birmingham/ Larrie Tiernan (021554-5068) W/D.

West Midlands Ethnic Minority Arts Service (Birmingham) (021523-7544).

Dudley Central Museum and Art Gallery, St. James Road, Dudley, West Midlands (0384-56321).

Wide-Angle, Film and Photography Workshop, Birmingham Community Association, Jenkins Street, Birmingham/Hussein Mirshahi (021772-2889) W/D.

Coventry Resource and Information Service, Unit 15, The Arches Industrial Estate, Spon End, Coventry/Roshini Kempadoo (0203-77719) W/D.

Edgewick Community Centre, Crossroads, Coventry/Rosemary Shonor (0203-663) W/D.

Hereford Arts Project, 89 East Street, Hereford/Angie Kelly, Jenni Morgan (0432-278226) W/D.

Kidderminster and District Youth Centre, Bromsgrove Street, Kidderminster/Bob Broadway (0562-752711) W/D.

Bath Place Community Venture, Bath Place, Leamington Spa, Warwickshire/Barbara Weed (0926-38421) W/D.

Maypole Photography Project, Maypole Centre, Dinids Heath, Birmingham/Ken White (0204-30622) W/D.

Community Action Project, 8 Beech Way, Smethwick, Birmingham/ Errol Walker (021565-3273) D.

Building Sights, Photography and Education Project, Tindal Rooms, Tindall Street, Birmingham/Stuart Daniels (021440-4026) W/D.

Worcester Arts Workshop, c/o The Old Quilt Factory, Angel Place, Worcester/Jane Hytch (0905-21093) W/D.

Jubilee Community Arts, Whitehall Road, Greets Green, West Bromwich, West Midlands/ Sylvia King (021557-1569) W/D.

Telford Community Arts, The Fighting Cocks, 48 Market Street, Oaken Gates, Telford, Shropshire/Graham Woodruff (0954-619055) W/D.

Penthouse Community Project, Whitehall House, Webly, Herefordshire/Heather Langridge (054431-8161) W/D.


YORKSHIRE

Yorkshire Arts, Glyde House, Glydegate, Bradford/Paul Brookes, Sara Worrall (0274-723051).

The Pavilion Project, 235 Woodhouse Lane, Leeds/Jill Hipkins, Debbie Best (0532-431749) G/W/D/E.

South Leeds Photographic Project, 2 Wharf Street, Leeds/Matt Winterlich (0532-468807) G/W/D.

Untitled Gallery (plus South Yorkshire Photography Project), 171–175 Howard Road, Walkley, Sheffield/Stephen Barnett (Chrissie Rawnsley) G/W/D.

Impressions Gallery of Photography, 17 Colliergate, York/Frances Middlestorb (0904-54724) G/W/D/E/B.

Piece Hall Art Gallery, Piece Hall, Halifax/Barry Sheridan (0422-54823) G.

National Museum of Photography, Princes View, Bradford 5/ Colin Ford, Terry Mordern (0274-393907) G/W/E/B/A.

The Arthouse, New Street, Farsley, Pudsey, West Yorkshire/Graham Hardy (0532-560637) g.

Crescent Art Workshops, Art Gallery Basement, The Crescent, Scarborough/Mick Fattorini (0723-351461) G/D.

Graves Art Gallery, Surrey Street, Sheffield/David Alston (0742-734781) G.

Mappin Art Gallery, Weston Park, Sheffield/Mike Tooby (0742-754091) G.

Bradford Mobile Workshop, 3 Hallfield Road, Bradford/Jenny Wilson (0274-722425) D.

Handprint, Old Stewards House, Northgate, Huddersfield/Huw Thomas (0484-516804) W/D.

Woolley Colliery Writers and Photographers, 71 Low Road, Woolley Colliery, Near Barnsley /Pauline Watkin (0226-382103) D.

Yorkshire Arts Association Photo Archive, Faculty of Art and Design, Sheffield City Polytechnic, Brincliffe, Psalter Lane, Sheffield/John Kirby (0742-556101) A (plus Arts Council of Great Britain Photo Collection).

Artivan, 8 Bankfield Terrace, Armitage Bridge, Huddersfield, West Yorkshire/Brian Cross (0484-665410) W/D.

Bannerworks, 9 Spinkfield Road, Birkby, Huddersfield/Graham Marsden (0484-513772) W/D.

Common Ground, 87 The Wicker, Sheffield/Maria de Souza (0742-738572) W/D.

Yorkshire Art Space Society, Sydney Works, 111 Matilda Street, Sheffield (0742-71769) D.

# Bibliography

## General Bibliography


Belsey, Catherine, *Critical Practice*, Methuen, 1980.

Benjamin, Walter, 'A Short History of Photography', *Screen*, vol.13, no.1.

Berger, John, *Ways Of Seeing*, Penguin, 1972.

Bezencenet, Stevie, 'What is a History of Photography?' *Creative Camera*, no.208, April 1982.

Victor Burgin (ed.), *Thinking Photography*, Macmillan, 1982.

Davis, Howard and Walton, Paul (eds.), *Language, Image, Media*, Basil Blackwell, 1983.

Dennett, Terry and Spence, Jo, 'Remodelling Photo-History', *Screen*, vol.23, no.1, 1982.

Downing, John, *The Media Machine*, Pluto, 1980.

Doy, Gen, 'Women, History and Photographic Imagery', *Camerawork* no.19.

Ecker, Giselda (ed.), *Feminist Aesthetics*, The Women's Press, 1985.

Enzensberger, H. M., 'Constituents Of A Theory Of The Media', in *Raids and Reconstructions*, Pluto, 1976.

Freund, Giselle, *Photography and Society*, Gordon Fraser, 1980.

Gardner, Carl (ed.), *Media, Politics and Culture*, Macmillan, 1979.

Green, David, 'On Foucault: Disciplinary Power and Photography', *Camerawork* no.32.

Hall, Stuart, 'Culture, the Media and the Ideological Effect', in *Mass Communication and Society*, Curran, J. (ed.) et al., Edward Arnold, 1977.

Hall, Stuart, 'The Culture Gap', *Marxism Today*, January, 1984.

Hall, Stuart (ed.) et al., *Culture, Media, Language*, Hutchinson, 1980.

O'Sullivan, T. et al., *Key Concepts in Communication*, Methuen, 1983.

Pearson, Nicholas, *The State and the Visual Arts*, Open University Press, 1982.

Rees-Mogg, William, 'The political economy of art in 1985', in *The Economist*, 9/3/1985.

Root, Jane, *Pictures of Women*, Pandora, 1984.

Tagg, John, 'The Currency of The Photograph' in *Thinking Photography*.*

Taylor, Brandon (ed.), *Art and Politics*, Winchester School of Arts Press, 1980.

Webster, Frank, *The New Photography*, John Calder, 1980.

Williams, Raymond, *Keywords*, Flamingo, 1983.

Williams, Raymond, *Culture*, Fontana, 1981.

Williamson, Judith, 'The History That Photos Mislaid', in *Photography/ Politics: One*.*

Williamson, Judith, *Decoding Advertisements*, Marion Boyars, 1978.

Williamson, Judith, *Consuming Passions: The Dynamics of Popular Culture*, Marion Boyars, 1986.


*Culture and the State*, Institute of Contemporary Arts (ICA), 1984.

*Photography*, FAN (Feminist Art News), no.6.

*Photography/Politics: One*, Photography Workshop, 1979.

*Photography/Politics: Two*, Photography Workshop, Comedia, 1986.

*Popular Culture*, Readers for Course U203, Open University Press.

*The Glory of the Garden*, The Development of the Arts in England, Arts Council, 1984.


**Journals and magazines**

*Artists' Newsletter, Block, Creative Camera, Camerawork*, Camera Obscura**, Exposure****, FAN, Formations Of…, Framework, October****, Schooling & Culture* (Cockpit), *Screen, Screen Education***, Ten.8, Undercut* (London Film-makers' Co-op).

*       no longer published. Back issues available from *Camerawork*, London.
**      UK distributors – National Film Theatre Bookshop, London.
***     no longer published – back issues from SEFT, 29 Old Compton Street, London W1.
****    UK distributors – SEFT, 29 Old Compton Street, London W1.


# Education Bibliography

Bethell, Andrew, 'Teaching about Power and Photography', in *Camerawork*, no.22.

Carter, Paul, 'The Photographic Gallery: Survey of its Education and Community Programme', *The Photographic Gallery*, Southampton, 1980.

Hornsby, Jim, *Independent Photography and Photography in Education*, Arts Council of Great Britain, 1985.

'Educational Sell-out?', response to Arts Council conference on *Photographers in Education* (March 1985), *Camerawork*, no.32 (Hornsby text above was a key conference item).

Instrell, Rick, 'Media Studies – A return to the democratic intellect?'

Lusted, D. and Drummond, P. (eds.), *T.V. and Schooling*, British Film Institute (BFI) Education Department, 1985.

Mann, Stewart, 'Photography in Schools', *British Journal of Photography* (BJP), July/Aug., 1983.

Nowell-Smith, Geoffrey, 'Common-Sense', *Radical Philosophy* 7, 1974.

Powell, Rob, *The Manpower Services Commission and Photography*, Arts Council, 1984.

Warren, Tony, 'The MSC – What goes up . . .', *NATFHE Journal*, April, 1985.

Williamson, Judith, 'How Does Girl No. 20 Understand Ideology?', *Screen Education*, no.40, Winter, 1981/2.

Wolpe, AnnMarie and Donald, James (eds.), *Is There Anyone Here From Education?*, Pluto, 1983.

*The Arts Council and Education: A Policy Statement*, Arts Council of Great Britain (ACGB), 1983.

*The Arts in Schools*, Calouste Gulbenkian Foundation, 1982.

*Cultural Studies in Schools*, Department of Cultural Studies, Cockpit Arts Workshop, London, 1985.

*GEN* (quarterly journal), Women's Education Group, WeD Collective.

*Initiatives*, Society for Education in Film and Television (SEFT), newsletter on media and education.

*Journal of Art AND Art Education*, AND, 10 Swanfield Street, London E2.

*Photography and Education* – Strategies for Arts Organisations (seminar report from Birmingham, March, 1983), ACGB, 1984.

'Photography and Education', *Ten.8*, no.21, 1986.

*Unjustified, Unwanted – Unworkable* (response to Government White Paper on Education), *NATFHE Journal*, June, 1984.


# Publishing/Distribution Bibliography


Ellis, Ainslie, 'The Magazines – Where Next?' (report of a seminar held in Newcastle), *British Journal of Photography*, 23.3., 30.3., 6.4., 1984.

Format Picture Agency, articles in: *Spare Rib*, June, 1983; *BJP*, May 11, 1984; *Creative Camera*, November, 1984.

Kelly, Owen, *Community, Art and the State*, Comedia, 1984.

Landry, Charles, *Current problems of magazines funded by the Arts Council and the BFI; distribution, promotion and marketing*, Arts Council, 1984.

Lomax, Yve and Slater, Don, 'Poster Film Collective', *Camerawork*, no.24.

Trevor, Paul, 'Self-Publishing', *Camerawork*, no.1.

'Lewisham: What are you taking pictures for?', *Camerawork*, no.24.

'Art Magazines', *Studio International*, Sept./Oct., 1976.


# Exhibition Bibliography


Barber, Ed, 'Doing it yourself – touring exhibitions', in *Camerawork*, no.10.

Barthes, Roland, 'Death of the Author', in *Image, Music, Text*, Fontana, 1977.

Barthes, Roland, *S/Z*, Cape, 1975.

Barthes, Roland, *The Pleasure of the Text*, Cape, 1976.

Benjamin, Walter, 'Author as Producer', in *Understanding Brecht*, New Left Books (NLB), 1973.

Benjamin, Walter, 'Work of Art in the Age of Mechanical Reproduction', in *Illuminations*, Fontana/Collins, 1970.

Burgin, Victor, 'Looking at Photographs', in *Thinking Photography*.*

Dunn, Peter and Leeson, Lorraine, 'Towards a Political Practice', in *Camerawork*, no.21.

Dunn, Peter and Leeson, Lorraine, 'The Fire & The Fireplace', in *Block*, no.1., 1979.

Evans, David and Gohl, Sylvia, 'Political Photomontage – Heartfield to Staeck', *Camerawork*, no.20.

Florence, Penny, 'Step by Step – Photographs, Text and Collage, Sirkka – Liisa Konttinen', in *Creative Camera*, no.242, February, 1985.

Foster, Hal (ed.), *Postmodern Culture*, Pluto, 1985. (Especially essays by Craig Owens, 'The Discourse of Others: Feminists and Postmodernism' and Edward Said, 'Opponents, Audiences, Constituencies and Community'.)

Foucault, Michel, 'What is an Author?', *Screen*, vol.20, no.1, 1983.

Glass, D. D. (et al.), 'Feminist Film Practice and Pleasure', in *Formations of Pleasure*, Routledge and Kegan Paul (RKP), 1983.

Hall, Stuart, 'Left in Sight', in *Camerawork*, no.29.

Hanson, N. and Jones, S. (eds.), *Directory of Exhibition Spaces*, Artic Publishers, 1983 (includes a collection of useful articles, especially N. Pearson's 'Alternatives').

Lovell, Terry, *Pictures of Reality – Aesthetics, Politics and Pleasure*, BFI, 1980.

MacDonald, Irene, *The Photographers' Gallery Education Report*, ACGB, 1984.

McGrath, Roberta, *Re-reading Edward Weston* (exhibition notes), Watershed, 1984.

Morley, Dave, 'Texts, Readers, Subjects', in *Culture, Media, Language*, Hall (et al.), Hutchinson, 1984.

Mulvey, Laura (catalogue essay), *Magnificent Obsession* – exhibition work by Karen Knorr, Mark Lewis, Geoff Miles, Olivier Richon, Mitra Tabrizian, British Council, 1985.

Pollock, Griselda, 'Issue – an exhibition of social strategies by women artists', *Spare Rib*.

Pollock, Griselda, 'Three Perspectives on Photography', *Screen Education*, no.31, Summer, 1979.

Sekula, Allan, 'Dismantling Modernism, Re-inventing Documentary', in *Photography/Politics:1*.

Spence, Jo., *Beyond the Family Album*,

Stoneman, Rod (ed.), *South West Film Directory* (useful sections on production, exhibition and education), South West Arts, 1980.

Tabrizian, Mitra, 'Governmentality – a Photo-Text Work on Advertising', *Screen*, vol.24, no.4/5, July/October, 1983.

Tagg, John, 'A Socialist Perspective on Photographic Practice', in *Three Perspectives on Photography*, Arts Council of Great Britain, 1979.

Tisdall, Caroline and Nairne, Sandy (eds.), *Conrad Atkinson, Picturing the System*, Pluto, 1981.

Walker, John, *Art in the Age of Mass Media*, Pluto, 1983.

Worpole, Ken, 'Do you ever wish you were better informed?' (article on Klaus Staeck and Peter Kennard), *New Statesman*, 19/26 December, 1980.

*Creative Camera*, no.232, April, 1984 (work by Burgin, Lewis and Tabrizian).

'Restricted Practices – Documentary Photography in Britain Today', *Ten.8*, no.7/8.

*Studio International*, 'Art and Photography', July/August, 1975.

*Studio International*, 'Art and Social Purpose', March/April, 1976.

*Studio International*, 'The State of British Art', no.2, 1978.

Watney, Simon, 'Making Strange: The Shattered Mirror', in *Thinking Photography*.*

* See general bibliography for details.

# Community Bibliography

Barthes, Roland, *Mythologies*, Cape, 1972.

Braden, Sue, *Committing Photography*, Pluto, 1983.

Kelly, Owen, *Community, Art and the State*, Comedia, 1984.

Kelly, Owen and Killip, Dermot, 'The Second Photography: Cameras as Convivial Tools', *Camerawork*, no.22.

Lee, Gwen and Griffin, Simon, 'Easington: the case for a socialist photography', *Camerawork*, no.31.

Nettleford, Rex, *Participation in Cultural Life and Social Reconstruction*, City Arts.

Nigg, Heinz and Wade, Graham, *Community Media*, Regenbogen-Verlag (Zurich), 1980.

Slater, Don, 'Marketing the Medium – an anti-marketing report', *Camerawork*, no.18.

Willats, Stephen, *Art and Social Function*, Latimer, 1976.

Worpole, Ken, 'Who's in the Community', *City Limits*, March 12/18, 1982.

*Art for Whom*, Serpentine Gallery catalogue, London, 1978.

*Camerawork* magazine, particularly: no.1, 'The Politics of Photography', Jo Spence; no.11, 'Oppositional Culture: Yesterday & Today', Ken Worpole; no.13: 'Photography in the Community' (whole issue); no.18, 'Photography in Opposition', Philip Wolmuth; no.20, 'Community Photography', Don Slater; no.21, 'Towards a Political Practice', interview with Peter Dunn and Lorraine Leeson.

*Another Standard*, the journal of the Shetton Trust for Community Arts, The Old Tin School, Collyhurst Road, Manchester.

*Community Arts* (The report of the Community Arts Working Party, June, 1974), ACGB, 1974.

*Community Arts Bulletin* (Quarterly), South East Arts, 9/10 Crescent Road, Tunbridge Wells, Kent TN1 2LV.

*Community Arts Training – new opportunities*, (Steve Trow, discussion paper) ACGB, 1983.

*Culture and the State*, ICA conference papers, 1984.

*Facts about the Arts*, Policy Studies Unit, 1983.

*On Ideology* (Centre for Contemporary Cultural Studies), Hutchinson, 1978.

*Photography/Politics: One*, Photography Workshop, 1979.

*A Reading List on Community Arts*, Information & Research, Ref. sheet no.3, ACGB.

*Step Forward*, Mount Pleasant Photography Workshop News Journal, Southampton.

*Streamlining the Cities*, response by the GLC Conservative Group, GLC, 1984.

*Strangling the Cities* (discussion paper), Independent Film and Video-Makers' Association.

*Ten.8* magazine – particularly issues nos. 1, 4, 7/8, 13, 14.

*Thatcher's Britain 1984*, Labour Party Research Department, 1984.

# Notes

*Introduction*
1.   John Tagg, The Burden Of Representation, *Ten.8*, no.14, 1984.
2.   A *Directory* of groups and organisations throughout England, Scotland and Wales is contained at the end of the book. There is also an article about the Tondu Photo Workshop in Wales in Section Four.
3.   The development of photographic practices in the North-East of England was intended to be a specific study in this book. The growth of production/exhibition centres paralleled by extensive debate on concepts of documentary, aesthetics and community, have established the region as particularly significant for photographic culture. Ironically, the volume of material became too substantial to be contained here. It is therefore intended for publication elsewhere in the near future. Meanwhile, I would like to acknowledge the help given by the following: John Bradshaw, Wendy Brown, Graham Evans, Peter Fryer, Brian Hoey, Bushy Kelly, John Kierney, John Kippin, Sirka-Liisa Kontinnen, Sarah McCarthy, Murray Mastin, John Rigby, Janine Struk, Ian Tinwell, David Watt and (especially) Chris Wainwright. (Stevie Bezencenet).

*Section 1: Photography and Education*
1.   The School of Communication of Ryerson Polytechnical Institute, Toronto, is in the process of introducing courses in the theory of photography into its syllabus. Ryerson invited four speakers – Victor Burgin, Hollis Frampton, Allan Sekula, and Joel Snyder – to give public talks on the topic, 'Theory of Photography'; the talks were followed by a panel discussion. What follows is a transcript of Victor Burgin's contribution, given on 30 September, 1983.
2.   Raymond Williams, 'The Writer: Commitment and Alignment', *Marxism Today*, Vol. 24, No. 6, June, 1980, p. 24.
3.   John Berger, 'Understanding a Photograph', *Selected Essays and Articles*, London, Pelican, 1972, p. 181.
4.   Peter Fuller, 'The Fatal Facility', *New Society*, Vol. 64, No. 1066, 21 April, 1983, p. 107.
5.   Walter Benjamin, 'A Short History Of Photography', *Screen*, Spring, 1972, Vol. 13, No. 1, p. 25.
6.   Pierre Bourdieu, 'Intellectual Field and Creative Project', in MFD Young (Ed.), *Knowledge and Control*, Open University Press, 1971, p. 161.

*Section 2: Distribution and publication*
1.   For further reading on this topic see *Spare Rib*, June, 1983, *British Journal of Photography*, 11 May, 1984, *Creative Camera*, November, 1984.
2.   Myers, K. (1984), 'The Alternative Picture Agencies', *Camerawork* no.29.
3.   The figures are taken from 'Directory of Publishers and Distributors of Photographic Books in the United Kingdom', *British Journal of Photography*, 20 January, 1984.
4.   Figures taken from (1984) *Report on Provision for Photography in London*, Greater London Arts Association.
5.   Landry, C., *Current Problems of Magazines Funded by the Arts Council and the British Film Institute: Distribution, Promotion and Marketing*, Chapter IV, Recommendations, p. 25, ACGB, 1984.

*Section 3: Exhibition*
1.  *British Journal of Photography*, 21/5/1982, Interview with Colin Ford by Margaret Harker.
2.  *Creative Camera*, no.175, January, 1979, Editorial; *Creative Camera*, no.202, October 1981, Interview with Roy Strong by Chris Killip. See also: *Creative Camera*, no.213, September, 1982, two interviews by Colin Osman; *British Journal of Photography*, 5/3/1982, Editorial; *British Journal of Photography*, 11/11/1983, Article by Margaret Harker.